REAL
OPTIONS

Financial Management Association
Survey and Synthesis Series

The Search for Value: Measuring the Company's Cost of Capital
Michael C. Ehrhardt

Lease or Buy? Principles for Sound Decision Making
James S. Schallheim

Derivatives: A Comprehensive Resource for Options, Futures, Interest Rate Swaps, and Mortgage Securities
Fred D. Arditti

Managing Pension Plans: A Comprehensive Guide to Improving Plan Performance
Dennis E. Logue and Jack S. Rader

Efficient Asset Management: A Practical Guide to Stock Portfolio Optimization and Asset Allocation
Richard O. Michaud

Real Options: Managing Strategic Investment in an Uncertain World
Martha Amram and Nalin Kulatilaka

REAL
OPTIONS
Managing
Strategic Investment in
an Uncertain World

**Martha Amram and
Nalin Kulatilaka**

Harvard Business School Press
Boston, Massachusetts

To our families—
Aurelle, Oz, and Yosi
Nishan, Ishika, and Mandy

Copyright © 1999 President and Fellows of Harvard College
All rights reserved
Printed in the United States of America

03 02 01 00 99   5 4 3 2 1

Library of Congress Cataloging-in-Publication Data

Amram, Martha, 1957–
    Real options : managing strategic investment in an uncertain world
/ Martha Amram and Nalin Kulatilaka.
        p.   cm. — (Financial Management Association survey and
synthesis series)
    Includes bibliographical references and index.
    ISBN 0-87584-845-1 (alk. paper)
    1. Options (Finance)   2. Institutional investments.
I. Kulatilaka, Nalin, 1953–   . II. Title. III. Series.
HG6024.A3A47 1999
332.64'5—dc21   98-22392
                                                                        CIP

The paper used in this publication meets the requirements of the American
National Standard for Permanence of Paper for Printed Library Materials
Z39.49-1984.

Text design by Wilson Graphics & Design (Kenneth J. Wilson)

Contents

Preface

Many managers believe that uncertainty is a problem and should be avoided. Uncertainty is frequently omitted from important corporate thinking.

We hold the opposite view. If your firm is properly positioned, you can take advantage of uncertainty. Your strategic investments will be sheltered from its adverse effects while remaining exposed to its upside potential. Uncertainty will create value and take you to market leadership. This book is about the real options approach to strategic investments, showing you how to capitalize on uncertainty through strategic investments, contracts, and use of the financial markets.

The Nobel Prize–winning work of Fischer Black, Robert Merton, and Myron Scholes on the pricing of financial option contracts is the foundation of the real options approach. Their breakthrough showed how to value complex contracts that give holders an *option* (the right, but not the obligation) to buy or sell a stock. Together with their colleague at MIT, Stewart Myers, they recognized that option-pricing theory had important applications for *real* or nonfinancial investments. The *real options approach* is the extension of option-pricing theory for managing real assets.

We wrote this book to bring the power of the real options approach to managers. Our own experience is that the approach goes beyond the tool kit and is a way of thinking. Uncertainty and risk create the worries that keep managers up at night, and the real options approach provides a framework of how investments can be managed to address these concerns. It also brings a discipline to internal investment decisions and corporate strategy, aligning them with financial market valuations.

This book is for a broad managerial audience. Although the application of option-pricing theory has led to dramatic changes in the financial markets, it has not reached its full potential for real options. Often the numerical details have prevented managers from seeing the big picture—the new way of thinking. To make the ideas accessible to a broad range of managers, we use only a few equations in this book.

In addition, this book lays out the path from financial options to real options. Managers who might be comfortable trading options in the financial markets may not know how to identify and value real options. Financial market applications of option pricing are generally well-posed, tight questions, with the terms of an option written in the contract. Real options applications are usually more open-ended, buried in the corporate decision-making process, with complicated real-world features. The first step in a real options analysis is to identify the strategic investment option, which requires some probing. We focus on the real options *solution process*, taking readers through this new territory.

Who Should Read This Book

Many industries are experiencing changes that require large investments with substantial risk. This book is intended to answer such questions as: "This investment has so many sources of uncertainty— which ones are critical to its success?" or "I know my company operates in a very fast changing and uncertain market. Can we do better by redesigning how we make and manage our strategic investments?" or "This decision seems to lead to a lot of risk—where is the value and how can I best communicate it to Wall Street?"

Putting job titles aside, this book should serve several kinds of managers.

- **Builders and Creators.** Managers can identify which costs to cut but find it harder to create a path forward. Where are the valuable strategic investments for growth? How can you use infrastructure investments to your strategic advantage? This book contains the tools needed to value growth opportunities, investments that capitalize on uncertainty.

- **Program Managers.** Anyone involved in managing an investment program knows that things seldom work out as expected. "Final" decisions are revisited, plans are modified, and certain types of internal investments always seem to take longer to implement than planned. This book shows why and when to revisit projects and how to design valuable opportunities for reassessment.

- **Coordinators.** Managers with multiple projects under development or a portfolio of projects should read this book. The real options approach recognizes and values the spillover from one project to its follow-on projects and provides consistent valuations, allowing an "apples-to-apples" comparison of the variety of internal and external opportunities.

- **Evaluators.** Some managers are the gatekeepers. They must judge the value and the risk of each project. Standard valuation tools frustrate them every day. The gatekeeper struggles to keep the numerical results in line with business intuition. The real options approach has much to add in such situations, and this book contains the technical details and practical suggestions to get started.

- **Communicators.** Investments must be understood throughout the company and by the financial markets. Communication of some investments, such as information technology, is hard because the benefits are elusive and uncertain. Using this framework, senior managers can better organize, evaluate, and communicate the costs and the benefits of a strategic investment program inside their organization and externally.

Organization of the Book

Interest in the real options approach comes from two perspectives. Senior managers want strategic investments to align with their strategic vision. The first six chapters of this book introduce the power of the real options approach for a wide range of applications and introduce a new way of thinking that builds on financial market discipline to strategic investments.

A second group of managers are familiar with standard evaluation tools and recognize that those tools don't work very well in a world of uncertainty. They want to introduce real options into their company's decision-making process, but they lack an accessible source that will put technical details of implementation in context and will help them communicate the benefits of this approach to senior management. The middle section of this book, Chapters 7–9, is an executive-level view of the real options solution process.

Finally, everybody wants to see how real options can really work. Chapters 10–19 are a portfolio of applications, illustrating real options thinking for a wide range of strategic investments. The book concludes with Chapter 20, a set of questions to guide you through the key steps in the real options approach.

Acknowledgments

In writing this book, we have benefited from the input of many people. We begin by thanking three of our teachers, who have developed this field and the language we use to describe it. Robert Merton of Harvard Business School has laid the foundation for the path from financial options to real options and for the real options way of thinking to be disciplined by the financial markets. A lunch conversation with Bob three years ago fundamentally shaped this book. Robert

Pindyck of MIT has given us much encouragement and has influenced our thinking through his own important contributions, including the synthesis of the academic literature in his pioneering book *Investment Under Uncertainty*. And Stewart Myers, who coined the term "real options," was the first to see the many corporate applications, and has guided us in so many ways. These teachers have had a lifelong influence on our way of thinking.

We also would like to thank colleagues who have generously shared their research and perspectives on real options, financial engineering, and corporate strategy: Carliss Baldwin, Zvi Bodie, Manuel Hernandez, Blake Johnson, Bruce Kogut, Alan Marcus, Bob McDonald, and Peter Tufano.

During the past few years, we have benefited from many conversations about real options with a talented group: Scott Albertson, Almudena Arcelus, Ron Bain, Roger Bohn, Joseph Cherian, Adriana Chiocchi, Mike Cochran, Roy Epstein, Paul Greenberg, Richard Homonoff, Alex Kane, Mike Koehn, John Landon, Jesse Langston, Sherman Lee, Donald Lessard, David Luenberger, Mike Manove, Finbarr McGrath, Jay Patel, Enrico Perotti, Brett Reed, Ron Rudkin, Steven Rutherford, Martha Samuelson, Ron Simenauer, Bruce Stangle, Lenos Trigeorgis, Ed Tuttle, and N. (Venkat) Venkatraman. We also have received valuable feedback from participants at a real options conference hosted by Analysis Group/Economics, participants at the Boston University Systems Research Center meetings, and Boston University Executive MBA students. We especially would like to thank John Henderson of the Systems Research Center for his continued support of this work.

To colleagues, family, and friends who carefully read earlier drafts: Thank you! Your time and energy helped us improve this book enormously: Bruce Ambrose, Ron Bain, Carliss Baldwin, Zvi Bodie, Lucy El-Hage, Ken Hatten, Blake Johnson, Bruce Kogut, Tudor Kulatilaka, Tim Luerhman, Kevin McCurry, Lloyd Nirenberg, Dana Rowan, Claire Schary, Philip Schary, and Peter Tufano.

Our editor, Kirsten Sandberg, shared our vision for this book and gave us her support, enthusiasm, and wise counsel. Thanks. Sarah Merrigan of HBS Press gently guided us through the many issues of turning a manuscript into an elegant book. And applause for the many others at HBS Press who helped to bring this book forward. Thanks also to Ward Winslow, who provided timely and sensible editorial services with good humor.

Our final thanks go to our families. For many weeks they made the enormous contribution of adjusting their lives so that we might write this book.

PART *I*

THE
REAL OPTIONS
POTENTIAL

Part I of this book introduces the real options way of thinking and demonstrates how it can be used in a wide range of applications. Because the real options approach is disciplined by the financial markets, we spend time showing the logic behind the Nobel Prize–winning breakthrough and how that logic can be used for real assets. The real options approach has a broad reach, including important implications for corporate strategy. Part I closes with a chapter on immediate lessons, quick reference points for evaluation of new investment opportunities.

Chapter **1**

Introduction

> The current set of valuation and decision-making tools just doesn't work for the new business realities: strategic investments with lots of uncertainty and huge capital requirements; projects that must adapt to evolving conditions; complex asset structures through partnerships, licenses, and joint ventures; and the relentless pressure from the financial markets for value-creating strategy. Real options is an important way of thinking about valuation and strategic decision making, and the power of this approach is starting to change the economic "equation" of many industries.

We live in an uncertain world. Managers who make strategic investment decisions often view uncertainty as costly; they also recognize that the most valuable opportunities may come with a great deal of uncertainty. A successful pharmaceutical product such as Prozac can earn a billion dollars annually, yet half of newly introduced drugs earn less than $100 million per year, while development costs are over $300 million.[1] The cost of a semiconductor manufacturing facility is now approaching $2 billion, but the product made there will be obsolete in five years.[2] We all have watched the emergence of the Internet: hundreds of new businesses and huge financial market valuations, yet only a handful of the publicly traded Internet companies are making a profit.[3] And some of the most visible businesses on the Internet, such as the on-line bookstore Amazon.com, retain their high valuations while being years away from profitability. According to John Seely Brown, Director of Palo Alto Research Center:

> Fundamental changes are under way in the world of business. . . . The accelerating pace of change is real. . . . With this shift, we are finding

many of our background assumptions and time-honored business models inadequate to help us understand what is going on, let alone how to compete.[4]

The Gap Between What Managers Know and Current Tools

Business growth requires making investment decisions fraught with uncertainty. Managers intuitively know that they must undertake and proactively manage investments by changing subsequent plans in response to market conditions. Managers also know that standard financial tools don't work in these situations. For example:

- *For strategic investments,* standard tools don't get managers asking the right questions. Which options do managers have to guide the project to success? What must happen for a follow-on investment to make sense?

- *For transaction valuations,* such as the pricing of acquisitions and the sale or licensing of assets, standard tools rely on subjective inputs, so the results are not consistent with valuations in the financial markets.

- *For strategic vision,* standard tools don't provide the integrated framework to link project analysis and the market value of the firm. Do you know why and when your strategy is value-increasing?

In fact, strategically important projects often fail internal financial tests. Analysts, in a quest to justify their "gut feel," tend to manipulate the evaluation process, raising cash flow forecasts to unlikely levels. Key managers make decisions colored by optimism and bounded by their degree of risk aversion. Everyone recognizes the limitations of the quantitative analysis and discounts it heavily with a dose of judgment. Meanwhile, after struggling to finish one planning cycle, the project manager ends up grappling with a new (but not unexpected) change in market conditions and must revisit the investment decision. The result is that the decision-making process lacks credibility.

Higher in the organization, a fragmentation exists that prevents senior management from identifying value-increasing investment opportunities. Current tools do not link internal strategic investment criteria and transaction opportunities in product and financial markets. For example, a contract to shelter profit margins against input price volatility could lay a base of predictable cash flows for use in product

---

What Is an Option?

An option is the right, but not the obligation, to take an action in the future. Options are valuable when there is uncertainty. For example, one option contract traded on the financial exchanges gives the buyer the opportunity to buy a stock at a specified price on a specified date and will be *exercised* (used) only if the price of the stock on that date exceeds the specified price. Many strategic investments create subsequent opportunities that *may* be taken, and so the investment opportunity can be viewed as a stream of cash flow plus a set of options.

---

development. Senior management misses important strategic opportunities because tactics, strategy, and valuation are considered separately.

> As a practical matter, many managers seem to understand already that there is something wrong with the simple NPV rule [a standard valuation tool] as it is taught—that there is value to waiting for more information, and that this value is not reflected in the standard calculation. In fact, managers often require that an NPV be more than merely positive. . . . It may be that managers understand a company's options are valuable, and that it is desirable to keep these options open.[5]

The Real Options Approach Is a Way of Thinking

We are not the first to see the enormous advantages of the real options approach. The power of the ideas underlying the approach has created high expectations, particularly in the academic world, but the rate of adoption in the corporate world has been slower than expected. We believe that this is largely because introductions of the real options approach have overly focused on the technical aspects of modeling, neglecting that real options is a *way of thinking*.

In this book, we take a broad look at the real options approach, laying out how it provides an immediate and important perspective on value creation in an uncertain world. The real options way of thinking has three components that are of great use to managers:

1. *Options are contingent decisions.* An option is the opportunity to make a decision after you see how events unfold. On the decision date, if events have turned out well, you'll make one decision, but if they have turned out poorly, you'll make another. This means the payoff to an option is nonlinear—it changes with your decision. Fixed (noncontingent) decisions have linear payoffs because no matter what happens, you'll make the same decision.

2. *Option valuations are aligned with financial market valuations.* The real options approach uses financial market inputs and concepts to value complex payoffs across all types of real assets. The result is an "apples-to-apples" comparison of managerial options, financial market alternatives, and internal investment opportunities and transaction opportunities, such as joint ventures, technology licenses, and acquisitions.

3. *Options thinking can be used to design and manage strategic investments proactively.* The nonlinear payoffs can also be a design tool. How

---

What Are Real Options?

In a narrow sense, the real options approach is the extension of financial option theory to options on real (nonfinancial) assets. While financial options are detailed in the contract, real options embedded in strategic investments must be identified and specified. Moving from financial options to real options requires a way of thinking, one that brings the discipline of the financial markets to internal strategic investment decisions.

The real options approach works because it helps managers with the opportunities they have to plan and manage strategic investments. Stewart Myers of the Sloan School of Management at MIT coined the term "real options" to address the gap between strategic planning and finance:

> Strategic planning needs finance. Present value calculations are needed as a check on strategic analysis and vice versa. However, standard discounted cashflow techniques will tend to understate the option value attached to growing profitable lines of business. Corporate finance theory requires extension to deal with *real options*.[6]

can I reduce my exposure to uncertainty? How can I increase the payoff if there is a good outcome? The first step is to identify and value the options in a strategic investment. The second step is to redesign the investment to better use the options. The third step is to manage the investment proactively through the options created.

The Real Options Approach Can Help Form the Strategic Vision

Integrating valuation and decision making across uncertainty and over time, the real options approach addresses many of the same questions as corporate strategy. The real options approach creates a way to learn from past performance because it distinguishes the contributions of luck from those of foresight—the contribution of a particular outcome of uncertainty from the contribution of investments thoughtfully put in place to capitalize on unfolding events. The real options approach expands the set of strategic alternatives managers consider, so

---

Examples of Real Options

- Suppose Snow Inc. is considering producing skis. Once in production, it will acquire information useful in making and selling ski boots, so it may want to expand to this second product; in other words, there is an option to expand. To calculate the value of that option, information is needed about the volatility of the ski boot business. Contrary to what most managers believe, the real options approach shows that the option to expand into ski boots is more valuable when there is greater uncertainty about the ski boot business.[7]

- Recently AT&T spun off Lucent, a technology-based company. Based on current earnings, Lucent's stock would be priced at just over $8 per share.[8] Since its spinoff, Lucent has consistently traded above $60 per share. The difference reflects the market's pricing of Lucent's growth options—the business opportunities that may arise from its technology base and R&D portfolio—and management's signals that it can execute to realize the value of these options.

---

that managers also identify and value opportunities to contract in the financial and product markets.

The real options approach also creates two links between project-level analyses of strategic investments and the corporate strategic vision. In a top-down perspective, the real options approach hammers at these questions: What value-creating opportunities are unique to this firm? What amount and type of risk must be borne to create this value? What risk can be shed?

In a bottom-up perspective, the real options approach provides the framework in which to aggregate project value and risk and the structure to manage the company's net exposure to risk. The bottom-up aggregation also raises the visibility of how uncertainty affects value at the project level, useful information for senior managers creating the vision. As Andy Grove, the former CEO of Intel wrote, "Time and time again, it is the product managers who are the first to know what is going on in the market, and where the 10X [huge] uncertainty is."[9]

Uncertainty, Exposure, and Risk

Throughout this book, we use the terms "uncertainty" and "risk," but not interchangeably. Uncertainty is the randomness of the external environment. Managers cannot change its level. Uncertainty is an input into the real options analysis. A firm's exposure to uncertainty—the sensitivity of the firm's cash flows and value to a source of uncertainty—is determined by a number of factors, including the line of business, the cost structure, and the nature of contracts to obtain inputs and sell outputs. Managers change asset exposure through investment, after they analyze the external uncertainty. The adverse economic consequence of a firm's exposure is risk.

For example, an oil-burning industrial furnace and one that can burn either oil or gas have quite different exposures to oil price uncertainty. The risk for each furnace—in this case, the chance of negative operating profits—is determined by the combination of oil price uncertainty, the exposure of the furnace's profits to that uncertainty, *and* the plant manager's ability to respond to unfolding events.

Real Options and Derivatives Thinking Will Change the Structure of Many Industries

The energy industry and many commodity industries already have been invaded by "derivative thinkers," new players who bring the power of option-pricing perspectives to create new contracts and markets for the exchange of assets. For example, a modern oil refinery uses opportunities to trade and hedge the crack spread (the difference between input and output prices) to avoid temporary refinery shutdowns when the crack spread is low. The financial strategy can be cheaper because it avoids the larger cost of a physical shutdown. (We discuss the financial strategy for that refinery in more detail in Chapter 17.)

In the biotech industry, many companies are finding the need to write contingent contracts with pharmaceuticals as they establish joint ventures and license products. (A contingent contract contains a menu of decisions that can be made in the future after events have unfolded.) How the contract is written determines the asset and its payoffs, an issue better illuminated by the transparent payoff structure of the real options approach. A valuation model that is clear and anchored by financial market inputs and perspectives will make transactions much easier to accomplish, further increasing the number of transactions in the industry. We see opportunities for this self-reinforcing process in industries that require complementary inputs to large capital investments, such as biotech and pharmaceuticals, and in industries that require the aggregation of a number of components, such as the system-on-a-chip segment of the semiconductor market.[10]

One quick lesson from the real options approach is that there is great value in breaking up large projects in uncertain markets. As semiconductor fabrication plant costs increase beyond their current $2 billion level, monolithic investments in capacity will be replaced by staged expansions and more flexible production capabilities. The real options approach values the tradeoffs involved, including the cost of production delays in this fast-paced market. Telecommunications and oil and gas exploration are two other industries that offer significant opportunities to create options by staging large capital investments.

In sum, we see evidence that many large industries are ripe for derivatives thinking. Adopting the real options approach accelerates that change. With it, market leaders will understand how value is created in an uncertain environment and will know how much risk they are bearing.

How the Real Options Approach Changes Common Business Decisions

Throughout this book, we use examples to illustrate real options concepts. Our experience is that, although each application must be tailored to the specifics of the industry and the market, insights from the real options way of thinking are relevant across a number of industries. As you read on, try to draw the parallels to your company and your market in how the application is structured, the key decision-making triggers, and the consequences of adopting the real options thinking. Here are some common business decisions that are changed by a real options analysis.

Waiting-to-Invest Options

Sales of healthy, low-fat ice cream are surging. The Big Black Cow Creamery can't tell if the sales increase will persist, but traditional tools suggest that a plant expansion is worthwhile. A real options analysis incorporated possible future sales outcomes and quantified the trade-offs between the increased revenues from immediate expansion and the losses avoided by waiting to resolve uncertainty. The analysis identified the best strategy, showing that the value of waiting exceeded the value of immediate expansion.

Growth Options

Friend-to-Friend sells cosmetics through a network of independent saleswomen and is considering whether to enter the market in China. The initial investment in local manufacturing and the sales organization is large, but it *may* lead to opportunities to sell a whole range of products through an established sales network. A traditional analysis indicated that costs exceeded forecasted profits. A real options analysis showed that the entry investment should be made because it created growth options, options to take on the follow-on projects if the initial investment worked out well.

Flexibility Options

Cell Inc. must build a new plant for the production of its latest cell phone product. The forecast for the new product showed that sales are highly uncertain and spread across two continents. A traditional manufacturing analysis suggested that one plant would be cheaper to build and operate. A real options analysis showed a greater value in building two plants, one on each continent, creating an option to switch production as needed. The traditional analysis missed how investing in an option to switch creates value out of uncertain events.

Exit Options

PetroChem might begin development of a new product, but it is worried about the size of the market opportunity and whether the manufacturing process can meet government regulations regarding toxic chemicals. Traditional tools suggested that the project should not be started. A real options analysis valued the exit option held by PetroChem, the option to walk away from the project if it receives bad news about the market opportunity or the clean-up liability. By including the abandonment option, the project value increased and PetroChem began development.

Learning Options

Hollywood Inc. is planning the release of three new movies for the Christmas season. Before the first showing, the executives can't tell which movie will be the biggest hit, so they plan their advertising budgets as staged investments. Each movie is released to a limited number of screens in selected cities. The movie with the strongest performance will get a national rollout and a large advertising budget. During the national rollout, management will decide how much to spend on advertising for the video and international markets. Traditional tools would have missed how each stage of investment creates better information about the movie's total profits and an option to make the next investment decision. The real options approach valued the contingent decisions and showed how to structure each stage for higher value.

In Sum

This book lays the foundation for using real options thinking in the design and management of strategic investments and in the development of the strategic vision. Our message to managers is about:

- How to think about uncertainty and its effects on valuation over time
- How to bring the discipline of the financial markets to internal valuation and decision making

- How to frame real options applications, especially with regard to the nature of uncertainty and contingent decision-making opportunities
- How to manage strategic opportunities to best take advantage of the options that come with investment, including creating options in the original project design for increased value
- How real options thinking can be used across an organization
- How to crunch the numbers

We recognize that real assets are more complicated than financial assets and that real options are harder to identify and describe. Throughout this book, we point out how to deal with these complexities, when and where the real options approach can add value, and when and where it cannot. Some applications don't fit any objective valuation model very well, but our experience is that by maintaining the discipline of the real options way of thinking, we can push these applications a lot further and obtain better results.

Changing how you think is a great opportunity. Use your options!

The real options approach gives managers a decision-making and valuation tool that reflects good project management, ensuring that these decisions lead to the highest market valuation of corporate strategy. The real options approach is a way of thinking and is part of a broad wave of change in financial and product markets, a change that requires executives to create value through their management of strategic investments in an uncertain world.

Chapter **2**

Uncertainty Creates Opportunities

Managers anticipate and respond to uncertainty when they make mid-course corrections, abandon projects, or build in reviews at milestones for projects and licenses. In the language of real options, managers are making contingent decisions—decisions to invest or disinvest that depend on unfolding events. This chapter lays out the nature of contingent investment opportunities in an uncertain world.

*T*oday's markets require that important strategic investment decisions be made in very uncertain environments—when market size, time to market, costs of development, competitor moves, and so on— simply are not known. The circumstances evoke fear and caution, and frustration with the available decision tools only heightens the sense of operating in the dark. Because a large gap exists between what managers want to do and what their tools were designed to do, managers often make decisions without relying on a quantitative analysis.

Two particular features of current practice stand out as significant problems. The first problem is that some tools require a forecast of future cash flows. Because only a single forecast is used in the analysis, it receives much scrutiny. Is it an overoptimistic projection by a project advocate? What are the growth rate and profit margin assumptions in the forecast? Too often, managers treat the forecast as reality, creating an illusion of certainty about the numbers. To compensate, some companies try to expand the analysis to a range of forecasts or scenarios. These efforts appear rigorous to their author but arbitrary to others. Whether a single scenario or a set of scenarios, the cash flow forecast becomes a subjective input.

The second problem with the tools most often used is that future investment decisions are fixed at the outset. Managers update and revise investment plans, but the analysis, as structured by most tools, includes only the initial plan. The world changes, but your model doesn't. As the gap between tools and reality widens, the tools are discarded, and the important decisions are made by "strategic considerations" and "managerial charisma."[1]

No one believes that this process works well for investment decisions in certain industries—such as high tech, pharmaceutical, and oil exploration—or for certain large investment decisions—such as information technology, research and development, and major capacity expansion. Current practice works well for some projects but not for those most closely connected to business growth.

Managing Strategic Investments in an Uncertain World

Once your way of thinking explicitly includes uncertainty, the whole decision-making framework changes. Figure 2.1 illustrates one of the most important shifts in thinking from the real options approach: Uncertainty creates opportunities. Managers should welcome, not fear uncertainty. In rethinking strategic investments, managers must try to view their markets in terms of the source, trend, and evolution of uncertainty; determine the degree of exposure for their investments (how external events translate into profits and losses); and then respond by positioning the investments to best take advantage of uncertainty.

The Resolution of Uncertainty

When a future decision depends on the source of uncertainty, managers care about the range of possible outcomes that the uncertain variable might have when the decision date arrives. The key is the link between time and uncertainty. Figure 2.2 introduces a simple picture that we have found very helpful, the *cone of uncertainty*.[2] The figure illustrates how a straightforward question could be answered, one that does not involve options. Suppose the current value of a company is $1 million. What possible values might it have in two years?

The left point of the cone shows today's value of the firm, and as we look out into the future, the range of possible outcomes grows wider. The width of the range of outcomes depends on the length of the time horizon. The cone tilts upward, reflecting the expectation that the firm's value will grow during the two years.

Figure 2.1 Uncertainty Increases Value

In the traditional view a higher level of uncertainty leads to a lower asset value. The real options approach shows that increased uncertainty can lead to a higher asset value if managers identify and use their options to flexibly respond to unfolding events.

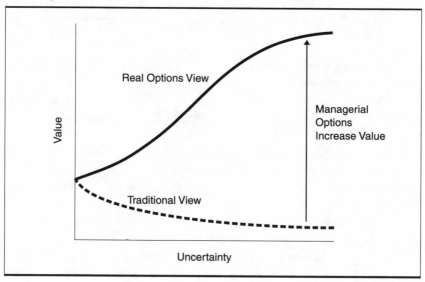

Figure 2.2 The Cone of Uncertainty

The cone of uncertainty is a simple picture of how value might evolve over time. In this example the range of uncertainty increases with the time horizon. The positive rate of return expected over the next two years gives the cone an upward tilt.

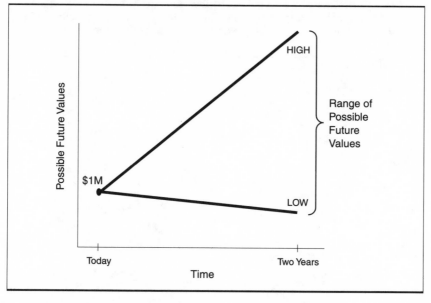

There is no magic to what we do. It's just applied common sense. My job is to forecast, not to predict. Forecasting accepts that at any one time there are multiple possible outcomes. That is the cone of uncertainty. My job is to map that, to reveal the options and opportunities, and to convince my clients that if they think about uncertainty, they can make better decisions, and depending on the circumstances, even influence the ultimate outcome.[3]

As the value of the firm evolves, or changes over time, the highest and lowest values marked on the cone are rather unlikely. Figure 2.3 shows how the evolution of an uncertain variable over time is related to the distribution of outcomes at the end of the time horizon. As Figure 2.3(b) shows, in two years it is likely that the value of the firm will be near the middle of the range.[4] Many strategic investments come with a series of options, which have decision points in the interior of the cone of uncertainty, before the cone ends at the decision date of the final option. For each interior decision point, the distribution of outcomes for that date is found by "slicing" off the remainder of the cone of uncertainty.

During the two years, the value of the firm is expected to grow at some rate. There is uncertainty about the actual growth rate that will be realized each year, and this is measured by the volatility, the standard

Figure 2.3 Two Views of the Resolution of Uncertainty

(a) The cone of uncertainty contains a range of possible future values at the end of two years. (b) This range is part of the distribution of outcomes. The expected value at the end of two years is measured by the mean of the distribution and its standard deviation is a measure of the range of outcomes. (See the appendix for more details.)

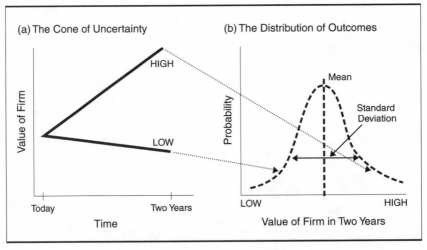

deviation of the expected return.[5] (Standard deviation is a measure of the range of outcomes. Volatility is usually expressed in annual terms.) The real options approach interweaves the effects of time and uncertainty on valuation and decision making, so it naturally focuses on volatility, the range of uncertainty about growth rates.

Here are two examples of how option values depend on volatility:

- *Stock options.* The value of the stock option contract depends on the uncertainty of the stock price, which can be estimated as the standard deviation of the stock's return.

- *An option to develop a parking lot into an office building.* The value of the option depends on the value of office space in the local market and its volatility, which can be estimated as the standard deviation of the return to a local real estate investment trust. (REITs are portfolios of office buildings whose shares are traded on the financial markets.)

Before moving on, let's link the cone of uncertainty to the concept of exposure introduced in Chapter 1. Figure 2.4 shows how external uncertainty is passed through the firm's assets. The exposure, or sensitivity, of the assets determines the magnitude and form of uncertainty

Figure 2.4 The Presence of Real Options Modifies the Exposure to External Uncertainty

External uncertainty is transformed through the firm's assets to uncertainty about the value of the strategic investment. In the traditional view the firm's exposure to external uncertainty remains large. Real options present in strategic investments allow managers to reduce exposure to bad outcomes and enhance exposure to good outcomes, modifying the exposure to uncertainty and increasing the value of the strategic investment.

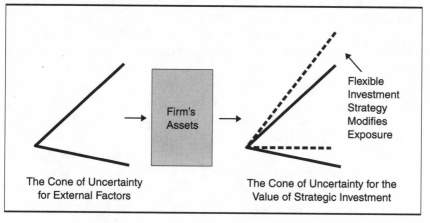

The Cone of Uncertainty for External Factors

Firm's Assets

Flexible Investment Strategy Modifies Exposure

The Cone of Uncertainty for the Value of Strategic Investment

for the value of the strategic investment. As the real options in the investment are identified and managed, the cone of uncertainty generated by the firm's assets tilts farther upward, increasing the value expected from the strategic investment.[6] Figure 2.4 highlights how the real options approach can be used to modify (but not necessarily eliminate) the exposure of assets to increase the value of the real options they contain.

The Consequences of Contingent Investment Decisions

Managers intuitively use options, such as when they delay completing an investment program until the results of a pilot project are known. The decision about whether to complete the investment program is a contingent investment decision, one that depends on an uncertain outcome. Valuing investment opportunities that contain future contingent decisions is hard, but it can be done with the options approach to valuation.

Let's use an example. Forest Products Inc. wants to buy an option from a private landowner to harvest the timber on a tract of land in three years. If the timber is not harvested at the end of three years, Forest Products obtains no revenues and has no further rights to the timber. An investment of $750,000 is needed to build roads and other infrastructure for the harvest. Clearly the harvest decision depends on the price of lumber.

Figure 2.5, the payoff diagram for the contingent harvest decision, shows how the harvest payoff (revenues less costs) is exposed to the price of lumber in three years. For lumber prices below a certain level (L*), it is not worthwhile to invest the $750,000, and the optimal strategy is to do nothing. The cash flow is zero. For lumber prices above L*, the cash flow payoff increases with the price of lumber. The dashed line is the payoff assuming the timber is harvested regardless of the price of lumber. It is the payoff to the fixed investment strategy discussed in Chapter 1 and is how standard tools diverge from actual practice. No manager would undertake a money-losing harvest, but standard tools don't capture the manager's option not to harvest.

Although the exact shapes vary, options always have kinked payoff functions. The nonlinear shape is how uncertainty creates value. For example, in the harvest option, losses are limited to the original payment made to the private landholder. Once the option is in place, high levels of volatility translate into a wide range of outcomes on the harvest decision date. The kink in the payoff function makes this a one-

Figure 2.5 Payoff Diagram for Forest Products

Below L*, revenues are less than costs so Forest Products will not harvest, and the payoff is a flat line at $0. Above L*, profits can be made and the payoff increases with the price of lumber. The decision to harvest is contingent on the price of lumber in three years, so it has a kinked payoff function. The dashed line shows the payoffs to a decision to harvest regardless of the price of lumber, the strategy implicit in standard tools.

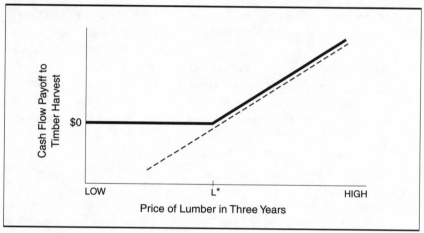

sided effect: There is an increase in the upside potential, the chance of a very high payoff, but no increase in potential losses. Investments with a kinked payoff function benefit from uncertainty.

Identifying the Options: Three Examples

Here are three examples to get you started on seeing investment opportunities through the real options approach. The numerical calculations for these and other examples in this book are at our Web site: www.real-options.com.

The Growth Option of Luxury Auto

Luxury Auto plans to expand to a suburb near Redmond, Washington, which has recently experienced a rise in household income, largely from the exercise of stock options by employees of Icon Inc. Luxury Auto has two alternatives:

- Build a large showroom now for $5.8 million
- Build a smaller salesroom now for $3 million, with room, zoning, and permits for a later expansion for an additional cost of $3.5 million

Over the years, Luxury Auto has found that sales follow the local level of disposable income, which is best predicted by the price of Icon stock. Uncertainty about the stock price translates into uncertainty about showroom profits on an approximately one-to-one basis and determines the value of the expansion strategies. Icon's stock price volatility is estimated to be 35% per year.

Figure 2.6 shows the payoffs from the two expansion strategies. The payoff to the one-stage strategy is not contingent—it is fixed, as indicated by the straight line. The payoff to the one-stage strategy breaks even (crosses the $0 line) when the value of the expansion exceeds its cost, $5.8 million. The initial investment in the alternative expansion strategy has two components: a fixed payoff and an option for the second investment, an opportunity to grow if the local economy remains strong.

The value of the one-stage expansion is only $200,000, while the value of the two-stage expansion is over $1 million. Hence, the optimal investment strategy is to not go ahead with the full expansion but to start small. The real options analysis included the option of making the second investment and identified the higher-valued expansion strategy.

Figure 2.6 Two Expansion Strategies for Luxury Auto

(a) The decision in the one-stage expansion strategy is fixed for all outcomes, and hence has a linear payoff function. (b) The two-stage strategy consists of a fixed decision to make a smaller initial investment and an option to expand later. Although the one-stage strategy is valuable, the value of the two-stage expansion strategy is greater because of the flexibility of the second-stage option.

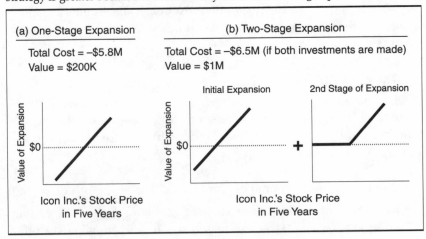

Growth Options and Investment Platforms

Luxury Auto's strategy is based on growth options, investments that create the opportunity to participate in a fast-growing firm or business industry or investments that create additional growth in standard business situations, such as investments in advertising and improved customer service. Investments in R&D also contain growth options because they create a platform of knowledge for future products.

Traditional valuation tools undervalue investments that contain growth options, and companies that rely on those tools may be limiting their growth by underinvestment.[7] Such myopia is corrected by accounting for the value of growth options in strategic investments.

What is the source of value in growth options? Uncertainty, and the firm's ability to respond to it. Growth often takes place in a highly uncertain environment, and strategic investments are most valuable when they are accompanied by options. For example, losses can be avoided using the option to postpone investment or the option to abandon the project.[8] Such downside protection leaves the upside potential intact, positioning the firm to capture the value of growth.

Purchasing Flexibility at Mutual Life

Mutual Life is developing an office complex in Phoenix. It is evaluating three systems for its cooling needs:

- Equipment that burns natural gas to cool water
- Equipment that receives chilled water from a neighboring cogeneration facility
- Equipment that can switch between burning natural gas and receiving chilled water. The flexible system is 20% more expensive than the alternatives.

The flexible equipment is an investment that contains a sequence of options. Once operations are under way using one source of chilled water, the building manager has the option to switch to the other source. Then, having switched, the manager has the option to switch back. The additional cost of the flexible system is justified if the sequence of switching options has greater value than the fixed operating mode of either alternative. (The real options approach compares the values of the alternatives, not just the costs.)

The purchase decision rests largely on the frequency in fluctuations in the costs of chilled water. Figure 2.7 shows two possible cases. When costs are stable, one of the fixed systems will dominate. When costs fluctuate and the cost of switching is sufficiently low, the option to switch is valuable and the flexible system should be purchased.

The Option to Develop and Operate a Gold Mine

Au Mining Inc. (AMI) has a contract that gives it the right to develop a gold mine. Development costs are projected to be $50 million, and a traditional analysis shows that at current and projected gold prices the mine's value over development costs is marginal, only $1 million.

However, AMI recognized that the development contract gave it two important options. First, the contract allowed AMI the right to develop the mine at any time during the next 10 years. The decision to develop was not the now-or-never proposition captured in the traditional analysis. Second, once the mine was operational, AMI held the option to temporarily shut it down if gold prices fell and the option to start it up again if gold prices recovered. (The second option is similar to the

Figure 2.7 Purchasing Flexibility at Mutual Life

(a) The relative costs of chilled water are stable, so the option to switch has little value. (b) The relative costs of chilled water fluctuate and neither source is consistently cheaper. If the cost of switching is sufficiently low, the option to switch could be valuable.

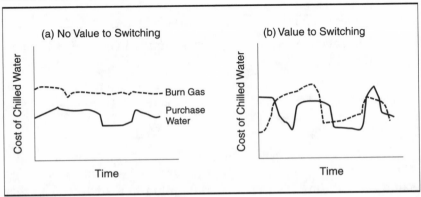

Predictable and Uncertain Changes

Some changes are predictable. For example, suppose demand suddenly drops. Every player in the industry expects the price to fall; the only questions are when and by how much. In another case, consider the situation in a commodity industry in which there is an unexpected price spike but also a slow reversion back to a long-term average. A trend can be predicted; hence, uncertainty should be measured as the deviation from the expected trend.

Traditional valuation tools can be used when future changes are predictable; a real options analysis is needed when there is a significant level of uncertainty. In a real options analysis, separate inputs are used for the trend and uncertain fluctuations about the trend.

option in Mutual Life's cooling system; think of the mine as having the option to switch between being closed and being open.)

When should the mine be developed and how should it be operated? The real options approach answers these questions simultaneously because the value of a developed mine depends on how it is operated, and the value of an operating mine depends on when it is developed. The decisions to develop and how to operate both are triggered by observable gold prices and must account for future contingent decisions.

Consider the decision to shut down an operating mine. The decision rule must look ahead and determine the gold price at which the mine would open and the likelihood of obtaining that price. Now consider the option to develop. The decision rule must look ahead and determine the value of developing later, when the price of gold might be higher and the mine could be operated more profitably.

The real options way of thinking puts the focus in this analysis on the right issues, not on a single projected gold price trajectory but on the range of possible gold price paths, on the cone of uncertainty. The real options approach also brings financial market discipline to the development and operating decisions as market information is used about gold price volatility and the expected trend.[9] There is no subjective forecast of future gold prices.

The real options analysis showed that the opportunity to develop the mine was much more valuable than the traditional analysis showed. It also identified the changes required in labor and supply contracts that would allow the valuable shutdown options to be used.

When (and When Not) to Use the Real Options Approach

The real options approach is not always needed. Some decisions are "no brainers"—the investment is either incredibly valuable or a total dog, and a real options analysis won't change this result.[10] Many decisions fall into a gray area requiring hard-headed thinking, and the real options approach can help.

Traditional tools work well when there are no options at all, or there are options but very little uncertainty. Traditional tools correctly value the proverbial "cash cow" business—the one that steadily produces the same or gently declining cash flow each year without further investment—and products that have no follow-on opportunities. Although uncertainty is everywhere, the consequences of uncertainty for some projects are sufficiently small that they can be ignored. For example, the decision to close a manufacturing plant might be obvious, despite some uncertainty about the local tax consequences.

A real options analysis is needed in the following situations:

- When there is a contingent investment decision. No other approach can correctly value this type of opportunity.

- When uncertainty is large enough that it is sensible to wait for more information, avoiding regret for irreversible investments.

- When the value seems to be captured in possibilities for future growth options rather than current cash flow.

- When uncertainty is large enough to make flexibility a consideration. Only the real options approach can correctly value investments in flexibility.

- When there will be project updates and mid-course strategy corrections.

Strategic Investments in an Uncertain World

Let's put a real options perspective on some common strategic investments.

Irreversible Investments

Irreversible investments require good up-front analyses because, once the assets are in place, the investment cannot be reversed without losing much of its value. Irreversible investments often are managed by delaying a project until a significant amount of the uncertainty is resolved or by breaking the investment into stages. For example, irreversibility in nuclear power plant construction comes from construction costs and the clean-up liability. The option to halt the construction can be used to avoid the clean-up liability if warranted by new information.

The value of an irreversible investment with its associated options is greater than recognized by traditional tools because the options truncate the losses. Managers using the real options approach will make more irreversible investments, but in smaller stages, and after waiting for some uncertainty to resolve. (We discuss the irreversible investment to develop vacant land in Chapter 15.)

> Risk and time are the opposite sides of the same coin, for if there was no tomorrow, there would be no risk. Time transforms risk, and the nature of risk is shaped by the time horizon: the future is the playing field. Time matters more when decisions are irreversible. And yet many irreversible decisions must be made on the basis of incomplete information. Irreversibility dominates decisions ranging all the way from taking the subway instead of a taxi, to building an automobile factory in Brazil, to changing jobs, to declaring war.[11]

Flexibility Investments

Flexibility investments build options into the initial design. Flexible manufacturing equipment allows a production line to be easily switched across products; the option to switch is part of the capital equipment. Flexibility options can be purchased in equipment or created by internal investment, such as the labor and training practices of Japanese auto manufacturers that allow rapid model switching in the production line.[12] Chapter 16 contains additional analyses on the value of flexibility.

Companies can also invest to obtain flexibility in the time dimension. Opportunities to accelerate investment can be valuable when markets may be won by the early entrants. Opportunities to slow down are valuable when an important component of the uncertainty will be resolved during the investment process, such as waiting to see which technology platform is more widely adopted.

Flexibility is difficult to handle with traditional tools because the value of switching depends on your current status. Once you've switched, the value of switching depends on your new status and the switching options that it has. Traditional tools can't keep track of those interdependencies.[13] Managers using the real options approach are better able to select from alternative ways to achieve flexibility—equipment, contracts, or internal operations.

Insurance Investments

Insurance investments reduce exposure to uncertainty. Investing in excess capacity ensures against running out of product if demand surges, but with a cost or "insurance premium": the incremental costs of constructing and carrying the capacity built beyond immediate needs. Using off-the-shelf equipment in a plant rather than custom-built equipment creates insurance. If the plant has to be closed, off-the-shelf equipment will have higher salvage value.

Insurance pays off only in a few outcomes, so traditional tools that show the same payoff in all outcomes cannot value insurance. (Insurance has a kinked payoff function, but traditional tools incorporate only linear payoff functions.) Managers using the real options approach are able to value insurance and also check to see whether the value exceeds the cost. Buying insurance by modifying real asset or long-term contracts can be costly.

Modular Investments

Modular investments create options through product design. Each module has a tightly specified interface to the others, allowing modules to be independently changed and upgraded. A modular product can be viewed as a portfolio of options to upgrade. Modular designs also can be used to preserve a flexibility option, such as when the design of a particular component is left open to the last minute. The real options approach illuminates the trade-offs involved in modular designs between the up-front costs of developing a modular interface against the value of the options it creates. Examples of business strategies built around modular designs are given in Chapter 5.

Platform Investments

Platform investments create valuable follow-on contingent investment opportunities. R&D is the classic platform investment because its value comes from products it releases for further development that *may* lead to marketable products. An initial investment in modular design is a platform investment that *may* lead to follow-on opportunities to upgrade specific modules. Managers using the real options approach will increase their platform investments, sometimes by a significant amount, because traditional tools greatly undervalue these investments.

Learning Investments

Learning investments are made to obtain information that is otherwise unavailable. For example, oil exploration is a learning investment because it generates geological information. If the exploration investment is not made, no geological information is obtained. Learning investments are used in industries with several different kinds of uncertainty, and their value is determined by the simultaneous outcome of all sources. For example, the value of an oil exploration investment depends on the new geological information and the evolution of oil prices. If oil prices plummet, good geological data is much less valuable. Managers using the real options approach will increase the number of learning investments they make, but they also will quickly abandon them if warranted. We discuss learning investments for oil exploration and drug development in Chapters 12 and 13.

Focusing on What Managers Worry About: Total Risk

Our experience is that using the real options approach changes the way you think about the consequences of uncertainty. By investing in this approach for one strategic investment, you bring insights to other investments without crunching a single number. The real options approach becomes a frame of reference, allowing you to reinterpret existing metrics and analyses.

One example of this change in the frame of reference has to do with the nature of risk. In the real options approach, the focus is on total risk, the full range of outcomes. With standard financial tools, such as discounted cash flow, the discount rate is adjusted for the systematic risk of strategic investment. Systematic risk is a part of total risk and is the correlation of an asset's value with the broader economic system. For example, the systematic risk in a chemical plant expansion is the correlation of the plant's value with a broad-based stock market index such as the S&P 500. Many managers, frustrated with such an incomplete accounting of the risks, increase to their corporate discount rate. There are two problems with this ad hoc response: the traditional tools don't get managers thinking about the right issues, and the ad hoc adjustments increase the subjectivity of the results. In contrast, the real options approach focuses on total risk, which completely accounts for the outcomes that worry managers.

Laying Out Uncertainty and Options Is Not Enough

Identifying the options is the first step to managing strategic investments in an uncertain world, but it is not enough. Decision making must be based on the *value* of investment alternatives. How do you ensure that internal valuation results are consistent with valuation in the financial markets? Only this stringent criterion ensures that strategic investments increase shareholder value. In the next two chapters, we show how the real options approach produces values—and, consequently, decisions—consistent with financial market valuations.

Strategic investments include options that must be recognized by valuation and decision-making tools. The real options approach focuses on the total risk of the investment, which is exactly what managers worry about and act on.

Chapter **3**

Option Valuation: The Nobel Prize–Winning Breakthrough

> The option approach to valuation is very different from traditional tools. The value of an option is inferred from the value of a portfolio of traded securities which has the same payoff as the option, and which mimics its fluctuations in value over time. If the value of the option and the portfolio are not equal, an opportunity to profit from trading would exist. Financial markets move quickly, and arbitrage opportunities are fleeting, bringing discipline and precision to option valuation. The option approach to valuation earned its authors the 1997 Nobel Prize in Economics.

*T*he first half of the real options approach is about recognizing that uncertainty provides managers with investment opportunities. The second half is about how options are valued. Real options—and financial options—are valued relative to the prices of traded assets, adding discipline and objectivity. That allows the real options approach to provide consistent valuations across internal and external applications, making possible an "apples-to-apples" comparison of *all* strategic opportunities, including opportunities to use financial market transactions to better manage investments and risks. Initially, the concepts (and the associated mathematics) behind the options approach may appear complex, but using the options approach allows you to make great strides over competitors who are wedded to current practice.

Look at how quickly financial markets adopted the approach for the valuation of financial contracts. Within six months of the model's publication in 1973, Texas Instruments introduced a calculator with the option model preprogrammed, and within a year, options traders who ignored the model had lost money.[1] We expect a similar complete change in approach for the valuation of real assets. As financial and real asset markets evolve to provide more opportunities to manage risk, adoption of the options approach to valuation will be critical for competitive positioning of real assets.

Why Do We Care about Financial Market Valuations?

The options approach produces internal valuations of strategic business opportunities that are aligned with valuations in the financial markets. Why is this significant for managers?

- Financial market valuations are transaction prices and evidence of a willingness by parties to put money behind their forecasts. Sometimes the valuations are puzzling to outside observers, but it is hard to argue with the swift flow of money to and from misvalued assets.

- Managers are rewarded by growth in the value of the firm through stock holdings and stock options. Better alignment of business decisions with financial market valuations rewards everyone.

- Perception is important. By using a model so clearly based on pricing done in financial markets and identifying the value increase associated with an investment strategy, managers have an unbeatable way to communicate with the markets. Biotech firms, for example, must go to the capital markets several times during their early growth phase, each time requiring a full disclosure of recent product developments and alliances. Because the value of such firms is based largely on the recognition and execution of growth options, communicating a disciplined understanding of those corporate options should raise the market's perception of their value.

A Valuation Dilemma

Most companies use some form of discounted cash flow to value investment opportunities.[2] However, using the discounted cash flow approach to value contingent investment decisions—the kinds of decisions managers face—produces a "show-stopping" dilemma. Consider the option to abandon. If the option is used, the asset is abandoned and there is no further risk. If the option is not used, there is risk to holding the option and the asset. No single discount rate can bring those risky cash flows back to the present, and the problem has no remedy inside the traditional discounted cash flow framework.[3]

While managers might be tempted to ignore the discount rate problem, this won't work because the problem is actually larger. Traditional valuation tools fail managers because the tools don't focus consistently on where managerial decision making can shape outcomes.

Some tools, such as decision analysis and simulation models, also pose a practical problem: Where do you get the probabilities for each outcome? Typically, analysts estimate the probabilities based on prior experience, forecasting models, and subjective judgment. Experienced managers fear that opening up a project's uncertainty is just another way to manipulate the results.

The Breakthrough That Won the Nobel Prize

The discount rate dilemma stumped many sharp minds. Some academics, including the preeminent economist Paul Samuelson, recognized the kinked payoff to contingent investments and the need to bring the value of the uncertain payoffs back to the present. However, the work that he published in 1965 and previous work in the area by others did not solve the discount rate problem.[4]

The solution developed by Fischer Black, Robert Merton, and Myron Scholes was a radical departure from the discounted cash flow approach. The three focused on factors that would change the value of an option over time. What is the value of an option at the time of its purchase? What is the value a bit later when less time remains and the value of the underlying asset has changed? The original option pricing work was for the valuation of stock option contracts traded on a financial exchange and of warrants, which are option contracts issued by companies.[5] Stock options are written on a company's equity, so much thought was given to how the value of the option would change with fluctuations in the stock price.

The dynamics of the relationship between the option value and the stock price are captured by a partial differential equation, an equation that reflects the simultaneous rates of change of several variables.[6] Black recalled that "I stared at the differential equation for many, many months. I made hundreds of silly mistakes that led me down blind alleys. Nothing worked. . . . [The calculations revealed that] the warrant value did not depend on the stock's expected return, or any other assets' expected return. That fascinated me."[7]

In late 1969, Black wrote down the partial differential equation and together with Scholes found a single-equation solution that provided the option value, now known as the Black-Scholes formula. Black, Scholes, and Merton argued over the meaning of the solution during the spring of 1970. Then one Saturday afternoon, Merton added the final piece: arbitrage.[8]

Arbitrage is the process that enforces the Law of One Price, the buying of an asset at one price and simultaneously selling it (or an equivalent asset) at a higher price. Arbitrage opportunities are rare and fleeting because professional investors move their money around to quickly close any pricing gaps. What Merton recognized was that the value of the option produced by the model must be free of arbitrage opportunities. Black later said, "A key part of the option paper I wrote with Myron Scholes was the arbitrage argument for deriving the formula. Bob [Merton] gave us that argument. It should probably be called the Black-Merton-Scholes paper."[9]

In 1973, Black and Scholes published their solution, and Merton published a paper with a more generalized approach to option valuation. Merton and Scholes were awarded the 1997 Nobel Prize in Economics for their work; Black had died in 1995.

The Option Valuation Model

The Black, Merton, and Scholes breakthrough uses an entirely different approach to work around the discount rate dilemma. They established the value of an option by constructing a portfolio of traded securities, known as a tracking portfolio, which has the same payoffs as the option. By the Law of One Price, two assets that have the same future payoffs must have the same current value. The option valuation model uses that "no arbitrage" condition to dynamically ensure that the value of the option equals the value of the portfolio as the stock price evolves. This is known as dynamic tracking.

Figure 3.1 illustrates how dynamic tracking is used to value an op-

Figure 3.1 Dynamic Tracking

In each short time interval, the change in value of the option is exactly offset by the change in the value of the tracking portfolio, resulting in a constant risk-free return to the hedge position. Dynamic tracking maintains the risk-free return by updating the composition of the tracking portfolio. The dynamic relationships are captured mathematically in the partial differential equation.

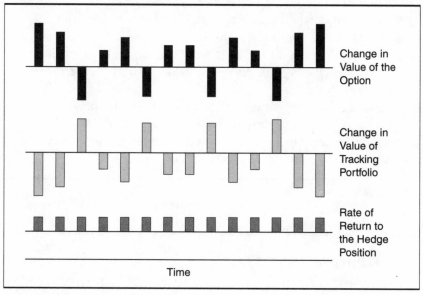

tion. Suppose the option payoffs are known and the tracking portfolio has been constructed to perfectly mimic the change in value of the option during a short time interval. The option and the tracking portfolio are combined in an offsetting manner into a hedge position. Suppose the value of the underlying asset changes. Because they are in offsetting positions, the change in value of the option will equal the change in value of the tracking portfolio. As a consequence, the value of the hedged position is independent of fluctuations in the underlying asset. The hedge position has no other source of uncertainty and so it earns a risk-free rate of return. (Risk-free return is the interest rate earned by entities that are entirely creditworthy during the period of a loan. The interest rate paid by the United States Treasury is considered risk free.) The value of the option determined by dynamic tracking ensures that there is no arbitrage opportunity between the option and the tracking portfolio.

Although we have been talking about option valuation relative to portfolios of traded securities, it is not necessary to actually buy them. Options, particularly real options, are most often valued by a pencil

Hedging and Insurance

Suppose you held two assets such that as one moved up, the other moved down by precisely the same amount. You would then be completely immune to price fluctuations, losses as well as gains. Hedging completely eliminates this risk. For example, a soft drink company can hedge the price of sugar by matching its planned purchases with offsetting sugar futures contracts. That ensures a fixed price of sugar.

An alternative strategy is to buy a financial contract that places a cap on sugar prices above a certain level. Now the soft drink company would profit if sugar prices fell unexpectedly, while being insured against losses if the price rose.

Derivatives Assets: Options, Forwards, and Futures Contracts

Options are one type of a derivative asset, an asset whose value depends on or is derived from the value of another, the underlying asset. Forward and futures contracts are also derivative assets and are frequently used in the tracking portfolio.

A forward contract is an agreement to buy or sell an asset in the future. The price is fixed at the time of the agreement, and payment is made at the delivery date. For example, a three-month forward contract for coffee sets the price at delivery three months hence. The value of the forward contract will change with fluctuations in the spot price of coffee.

A futures contract is a forward contract whose terms have been standardized for easier trading in the financial markets, including the daily settling up of the position. The market for futures contracts for a commodity is often more liquid than in the spot (or cash) market. Futures contracts are used in a number of markets, from interest rates to soybeans to electricity.

and paper exercise, "as if" the tracking portfolio was purchased and the riskless position established. Options are priced relative to the prices of the securities included in the tracking portfolio, relying on the financial market's valuation of the underlying asset.

Total Risk and Option Value

The option valuation model builds on the tools we introduced in Chapter 2. The value of an option depends directly on the payoffs to the contingent decision, the length of time to the decision date, and volatility.

Figure 3.2 shows how an increase in total risk increases the value of an option, all else being equal. In Figure 3.2(a), the payoff function is overlaid on two distributions of outcomes. When volatility is high, the distribution of outcomes is wider. Higher volatility results in a higher value of the option, as shown in Figure 3.2(b). The kinked payoff function creates a one-sided effect to volatility. Higher volatility leads to a higher chance of a bad outcome, but losses are limited. Higher volatility leads to a higher chance of a good outcome, creating value. Volatility, or equivalently, total risk is a critically important determinant of option value.[10]

Figure 3.2 Total Risk and Option Value

(a) An increase in total risk widens the distribution of outcomes, creating more outcomes with a positive payoff. (b) The one-sided effect increases the value of the option.

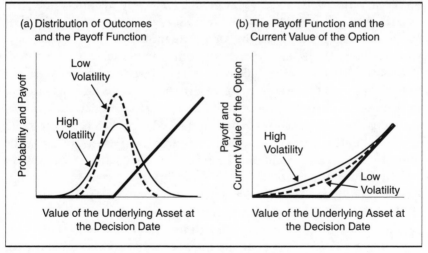

Getting Answers

We have just described the concepts behind a remarkable approach to valuation, but how do you get the number, the actual value of the option? The answer will depend on the particular features of the application that might restrict the solution method.

The partial differential equation that Black and Scholes studied mathematically defines the evolution of the value of the option in terms of the value of the underlying asset, its volatility, and the risk-free rate of return. As we discuss in Part II, different partial differential equations are specified to reflect the specific features of the option, and not all partial differential equations have an analytical solution. (In an analytical solution, the option value can be written as a function of the inputs.) The Black-Scholes equation is an elegant, single-equation solution to one particular partial differential equation. When an analytical solution is available, it is a simple matter to program the equation(s) into a spreadsheet. The Black-Scholes equation is well suited for simple real options, those with a single source of uncertainty and a single decision date.

When the application is more complex and includes particular features of a real asset, such as multiple sources of uncertainty or many decision dates, analytical solutions cannot be obtained. Specialized mathematical tools known as numerical methods are required.

One approach for handling complex real options, risk-neutral valuation, was introduced by John Cox and Stephen Ross in 1976 and later applied by these authors and Mark Rubinstein in a very useful manner in the binomial option valuation model.[11] The key insight of the risk-neutral approach is that because the option values are independent of everyone's risk preferences, the same valuations will be obtained even when we assume that everyone is indifferent to risk, or risk-neutral. This assumption simplifies calculations enormously because we do not need to estimate the premium for risk in the discount rate, because no investor requires compensation for taking on risk. A particularly simple, yet robust, implementation of the risk-neutral approach is the binomial option valuation model, in which the underlying asset moves up or down by a small amount in each short period. (See Chapter 8 for details.)

There are three advantages to the binomial option valuation model. First, it can span a large range of real option applications, including those with some complexity. Second, the approach is comfortable for many users because, although it is consistent with the option valuation breakthrough, it retains the appearance of discounted cash flow analysis. Third, uncertainty and the consequences of contingent

---

Valuing an Option: What You Need to Know

The following inputs are the only information you need to value an option.[12]

- *The current value of the underlying asset*, which is observed in the market
- *The time to the decision date*, which is defined by the features of the investment
- *The investment cost or exercise price (also called the strike price)*, which is defined by the features of the investment
- *The risk-free rate of interest*, which is observed in the market
- *The volatility of the underlying asset*, which is often the only estimated input
- *Cash payouts or noncapital gains returns to holding the underlying asset*, which are often directly observed in the market or sometimes estimated from related markets

An example: What is the value of an option to buy TV-Sat in six months' time at 125% of today's price? TV-Sat's stock is widely traded. The inputs required to evaluate the option are: the current price of TV-Sat; the length of time to the end of the option, six months; the guaranteed purchase price, 125% of the current price; the risk-free rate of interest, 5%; the annual stock price volatility of TV-Sat, 35%; and the dividends expected to be issued by TV-Sat during the next six months.

---

decisions are laid out in a natural way; the binomial model generates good visual images.

Important Implications of the Valuation Breakthrough

The power of the Black-Merton-Scholes breakthrough is easy to recognize. It is an elegant and objective way to characterize the relationship between risk and value. What does this amazing set of insights mean for strategic investments? Here's our short list:

- *Total risk matters for valuation.* This result fits with managerial intuition. Through dynamic tracking, the value of the option is updated for fluctuations in the underlying asset. The real options approach tracks the consequences of uncertainty on the value of the strategic investment.

- *Options can be riskier than the underlying asset.* Understanding option valuation gives managers a pair of glasses that allows them to identify and measure the risk exposure of their investments. When properly designed, small investments in options can be used to offset large exposures.

- *Very little information is needed about the underlying asset, often just the current value and its volatility.* This has an important implication for the typical "pinpoint" forecast of the future: Don't do it. Instead, the option value relies on the observed current value of the underlying asset and an estimate of volatility. Volatility is much more likely to be stable over time than any single forecasted variable.

- *Options are valued in a transparent, no-arbitrage manner.* Wall Street and the quant crowd fully understand the mathematics of dynamic tracking. There is no room for subjective inputs; when you use a subjective input, you've just created an arbitrage opportunity for someone else. This is how market discipline is imposed on valuation.

- *Option valuations can be done without trading.* The mathematical recipes for option valuation can be used without trading the option or purchasing the hedging portfolio. Thus, the approach can be applied to internal investment decisions as well as external transactions.

- *The whys and whens of imperfect tracking are transparent.* Trading opportunities replace the need for theoretical models about the price of risk and estimates based on subjective assessments about risk preferences. When dynamic tracking does not work perfectly, the option valuation model gives us the tools to understand why.

Going Head to Head: Comparing the Options Approach to Valuation to the Alternatives

Many corporations have a collection of tools to better understand the effect of uncertainty on large capital investments, and successful

---

Valuing an Option:
What You Don't Need to Know

What is *not needed* to value an option contributes greatly to its power. The following information is not used in the real options approach:

- *Probability estimates* of possible future stock prices are not needed because these are captured by the current value of the underlying asset and the volatility estimate.

- *The expected rate of return for the underlying asset* is not needed because the value of the underlying asset and the ability to form tracking portfolios already capture its risk/return trade-off.

- *The expected rate of return of the option* is not needed because the option is valued directly by dynamic tracking.

- *An adjustment to the discount rate for risk* is not needed because the valuation solution is independent of anyone's taste for risk.

---

consulting firms have been built to bring these tools to their clients. Many of these methods use discounted cash flow (DCF) and suffer from the discount rate dilemma mentioned earlier. Here's a quick rundown on how the methods compare to the real options approach on other dimensions.

- *DCF with scenario analysis.* Modifying a DCF analysis with scenarios is the first step to incorporating uncertainty, but each scenario remains fixed on a single future outcome and investment plan. There is no clear way to reconcile, aggregate, or choose between scenarios.

- *Decision analysis.* Often called decision tree analysis, decision analysis is a straightforward way to lay out future decisions and sources of uncertainty. Decision analysis, however, relies on subjective assessments of probabilities, subjective discount rates, and preferences about the objective.

- *Simulation analysis.* Simulation analysis lays out thousands of possible paths for the uncertain variables. It is very difficult to handle decision opportunities that arise before the final decision date in a simulation model. In addition, it is often hard to interpret the results of a simulation analysis because simulation models use a subjective discount rate and do not incorporate financial market information.

If carefully structured using the real options way of thinking, decision analysis, simulation analysis, and real options can be reconciled to produce identical results for some applications. In practice, however, the real options approach informs many details of framing the application, and we have found that getting the frame right is the critical determinant of success.

Changing the Practice of Corporate Investment

We have introduced the options approach to valuation at some length because we believe it is an important way of thinking about strategic investments. The following examples show how this way of thinking is used in practice.

Valuation of a Strategic Acquisition

C-Net is a large high-tech company that sells networking equipment. To fuel its growth, it is in constant need of new people and new products. C-Net's strategy is to obtain these by investing in smaller companies with good products and then, if things go well, to acquire a controlling interest. How much should C-Net invest in HotRing today in exchange for the option to acquire 51% of HotRing in two years for $33.2 million?

The option perspective recognizes that uncertainty drives the value of C-Net's option to acquire. The option has upside potential, and losses are limited to the size of today's investment.

The inputs needed to value the option are: 51% of HotRing's current market value, $30.6 million; the time to the decision date, two years; the cost to acquire 51% of HotRing, $33.2 million; the risk-free rate of return, 5%; and the annual stock price volatility, 45%. HotRing does not expect to pay dividends over the next two years. HotRing is a publicly traded company, so the tracking portfolio would be constructed from shares of HotRing and Treasury securities.

Figure 3.3 illustrates the valuation results. Using the Black-Scholes equation, the option to acquire is valued at $8.4 million, so C-Net

Figure 3.3 C-Net's Option to Buy HotRing

At today's stock price, 51% of HotRing is worth $30.6 million. Using the Black-Scholes equation, the current value of the option to acquire is $8.4 million. This is how much C-Net should invest in HotRing today in exchange for the option to acquire.

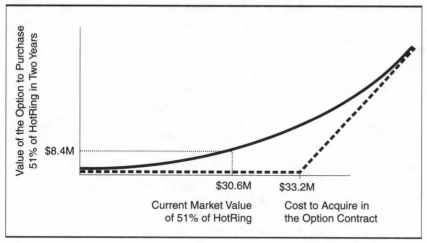

should be willing to invest up to this amount in HotRing. Only the option valuation model can value this common contingent investment.

Valuation of a Contractual Feature

Red & White, a soft drink company, buys a large volume of sugar each year from Big Beet, a farmers' cooperative. In the past, Red & White has paid the world spot price; however, Big Beet has offered a new supply contract that includes a price cap. The price cap in the new contract would limit the price Red & White pays to 10 cents per pound, if the world spot price is higher than this level. The proposed contract also has a 4-cents-per-pound annual up-front fee. Should Red & White take the contract with the price cap or just pay world spot market prices each month?

Figure 3.4 shows the payoff diagram for the price cap. When the price of sugar is above 10 cents per pound, Red & White's gain from the price cap increases with the price of sugar. A conventional analysis might be based on a forecast of the price of sugar, whereas an options analysis rests on volatility of sugar prices. The option valuation model is required to value the kinked payoff of the price cap; traditional tools cannot value the nonlinear payoffs.

Because Red & White takes deliveries and makes payments each month, the proposed contract actually contains 12 price caps. The in-

Figure 3.4 Payoff to Red & White's Price Cap

With the price cap in place, Red & White pays the world spot market price up to 10 cents a pound and 10 cents a pound for prices higher than this level. The gain from a price cap is obtained whenever the world price of sugar exceeds 10 cents a pound.

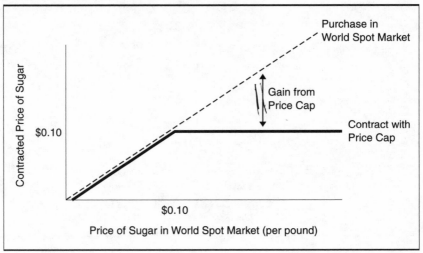

puts required for each cap are: the current price of sugar, 8 cents per pound; the length of time until the month of payment; the price cap at 10 cents per pound; the risk free rate of return, 5% per year; the volatility of the price of sugar, 37% per year; and the return to holding sugar inventories.[13] The tracking portfolio would be constructed from securities that depend on the price of sugar, such as sugar futures contracts.

The option valuation model shows that, at current prices, the value of the price cap to Red & White is 3.52 cents per pound, less than Big Beet's proposed up-front fee of 4 cents per pound. This means that the price cap is overpriced by 0.48 cents per pound, or $9.59 per ton. Red & White should buy sugar on the world spot market or ask an investment banker for a competitive quote for the cap.

The Option to Abandon

Classic Mill was a weaving mill in New England.[14] After World War I, cloth sales fell sharply, and the managers at Classic were considering closing operations. The only valuable asset was the looms, which had a scrap price of $25 per loom. The managers calculated that the value of future profits from continuing operations until the mill wore out was $21 per loom.[15] However, there was a great deal of uncertainty about continuing, because the profit margin between cloth prices and cotton prices fluctuated widely. The annual volatility of continued operations was 65%.

Traditional analyses suggest that Classic Mill should close its doors immediately. A real options analysis accounts for the uncertainty about the profit margin and suggests that the mill stay open. The option to abandon is shown in Figure 3.5. The underlying asset is the value of continuing. The figure shows that the payoff to abandonment has its highest value when the value of continuing is zero. As the value of continuing increases, abandoning requires giving up a valuable asset and so the payoff falls. The tracking portfolio can be constructed from a broad-based portfolio of New England textile mill stocks and U.S. Treasury securities.[16]

Figure 3.6 shows the optimal abandonment strategy for Classic Mill. The horizontal line is the scrap value of the mill ($25 per loom), and the curved line below it gives the critical values, the value of continued operations at which it is optimal to switch strategies and abandon. The critical value is below the scrap value because it is optimal to wait to see if profit margins will increase. As the physical life of the looms shortens, there is less value to waiting and the critical value converges to the scrap value.

The option to abandon shows that uncertainty makes it optimal for individual plants to operate until the value of continuing is well below

Figure 3.5 Classic Mill's Option to Abandon

The payoff from abandonment has its greatest value when the value of continued operations is zero. Uncertainty about the value of continued operations keeps the value of the option above its payoff in the area to the right of the salvage value.

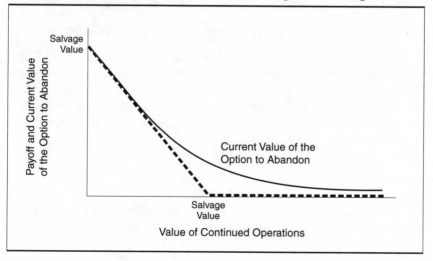

Figure 3.6 Classic Mill's Critical Values for Abandonment

The critical value of the underlying asset is the value at which it is optimal to change strategies. When many years remain, the critical value is well below the salvage value because uncertainty about the future makes it optimal to hang on to the looms. As time passes, there is less chance of a significant improvement in the value of continued operation and the critical value converges on the salvage value.

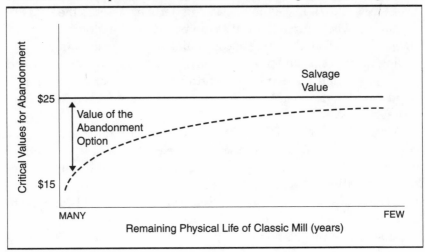

salvage values, leading to a persistence of excess capacity. The analysis can also be used to identify who will exit first, that is, the mill with the lowest-valued abandonment option. This type of real options thinking can be applied to modern industries, such as electric power generation, that have both excess capacity and tremendous uncertainty about future profits. Don't expect a quick exit by competitors.

The Discipline of the Option Valuation Model

This chapter has demonstrated how the financial market discipline permeates the real options approach. How do you know if you have a disciplined framing approach, if you have identified all the trends, sources of uncertainty, and managerial options? This is an important issue because the first step in a real options analysis is identifying and specifying the option.

> As Von Clausewitz craved the decisive battle, [then Intel Corp. Chairman Andrew S.] Grove hungers for the decisive risk, the bet that will guarantee Intel's future. "Are we missing something here?" Grove mused one day this spring over a lunch of tofu and ketchup, settling

his silverware into a moment of quiet. "Sometimes," he says in a rolling baritone, "the risk of omission is greater than the risk of commission.[17]

Our answer has two components. First, option valuation is based on objective inputs and a precise list of which inputs are needed and which are not. Those inputs are used in a way that produces market values, and the real options approach guides the user on where to look and why. Experienced users of the real options approach see the patterns, the types of options, and the important sources of uncertainty.

Second, the real options approach provides a framework for revising expectations. In the real options approach, investments are managed over time. The optimal exercise of managerial options requires frequent scans of the environment and updates of important information. Although it is impossible to always avoid the sin of omission, the disciplined thinking about the consequences of uncertainty in the real options approach can help.

There is no simple fix to traditional valuation tools—only the real options approach to valuation correctly values the managerial opportunities embedded in strategic investment. The alignment of valuation results with the discipline of the financial markets allows managers to use the real options approach for external transactions as well as internal evaluation of strategic investment opportunities.

Chapter 4

From Wall Street to Main Street: Options on Real Assets

> The option valuation breakthrough must be adapted for application to the real assets of strategic investments. Real options often depend on private risks as well as risks priced in the financial markets. However, continued innovation in the financial and product markets blurs the distinction between real and financial options, providing better valuations of real assets and creating more opportunities to manage the risks of strategic investments.

*T*he option valuation breakthrough described in Chapter 3 is a remarkable achievement, producing arbitrage-free valuations for financial option contracts. How should the option valuation model be adapted for options arising from real assets? How well does this approach actually work for real asset applications? Obviously our response is that it works very well—otherwise we would not have written this book!

One reason the framework works well for real asset applications is that the payoffs of the contingent investment decision can be tailored to virtually any situation. This is particularly important for the proactive design of products and contracts and is discussed in the first half of this chapter.

The second reason the framework works well for options on real assets is that it illuminates the nature of risk embedded in real assets. Managers know that although some of the risks they face come from market sources, others come from private sources shared by no one else. The real options approach extends the financial option valuation model to incorporate the effects of both market-priced risk and private risk in the valuation of strategic investment opportunities. In the second half of the chapter, we show why valuation errors might arise, how they are mitigated by financial market forces, and how firms can use the real options model to better understand and manage their risk profile.

Tailoring the Payoffs to Contingent Investment Decisions

As we've seen from the examples in Chapters 2 and 3, payoff diagrams come in several shapes. Real options can have fairly complex payoffs, but these payoffs can be built up from simple building blocks. Figure 4.1 gives the four basic shapes of the payoffs to contingent decision making. Figure 4.1(a) shows the payoff from an investment decision that takes advantage of potential good news or high values of the underlying asset. Known as a call option in the financial markets, this payoff arises from the right to buy the underlying asset at a fixed price. Figure 4.1(b) shows a payoff from a strategic investment that benefits from bad news, a payoff that reaches its highest value when the underlying asset is at its lowest value. Known as a put option, this payoff arises from the right to sell the underlying asset at a fixed price.

Pricing a Squiggle[1]

Question: How do you present this [option valuation] theory to your students?

Answer by Robert Merton: What the formula captures permeates many financial aspects of life. One way I present it in the classroom is to have the students design a security. They ask, "What's a squiggle?" I say, "I don't know yet. You're going to design it for me." And in real time, they design the payoffs to the security.

Then I say, "Now I'll show you how we price and analyze the risk of this just-created security." I take them through and apply the analysis, and boom—within a class session we've worked out how this thing has to be priced. So they see that even with an instrument that never existed before they came into the classroom that day, the theory allows us to price it and measure its risk.

Tailoring the Model for Employee Stock Options

Many companies reward employees for value growth by granting them stock options. A grant might consist of a number of options to buy the company's stock during the next 10 years at today's price, with the restriction that options can't be exercised until they are vested (transferred from the employer to the employee), which is done gradually over several years.

The standard option valuation model must be extended to account for several factors that affect how the options are exercised, including:

- *Lack of wealth diversification.* Employees typically are not well diversified, making them risk-averse, and they exercise their options early before the optimal exercise date.

- *"Blackout" periods.* There are significant periods of time in which key managers cannot exercise options because they hold insider information.

- *Taxes.* Tax considerations also change the value of exercising options and the optimal exercise date.

After parsimoniously adapting the option valuation model for these and other factors, academic research shows that the actual value obtained from employee stock options is less than would be predicted by standard option valuation models, such as the Black-Scholes equation. Two studies put the loss at 50% of the Black-Scholes value.[2]

Every transaction has two sides, and the payoff diagrams in Figures 4.1(c) and 4.1(d) are mirror images of the payoff diagrams in Figures 4.1(a) and 4.1(b). While one party realizes the payoff on the top row, the other party to the transaction realizes the payoff on the bottom row.

The *building-block approach* to option valuation breaks apart complex payoffs into simple-to-value and easy-to-understand components. All that is needed are the four option payoffs given in Figure 4.1 plus the payoffs to the two noncontingent investment decisions shown in Figure 4.2. Figure 4.2(a) shows a payoff from holding or purchasing an

Figure 4.1 The Building Blocks of Contingent Decisions

The top row shows the payoffs from holding an asset that confers the right (but not the obligation) to buy or sell at a fixed price. The payoffs in the bottom row are the mirror images and show the position of the party on the other side of the transaction.

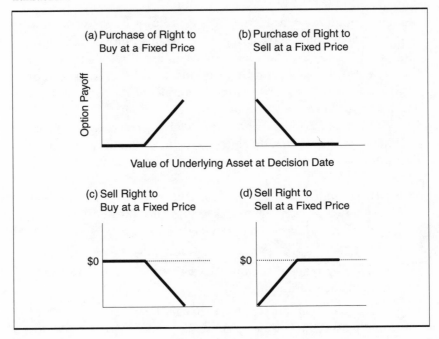

Figure 4.2 The Building Blocks of Noncontingent Decisions

A forward contract is the right to buy or sell an asset at a specified date in the future at a specified price. The payoffs to a forward are not contingent on a future decision (hence there is no kink) but do depend on the realized value of an uncertain asset (the line is sloped).

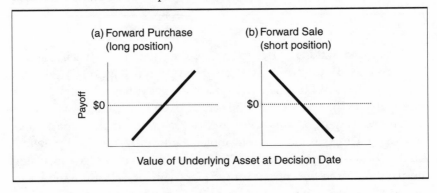

asset, known as a *long position* in the financial markets. Figure 4.2(b) shows a payoff from selling an asset, known as a *short position* in the financial markets.

For example, suppose Red & White, the soft drink manufacturer we discussed in Chapter 3, was offered a new sugar contract with a price floor of 90 cents per pound and a price cap of $1.10 per pound. Figure 4.3 shows the monthly payoff to these contract terms. Using the building-block approach, the contract can be seen as the sum of three parts:

1. Buy sugar on the world spot market.

2. Sell a put option with a strike price of $1.10.

3. Buy a call option with a strike price of 90 cents.

Figure 4.3 Identifying the Building Blocks in Red & White's Contract
(a) This contract requires Red & White to pay a minimum of 90 cents per pound and a maximum of $1.10 per pound. The building-block approach shows that the contract is equivalent to purchases in the world spot market (b) plus a put option with an exercise price at $1.10 per pound (c) plus a call option with an exercise price at 90 cents per pound (d).

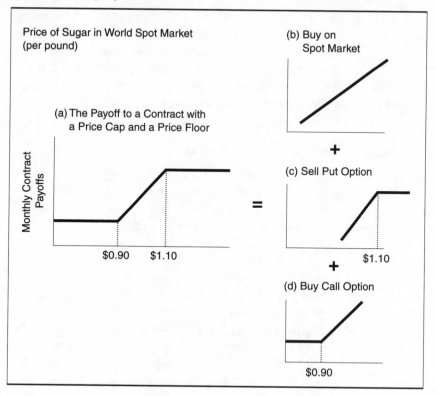

The building-block approach is also used to simplify the number crunching. The new contract can be valued using the Black-Scholes equation to separately value each option, and the calculations can be done from start to finish in just a few minutes.[3] This avoids developing a tailored numerical method to value nonstandard payoffs.

The option valuation framework has great scope because it can value virtually any type of contingent decision. In product development, for example, different design choices lead to different follow-on opportunities, to different contingent decisions. In large irreversible investments, the framework can be used to evaluate modifications to a construction schedule or the trade-offs between the cost of building in options to delay, abandon, expand, or accelerate against the additional value they create.

The building-block approach can be used to put together traded option contracts to obtain the complicated or tailored payoffs sometimes required by corporations. Investment bankers and sophisticated commodity dealers also develop tailored option contracts for their clients, known as proprietary or customized contracts. On many occasions, investment banks create a feature in the payoff that cannot be obtained in the financial markets, reflecting the bank's innovative recognition of the client's desired payoffs. Once they see the innovation, other banks reverse-engineer the contract by examining the payoffs, valuing the option, and then offering a competing product at a lower price. These services allow firms to better manage their risks by tailoring contract terms around the complex payoffs of real assets.

Valuing Options on Real Assets

Often managers wonder if the option valuation approach is applicable to real assets. We'll briefly introduce the wrinkles of real assets here and how they affect option valuation. The bottom line is that both financial and real option valuation can be less precise in practice than in theory because certain asset and market features can prevent the Law of One Price from holding. The consequences of the imprecision depend on the specifics of the firm and its industry.

The option valuation approach provides a clear visual image of the magnitude of imprecision in valuation. Perfect and imperfect tracking are illustrated in Figure 4.4. Recall from Chapter 3 that as the underlying asset fluctuates in value, the composition of the tracking portfolio is dynamically updated (the change in the value of the option is precisely matched by the change in the value of the tracking portfolio). In Figure 4.4(a) the option is perfectly tracked (or replicated) by the tracking

Figure 4.4 Perfect and Imperfect Tracking

Two sample paths for an option and its tracking portfolio are shown. (a) The option and the tracking portfolio move by exactly the same amount; the option is replicated by the tracking portfolio. (b) The tracking portfolio veers off the option value and there is imperfect tracking.

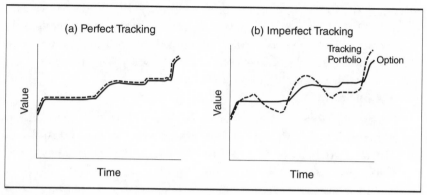

portfolio and the two lines are on top of each other. Figure 4.4(b) shows imperfect tracking. The tracking portfolio and the option clearly share some of the same sources of uncertainty, but the value of the tracking portfolio veers off the value of the option.

Two real asset features cause tracking error: the costs of tracking and the quality of the tracking (how closely the tracking portfolio moves with the value of the option). Perfect dynamic tracking requires frequent updates to the tracking portfolio. When it is costly to change portfolio positions, it may be optimal to let the value of the tracking portfolio wander away from the value of the option for a short time period.

For real options, the tracking portfolio may include commodities or even specific products and services. As Figure 4.5 illustrates, these and other real assets have three features that make dynamic tracking more difficult.

- *"Leakages" in value.* Real assets may generate cash payments, similar to a dividend, or require cash infusions. Convenience yield, an additional return, may be gained from holding a commodity inventory because it easily can be supplied to the market. Only the holder of the asset (not the holder of the option) obtains the convenience yield and cash flows from the underlying asset. To other parties, it appears that there is a "leakage" in the value of the underlying asset. An adjustment to the option valuation model is required because the holder of the option and the tracking portfolio do not get cash flows or convenience yields, they only experience the leakage in value. (These issues are discussed further in Chapter 9.)

- *Basis risk.* The traded securities in the tracking portfolio often are highly—but not perfectly—correlated with the value of the option. When the imperfect correlation is caused by differences in product quality, delivery location, or timing, the source of tracking error is known as basis risk. For example, an option on jet fuel for delivery in London may be imperfectly tracked by a portfolio containing heating oil futures or New York Mercantile Exchange (NYMEX) gasoline futures.

- *Private risk.* Real options have risks that are not contained in the available set of traded securities, risks that are not priced in the financial markets.[4] For example, risk of failing to develop a new technology is a private risk carried by a high-tech firm. The risk of not finding a large amount of oil in a particular prospect is a private risk borne by an oil firm. The effect of private risk in an option valuation model can be quantified, but it is not tracked by traded securities.

Figure 4.5 Tracking Error

When the tracking portfolio and the option have the same change in value during a short time interval there is perfect tracking. In all other cases there is imperfect tracking. Tracking error can be positive, as shown, or negative (the change in the value of the tracking portfolio exceeds the change in the value of the option.)

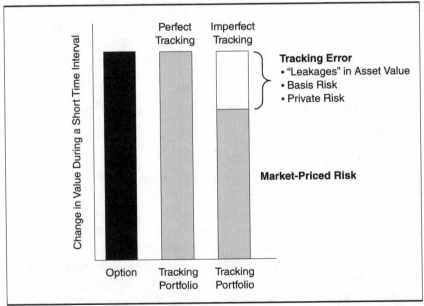

More about Convenience Yields and the Dynamics of Commodity Prices

Often commodity price fluctuations have a strong economic force behind them. For example, work stoppages in a major copper-producing country will create an unanticipated rise in world copper prices. Unusually warm winter weather will create a glut of heating oil, leading to a fall in heating oil prices. These economic forces affect the value of inventory and the value and volatility of commodity assets. When options are written on commodities or commodity-based securities, these forces change the dynamics of the underlying asset and require an adjustment to the option valuation model. The forces influencing commodity price fluctuations include:

- *The convenience yield.* In each short time interval the holder of a commodity inventory earns a return to capital (capital gains) and a convenience yield. For example, if you hold an inventory of aluminum, you expect a certain price appreciation plus you have the opportunity to feed the commodity into the market if there is an unexpected price rise. Only the holder of physical inventory can realize this convenience value and obtain the convenience yield.

- *Cost of holding a physical asset.* The magnitude of storage costs affects how quickly inventory is pushed into the market. For example, before the Gulf War, many parties wanted to store oil in or near the United States in anticipation of a supply interruption. Relatively inexpensive storage locations were quickly exhausted, and cost of storage soon became quite high. Small fluctuations in the world price of oil would then lead to movement in and out of the high-cost storage. Storage costs are paid only by the holders of the inventory, not by the holders of contracts tied to the price of oil.

- *Perishable or nonstorable commodities.* Some commodities (e.g., tomatoes and grapefruits) deteriorate in storage, and others can't be stored (e.g., electricity). These features are incorporated into the spot and futures market pricing.

More about Private Risk

Fast Sound is a modem company considering a radical new design, one that will require an expected $20 million in product development. There is worry about whether the product development can be completed on budget. During product development, Fast Sound will be learning more about its *private risk* and the value of the market for modems, which depends largely on sales of personal computers. (Consequently, uncertainty about the value of the product market is a market-priced risk.) Fast Sound may abandon the project if there is bad news about either or both its private risk and its market-priced risk.

The tracking portfolio for the option to abandon contains stocks in several personal computer companies, so although the value of the new design will depend on both market-priced and private risk, the tracking portfolio will only mimic the option's sensitivity to the value of the market opportunity. Private risk causes imperfect tracking of the option to abandon because the value of the option is greater than the value of the tracking portfolio. This is because private risk increases the range of possible outcomes. For example, Fast Sound might experience technical failure and a shrinking market, technical failure and a growing market, technical success and a growing market, and so on. There is no additional loss in value from the lose-lose combination of private and market-priced risk, and there is a gain in value from the win-win combination, so the value of the option to abandon is greater than the value of the tracking portfolio.

Many personal decisions are options with only private risk. Examples include the decision to bring an umbrella on a cloudy day (the option to have shelter from rain); the decision to bring skis and a snowboard on a mountain trip (the option to switch); and the decision to purchase additional collision coverage for your car (the option to limit losses if you have an accident). Information about private risk is gathered from historical experience, such as actuarial data, and is not inferred from market prices, so the real options approach has no particular advantage over other methods. Business decisions, however, are always affected by the price of some asset in the economy, and the real options approach extends financial market discipline to the valuation of options whose value depends on a mix of private and market-priced risk.

More about Basis Risk

Basis risk arises when differences exist between the standardized traded security and the true underlying asset, causing the values of the tracking portfolio to diverge from the value of the option. These differences are product quality (wheat vs. flour; high-sulfur coal vs. low-sulfur coal); geography (natural gas contracts specify delivery in Louisiana vs. the actual purchase takes place in Florida); and timing (a soybean futures contract specifies delivery in April vs. a planned purchase in mid-March). The consequences of basis risk depend on the specifics of the option and the firm. (Additional examples of basis risk are given in Chapter 9.)

For example, Sunnyside, a national chain of coffee shops, recently expanded into baking bread made from organic flour. It has entered into a long-term supply contract, with an option to cancel at some penalty. There are no traded flour contracts in the commodity markets, and the price of flour is not perfectly correlated with the price of wheat. The value of the option to cancel has tracking error caused by basis risk.

Suppose Sunnyside decided to buy a hedge on the price of wheat to protect itself against wheat price fluctuations. Because the price of wheat and the price of flour are highly correlated, Sunnyside believed it was purchasing flour price certainty. Things worked well for three years, until heavy rainstorms washed out key railroad lines between the Midwest and the flour mills. The price of flour shot up far more than the price of wheat, and Sunnyside suffered embarrassing losses, forcing the firm to slow its growth. The consequences of the basis risk event were high, so Sunnyside decided to eliminate the basis risk by purchasing a tailored hedge on the price of flour from its investment banker.

Tracking Costs

When there are significant tracking costs, the tracking portfolio is updated less frequently, creating tracking error. In addition to the direct fees and expenses, tracking costs include:

- *Infrequent trading.* Securities markets have nearly continuous trading, but trading in commodity, product, and service markets can be much less frequent. Dynamic tracking can be accomplished only infrequently.

- *Liquidity.* Low liquidity (a small daily volume of trades) increases the cost of dynamic tracking because it leads to wider bid-ask spreads and may cause the market price to move as the tracking portfolio is established and updated. Low liquidity is present in certain segments of the financial markets, so this is something Wall Street traders worry about as well.

- *Increased costs of monitoring, coordinating, and documenting.* The physical nature of real assets requires tailored infrastructures. For example, how do you track the ownership of electricity as it flows through the national market? How can it be used as an underlying asset for option contracts? Currently most real asset markets are not as standardized as financial markets, reducing the value obtained from the underlying asset and the option.

- *Infrequent observability.* The tracking portfolio for a real option may include securities that are traded off the exchange, with infrequent reporting. For example, early in the evolution of the deregulated natural gas market, the traded contracts were based on monthly settlements. Within the month, tracking errors were high and opportunities to exercise options at their highest value were missed. Enron stepped into this market opportunity and began offering natural gas securities based on daily prices.[5]

The Trade-off Between Tracking Error and Tracking Costs

Selecting securities for the tracking portfolio often requires a trade-off between a security that is weakly correlated with the underlying asset but with low tracking costs and a security that is highly correlated with the underlying asset but with high tracking costs. Either selection will cause tracking error. Characterizing and quantifying this trade-off is on the frontiers of financial market research.[6]

The recent history of failed products on commodity exchanges shows that market participants are willing to forgo quality of the tracking in exchange for low tracking costs. Examples include the introduction of a soft wheat futures contract for wheat grown in the Pacific Northwest. This product failed when market players continued to use the more liquid, but not highly correlated, hard wheat futures contract on wheat grown in the Midwest. Flour contracts have failed because the risk is more effectively hedged with wheat contracts; barley contracts have failed because the risk is more effectively hedged with corn; and so on.[7]

Financial Market Innovations Blur the Lines Between Real and Financial Assets

Two groups drive innovation in the financial markets: (1) market creators, investment banks, and commodity dealers who profit from new products and markets and (2) market participants, companies that benefit from transferring some of their risk to other parties. Market developments and risk management strategies are accelerated by the migration of derivatives thinkers—players from established markets who have seen the power of option pricing tools for pricing and identifying new business opportunities. For example, the electricity market is evolving toward a more deregulated commodity-like structure. Futures contracts have been introduced, quickly following the emergence of spot markets. Bankers and brokers migrating from other markets have introduced sophisticated derivative contracts for risk management and arbitrage across energy markets.[8]

There are powerful consequences to financial innovation, in the specific market and in related markets and technologies. First, financial market innovations reduce tracking error by increasing the range of risks priced in traded securities. Inflation bonds, for example, have payoffs that depend directly on measured inflation and interest rates. Before this security was introduced, inflation was treated as private risk or one imperfectly tracked by market-priced securities.

Second, the emergence of one market or security often sparks developments in other markets. The pollution allowance market created by the U.S. government is an example. In 1990, the U.S. government imposed a cap on total sulfur dioxide emissions nationwide through the year 2010. Each polluter was given an allocation of sulfur dioxide allowances, the right to emit one ton of pollutants in a designated year or any year thereafter. The cap declines each year, and polluters can either purchase allowances to continue polluting at current levels or install a technology, known as a scrubber, to physically remove pollutants. Analysts quickly recognized that the purchase of an allowance was the acquisition of the option to wait to install scrubbers.[9] The initial predictions were that the allowances would trade at over $500 per ton, reflecting the marginal cost of scrubber technology.[10]

In fact, sulfur dioxide pollution allowances have been trading below $100 per ton. The pricing of pollution made the trade-offs between low-sulfur (low-pollution coal) and high-sulfur (high-pollution coal) more explicit. As coal contracts came up for renewal, the utilities with the largest emissions switched to low-sulfur coal, reducing their emissions to below 1990 levels. The price of allowances fell, and the value of the option to wait to acquire a scrubber increased.

Third, financial innovations spark real asset innovations to support market trading. Recent changes in natural gas storage technology are an example.[11] In the early 1980s, before deregulation of the natural gas markets, gas storage facilities were used to hedge against delivery disruptions and to supply gas for peak demand. The gas storage technology was rather inflexible, because gas could be cycled in and out of storage only once per year. Under deregulation, the spot and futures market for gas experienced a great deal of monthly price volatility, and many players used the available monthly futures and forward contracts to create "synthetic storage." These contracts, however, could not be used to manage intramonth volatility, which could be large. Meanwhile, gas storage technology was developed that allowed more frequent and flexible withdrawals. This created the opportunity to physically arbitrage the intramonth market and led to the introduction of new financial contracts for managing intramonth volatility.

Fourth, financial innovations in established markets often lead to a huge growth in proprietary or off-exchange contracts. For example, 45 times more sulfur dioxide pollution allowances are transferred privately between polluters than are sold in the public markets, and there is virtually no difference in the private and public market prices.[12] This experience is typical. Investment banks typically find that the gains to financial innovation are not larger profit margins but greater market share in the market for proprietary contracts and trading services for standardized contracts.[13]

> The growth of the OTC (proprietary) market will continue to outstrip the growth of the exchange market. . . . The current growth path is to provide more client-focused structured solutions to problems. The clients most likely find it less expensive to execute a program through their financial service firm than to execute it themselves in the exchange market, and this is all the more so, if the positions must be adjusted frequently to hedge risks.[14]

Developing the Right Application Frame

Although the option valuation model vastly increases our ability to value financial and nonfinancial assets, it remains a model. Our experience is that model risk, caused by poorly structured inputs and a model framework, fails to capture the key drivers of option value and is the largest potential source of error in the real options approach.

This issue is significant for real and financial options. Investment banks receive quick feedback on the quality of their valuation models when the security has a short time to maturity or is widely traded. But for many long-lived and relatively illiquid securities, market feedback takes several years and the bank can evaluate the quality of the model and inputs only when the security has withstood a wide range of outcomes for the underlying asset.

Framing a model requires trade-offs. Novice users of the real options approach tend to include too many sources of uncertainty in the model framework, increasing the potential for tracking error. Over-specifying private risk increases model error. In many cases, direct modeling of private risk can be avoided, because the financial markets have priced the appropriate bundle of risk. For example, consider the value of an option to buy a start-up company, one facing product market and technology uncertainty. A good proxy for the underlying

---

The Importance of Model Risk on Wall Street

As we write this book, a pending merger between two Swiss banks highlighted the importance of model risk. United Bank of Switzerland (UBS) had a large presence in the equity derivatives market, creating options on stocks and other securities. *The Economist* explains: "Competitors and insiders alike were surprised that UBS won almost every deal it bid for. UBS did a particularly large amount of business selling long-dated options. Rivals openly wondered whether UBS was garnering so much business by selling its wares too cheaply. At least one bank went so far as to tell UBS informally of its worries. 'Either these guys had found a new way of pricing options, or they were just plain wrong,' reckons an executive there. . . . Derivatives contracts can run for several years. They can sit on a bank's books, all but unnoticed, while losses build up. And if a faulty computer model leads a bank to make deals at too low a price, the problem is likely to afflict an entire series of trades, rather than just a single transaction. This is why, when losses are reported, the amounts are often stunningly large."[15]

asset for the option is an index of high-tech companies that have recently gone public, companies that face the same bundle of risk as the start-up.[16]

The real options approach can be tailored for each application, including the specific features of real assets. Through continued innovations, financial markets are changing private risk and basis risk into market-priced risk and, as the next chapter shows, provide new opportunities for managing the risk of strategic investments.

Chapter **5**

Disciplined Strategy

A disciplined strategy fully uses financial market information and transaction opportunities to align corporate investment decisions with shareholder wealth creation. Fifteen years ago Stewart Myers of MIT wrote that corporate strategy and corporate finance address the same issue—obtaining the highest return on risky investments—and that including real options in the analysis could be a valuable bridge between the two disciplines.[1] This argument is immediate and compelling in today's business environment.

*T*his chapter takes a look at how the real options approach can be used to create, evaluate, and implement a disciplined strategy, a strategy that fully reflects the information, frameworks, and opportunities created by financial markets. The discipline keeps the firm on its value-maximizing trajectory and ensures that trade-offs and decisions are consistent for internal projects and external transactions. The real options approach can support the strategy creation process in two ways: The real options way of thinking expands the vision and alternatives considered in strategy creation, and the real options tool kit translates strategic vision into a tactical investment plan. These ideas are at the frontiers of the real options approach, and we expect the application of real options thinking to corporate strategy to be an active area of inquiry in the next few years. This chapter introduces frameworks we've found helpful and provides examples from various industries.

Disciplined Strategy Defined

Managers are increasingly required to make important decisions in the face of enormous uncertainty, and as the previous chapters have argued, uncertainty provides opportunities to gain. How should strategy be designed and implemented to capture these opportunities? Managerial options are valuable. What are the key points in which a managerial option will provide the most leverage?

Suppose three senior managers at a firm are wrestling with these questions. Using current tools and perspectives, they might use different information sets, make different assumptions about markets and products, and come up with three different strategies. How do they know which strategy is best? How do they know that another, not-yet-conceived strategy is not better? How do they communicate to the financial markets the wisdom of their choice? A disciplined approach to strategy addresses these questions about results by changing the process of strategy creation.

> Until we can distinguish between an event that is truly random
> and an event that is the result of cause and effect, we will never
> know whether what we see is what we'll get, nor how we got what
> we got.[2]

From both its tools and as a way of thinking, the real options approach infuses the strategy creation process with discipline because it:

- *Expands the menu of resources and strategic alternatives evaluated.* Options and value can be acquired in-house or through contracts and trades in the financial and product markets.

- *Expands the range of markets evaluated.* Markets are related, and the real options tool kit illuminates these links.

- *Illuminates the risk of strategic alternatives.* Corporate strategy must be aligned with corporate tolerance for risk. The real options toolkit can help frame this discussion.

- *Provides consistent "apples-to-apples" comparisons of internal projects, contracts, and market transactions.* Using the real options approach, all valuations are aligned with the financial markets. This allows the right trade-offs to be made across diverse sets of investment opportunities.

- *Illuminates the value and risk in contracts.* Licenses, joint ventures, and strategic alliances allow firms to share specialized resources and are key strategic levers in modern markets. These agreements can also lead to an enormous loss in value if they are poorly structured. The real options approach strengthens the agreements by linking the terms and conditions to the configuration of real assets needed for a successful implementation.

- *Focuses on the right questions.* This might be the greatest advantage of the real options approach; it gives managers a way of thinking about how to create value from uncertainty and how to identify the risks and potential pitfalls of the complex contingent business opportunities that are arising in rapidly changing markets.

- *Acknowledges the role of luck.* Firms get lucky. Look back at an industry and the competing firms. What was a good strategy? It was the one that worked. Was it the result of luck or foresight? It was both. The real options approach has the tools for positioning assets across the range of possible outcomes and for separating the roles of luck and managerial decision making.

The Need for Disciplined Strategy

Two economic forces create the need for the real options approach to strategy creation. First, in many industries the payoffs to investment are nonlinear. We provide examples of important business opportunities in which conventional tools fail to capture the upside potential and the trade-offs required in strategic decisions.

Second, in many industries there is a need to transact through alliances, joint ventures, licenses, and so on. Many technologies have become too complex and specialized for one firm to be the master of it all, and the only way to obtain best-in-the-class capabilities for each specialized resource is through transactions.

These transactions are also points of great exposure to the financial markets. For example, RamBus is a semiconductor firm with no manufacturing facilities. It lives or dies by its ability to license its designs to other companies. As a publicly traded company, RamBus must explain these transactions to Wall Street, and analyst reports on the firm reflect great familiarity with its licensing strategies and successes. Companies like RamBus recognize that licenses, licensing strategy, and strategic relationships move stock prices—there is not much distinction between internal and external alternatives. Hence, it becomes very important to ensure that all decisions are aligned with financial market valuations.

Using the Real Options Way of Thinking to Support Strategy Creation

As a way of thinking, the real options approach changes the strategy creation process and leads to different strategic plans. Figure 5.1 traces through this change in thinking for the electric generation industry. As electricity markets rapidly become deregulated, generation capacity is often spun off as a separate business unit. In the recent past, these assets generated electricity that was sold to captive local customers at a regulated price. Now the assets are exposed to competitive market forces of hourly spot prices in a regional wholesale market. The real options approach can help managers think through new strategies.

In the product market, a traditional industry and competitive analysis would quickly point to the commodity-like pricing structure of the new regional markets: generation capacity is used only when the hourly price of electricity exceeds the short-term marginal cost of generation. Short-term profits can be made by capacity with low marginal cost. Long-term profits require even higher profit margins, and many industry veterans wonder how they can maintain the capacity in the new ultracompetitive market. The real options approach adds two dimensions. First, it can be used to develop optimal generation-asset operating policies based on product market information. This ensures that capacity is operated in the value-maximizing manner, in a way that covers full long-term costs. Second, it can be used to expand the analysis to contracts and other transactions that complement the operating policy while creating value by managing price risk for end-users. These contracts can be tailored to match the operating and idling costs of particular units, creating pockets of profitability in the competitive market. (In Chapter 17, we show how the opportunity to mix physical and financial options changes the optimal operating strategy.)

If we look internally, a real options perspective complements traditional resource-based perspectives by identifying new capabilities needed, such as the ability to obtain and use financial and product market information for operations. Another set of new capabilities is required to create and trade financial contracts in the power markets in a way that complements the operating policies of the physical assets. A third set of capabilities is required to fully integrate physical and financial perspectives—generation capacity will not be rewarded for keeping risk that is more efficiently borne in the financial markets.

As the external and internal perspectives are combined, the real options approach adds new questions for the evaluation of strategic

Figure 5.1 The Real Options Approach and Strategy Creation

An illustrative example for strategy creation in the electric generation industry is shown. The white boxes are the analyses and factors identified by traditional tools, and the gray boxes are the expansion of alternatives and analyses provided by the real options way of thinking. The result is selection of a different set of investment choices.

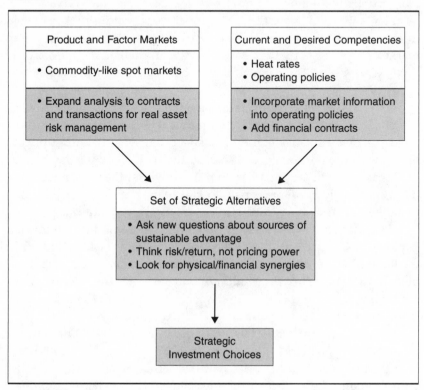

alternatives. Instead of looking for opportunities to increase pricing power, as might be suggested by traditional industry and competitive analyses, the real options approach identifies and values opportunities to create value through risk management. For example, can coal and gas contracts be restructured to reduce exposure of electricity-generating assets? And finally, real options tools help to sift through the set of strategic alternatives, make dollar comparisons across strategies, and identify the schedule of tactical investments. We'll give more detail on this last step toward the end of this chapter.

With this general framework in mind, we now turn to examples of how real options thinking provides new insights for corporate strategy creation and implementation.

Creating Markets to Profit from Risk Management at Enron

The Enron experience is a powerful example of how real options thinking can break down traditional industry structures and how real options tools allow comparison of contractual and physical investments. Enron is now the top electricity and natural gas marketer in the United States. Starting as a natural gas pipeline, then a gas marketer, Enron's current activities have been challenging the conventional wisdom that there is a boundary between the electricity and gas industries.

As a gas marketer, Enron gained market share by taking on natural gas price risk for its customers, offering them tailored contracts such as fixed prices for fixed volume or fixed volume at fluctuating prices. Enron's willingness to take on other parties' risk distinguished it from other gas marketing companies. Enron could offer these products only if it could get rid of the price risk, so it developed in-house capabilities to hedge and trade financial instruments based on natural gas prices.

For example, if Enron sold a five-year, fixed-volume, fixed-price contract at 65 cents per mbtu, it would offset this risk by buying a tracking portfolio of financial contracts and physical assets. The combined position (the hedge) would not fluctuate with the price of gas. If the tracking portfolio cost 63 cents per mbtu, Enron would lock in a risk-free profit of 2 cents per mbtu.

Developing capabilities to shed gas price risk allowed Enron to expand its marketing operations. Enron's 1992 annual report showed that its exposure to natural gas price risk was actually quite low—a 1% increase in natural gas prices would lead to a 0.12% increase in Enron's profits. By 1996, Enron had used this low exposure to expand its business in three areas: the day-to-day buying and selling of natural gas (cash and physical market), services to customers to hedge price risk and basis risk, and a financial services division offering financing for natural gas exploration and processing expansion.

In 1997, Enron consolidated its trading operations, putting electricity and gas traders in the same room. This reflected the company's ability to arbitrage the two markets. Through its vast network of physical transmission capacity, contracted capacity, and generation assets, Enron can offer cross-market contracts to customers that better meet their risk-management needs. Although it operates in competitive, commodity-like markets, Enron has been able to use its superior "derivatives thinking" to create profits through contracts that manage risk and return.

In sum, Enron has implemented a disciplined strategy by expanding the scope of markets in its industry by integrating physical investments, financial and product contracts, and trading functions.

R&D and Other Noncash-Generating Investments

R&D investments typify a critically important valuation problem: How much should you invest in a project that never generates cash? On a stand-alone basis, R&D has a negative value; it costs more than the present value of the direct cash flows it generates. But everyone recognizes that R&D is valuable—particularly R&D managers who want to justify their budgets! How can R&D be aligned with corporate strategy? Traditional tools fail to capture the value everyone sees.

The real options approach values R&D by linking the R&D investment to the opportunities it creates for follow-on investments. As most decision makers recognize, R&D is a platform investment, one that generates options. Consider a product that requires one round of R&D and one round of product development and then is launched. R&D creates options—the option to continue through to product development and the option to launch. For example, the option to start product development will be exercised, or used, if the value of the launch option exceeds the product development cost. (The cost of the launch is included in the value of the launch.) The value of R&D is the value of these follow-on opportunities, accounting for the fact that they may not be used. R&D is often called a platform investment because it creates many product development options from a single R&D investment. For example, basic research in materials may be applied in products used in several industries.

Platform investments are hard to value, even with the real options approach, because an important part of the future is "unknowable" and is easily omitted from the platform valuation. This means that, even with best efforts, we are likely to undervalue R&D. But a real options analysis is very useful when the question is turned around; instead of asking, "What is the value of my platform investment?" ask, "What does it take in terms of particular outcomes and payoffs from future investments to justify this initial investment?" The reversed analysis identifies the necessary events, the investments needed, and the required exposure to uncertainty. The reversed analysis also disciplines R&D investment strategy by aligning it with the end market, including end-market uncertainty.

Two features of R&D—an investment that does not generate cash and the platform of options created—are common to many other investment opportunities, including start-up ventures, redesign of product architectures, and so on. We give some examples below.

Platform Investments in Search of a Business Model: The Rough Road of Internet Start-ups

Internet start-ups are different from other "traditional" start-ups because of the large platform investments they require. The Internet is a young industry, still in search of profitable business models, with a rapidly evolving industry infrastructure. Internet start-ups are forced to continue making platform investments just to keep up. The evolving infrastructure creates market openings for competitors and new entrants, yet Internet start-ups must move on to the follow-on investments, such as marketing and business development, that convert business promise into cash flow.

What does it take to succeed in this environment? The platform investment will be wasted if there is no company left to execute the options created. Consequently, real options thinking identifies two critical capabilities for Internet start-ups: nimbleness and financial backing. As the company makes a series of attempts to arrive at the business model, it must be ready to change course and it must have the financial pipeline to do so. Financial backing tied to one strategy will cripple the firm. (The emerging industry for personal digital assistants has also required these capabilities, which we discuss later.)

The evolving nature of Internet business models makes the risk of an Internet start-up much greater than risks faced by start-ups in other industries.[3] From the real options perspective, Internet start-ups are options on options on options on options to generate cash flow. If you don't get started on the sequence, you won't resolve the uncertainty about your business model. If you don't start the sequence, you won't have the market intelligence needed to migrate with the shifts in business models. There is a role for luck, because there are a large number of options standing between current operations and profitability, and there is a role for disciplined strategy, to keep the firm's investments and strategy aligned with the Internet's growth potential.

Corporate Venture Capital Strategies to Resolve Private Risk

In the past few years, Intel Corp. has invested over $500 million in more than 50 companies that are developing products that will use

Life at the Conference Table

Red Howard is the coauthor of a comic strip about the venture capital business and the pen name of Robert von Goeben, a partner at a venture capital fund specializing in Internet investments. He is also a veteran of several pioneering Internet ventures and is all too familiar with the difficulties in valuing Internet start-ups before they generate revenues. Here's his humorous take on the valuation of start-ups, framed as a conversation between the CEO of the start-up and the venture capitalist:

> "Tell me, how do you value companies?"
>
> "Well, if they're on the hockey stick[4] it is usually a multiple of revenue."
>
> "But my company doesn't have revenue yet."
>
> "Oh. . . . Then it's typically a multiple of your last round."
>
> "But this is our first round of funding."
>
> "Hmmm. . . . For seed deals we apply our custom valuation matrix."
>
> "Valuation matrix?"
>
> "It's a complicated algorithm that factors in projections and potential. We'll run the model on your company and get back to you."
>
> Later that day, a dart hits the dartboard: "Bull's-eye—$3 million! Great shot!"[5]

Intel's chips. The real options way of thinking provides insights on how to manage these investments and when Intel should put additional funds into each. The start-ups have a mix of private (technical) risk and market-priced risk. Even though they are in the same industry, the start-ups differ in the relative magnitude of the two sources of uncertainty. For some start-ups, the biggest challenge is private risk, such as a product development bottleneck. Intel can throw dollars or software developers at this problem, increasing the value of the start-up by reducing uncertainty. For other start-ups, the biggest challenge is evolution of the product market, a market-priced risk. When Intel can't influence this outcome, it should stand back, let the market evolve, and make further investments only after market conditions exceed some critical level. Intel should be using two strategies to manage these corporate venture investments, sometimes at the same time. Without a discipline created by milestones and communication of expectations inside Intel and in the start-ups, it could be very easy to overinvest, to throw money at problems that money won't solve, and to have fruitless (and endless) negotiations with the start-up entrepreneurs.

Why would Intel, which has over 85% market share of microprocessors, start this new and seemingly unrelated strategic endeavor? Real options thinking identifies a key incentive: exposure. Historically there have been strong cycles in chip demand; now that Intel is the market, it is fully exposed to industry cycles and product market uncertainty. The commanding market share eliminates strategies based on holding revenues steady in a declining market by increasing market share. Intel must maintain volume to maintain revenues.

The investments in the potential chip-using start-ups help Intel increase growth in chip demand and remove volatility from the value of Intel. As the price of chips goes up, Intel's manufacturing division becomes more profitable, but the value of the chip-using start-ups falls because they must pay more for a key input. As the price of chips goes down, the value of the start-ups increases. Over time, demand from these companies will reduce Intel's exposure to fluctuations in volume. Texas Instruments is also making a large number of corporate venture capital investments in a segment of the chip business in which it holds a commanding lead, digital signal processing.

What is striking about the corporate venture capital strategy being used in the semiconductor industry is that it takes remarkably different corporate capabilities to achieve success. The traditional focus on volume and margin is replaced by the complex task of managing investments with many follow-on options.

Writing Contingent Contracts: Biogen and Merck

> The pharmaceutical industry's research and development operations are beginning to look more like venture capitalists—whereas in the past they had to manage a large portfolio of product development programmes, today they have to manage a large portfolio of biotech alliances.[6]

Pharmaceuticals and other industries are doing more and more business through licenses, joint ventures, and alliances. The real options perspective breaks open the problem of how to value these complex deals and how to discipline contract design to ensure that the terms are aligned with financial market pricing. For example, in December 1997, Biogen Inc. announced that it had signed an agreement with Merck & Co. to help it develop and bring to market an asthma drug.[7] Biogen received an up-front payment of $15 million from Merck, plus a potential $130 million in milestone payments over several years. If all works out well, Biogen will finish the development of the drug and Merck will market and distribute it. What is the value of the agreement to Merck? What is Merck's risk? What are the value and the risk of the agreement to Biogen?

To complete the drug development, Biogen must guide the potential product through clinical testing. During this process, the Food and Drug Administration (FDA) may require Biogen to refocus its development efforts, expand the tests, or possibly even abandon the drug for safety reasons. Also, the market for asthma drugs may change significantly during the years of testing. Drug development can be seen as a series of options, in which the payoff to one stage of development is the option to go on to the next.

The deal is worth more than $145 million to Merck and less than $145 million to Biogen. With each milestone payment, Merck obtains the option to continue, but it has downside protection because it can abandon the development effort. Merck's payments are capped by the agreement, but its upside potential is not; the value of the agreement to Merck is the value of the stream of options. These options were created through the joint venture agreement; they were "written," or sold, by Biogen to Merck.

The value of the joint venture to Biogen is the expected value of the milestone payments plus an option it obtained through an additional contract clause—an option to enter the Japanese market through a Merck affiliate. Because the milestone payments are received only if the development is continued, their expected value depends on the likelihood of Merck exercising all its options. The value of the license depends on options transferred from Biogen to Merck, and these cannot be valued using traditional tools.

The Nonlinear Payoffs of an Increasing Returns Industry: The Case of PDAs

If used correctly, the options method allows one to manage risk intelligently. It seems a particularly useful tool for risky situations like establishing de facto standards that relate to the increasing returns winner-take-all economy. In such situations, payoff distributions are exceedingly nonlinear with potentially counterintuitive results pertaining to the value of a particular set of technology options.[8]

The personal digital assistant (PDA) industry is a clear-cut example of a competitive industry dynamic known as increasing returns. Early investments in the industry were made by prominent companies—such as Apple and other consumer electronic firms—but were unsuccessful. Over a billion dollars was spent trying to develop and market a handheld electronic device to consumers.[9] The eventual winner, Palm Computing, also had some false starts before finding a product configuration that matched consumers' needs.

W. Brian Arthur, a leading author on increasing returns economics, characterizes competition in an increasing returns industry as series of quests for the next big winner, when winner takes all.[10] The real options view is that product development in an increasing returns industry is a sequence of options, with a nearly vertical payoff to the final option. This characteristic makes it worthwhile to invest enormous sums of money to search for a viable product. In contrast, investments made in a diminishing returns environment have less leverage, are less likely to preempt competitors, and show decreasing returns to further investment.

Most high-technology industries have some increasing returns strategies, such as "give away your Web browser, then charge the millions of dedicated users fees for related services" or "let anyone download Java for free and build applications, increasing the likelihood that it will become a standard." In these cases, the winner leverages its initial success with the energy and dynamics of resources supplied by other firms, accelerating the establishment of standards and making the product purchase decision more compelling.

The history of the PDA industry illuminates the need for a disciplined strategy based on nimbleness, a corporate flexibility in which many options during the search process and a base of resources allow execution of new options. Palm Computing's first strategy was to assemble a "virtual" company and define its product through partnerships with major players such as Tandy, Casio, Geoworks, Intuit, and America Online. The big players contributed manufacturing, the operating system, and so on. The first product, introduced in 1993, failed. Palm Computing had enough resources, however, to go out and get market data to redefine its product. In its second attempt, Palm kept control of the product design. Then, to obtain the resources to execute the option to market that had been created by the new design, Palm Computing sold itself to US Robotics. The PalmPilot, Palm Computing's second product, was a success and has started an industry. Now more than 5,000 programmers are working on software applications for PDAs, and more than 200 developers are designing hardware add-ons.

Another insight from real options thinking is about control of options. Palm Computing has created an opportunity for other firms to cluster around its design, and their products make the purchase of the PalmPilot more compelling. Palm Computing has created product development options and given them away to other companies. If Palm Computing makes these options more costly to exercise, fewer add-ons will be developed, and sales of the PalmPilot will fall. To preserve the options held by others, Palm Computing must carefully evolve its architecture. This constrains its strategy, but by giving away options Palm Computing has vastly increased the resources spent on development, making the product more attractive to the consumer.

Managing Portfolios of Options: Modular Software Development at Microsoft and Netscape

Modules are self-contained components that can be aggregated into a product. Many products can be designed in an integrated fashion with few components or in a modular fashion in which each component operates independently. The real options perspective views modular product design as the creation of a portfolio of options. Because the modules are independent, they can be used to evolve product features, such as to update this module, drop that module, divide up a third module, and so on. Good design rules allow the modules to evolve independently and create valuable options; poor design rules require coordination of changes and limit options.

Both Microsoft and Netscape have used modular software designs in their products. Microsoft has developed several organizational features that allow it to retain much of the value of the modules while constraining their independence. Teams are organized around product features or modules and are allowed to develop their feature independently. Coordination and consistency across the product are obtained by requiring modules to be reintegrated into the product each day. Microsoft reduces performance uncertainty by assigning a "testing buddy" to each programmer, someone who tests the code as it is being written. Finally, Microsoft constrains the independent development of modules by establishing a fixed product budget. This requires trade-offs across modules and keeps independent groups focused on the integrated product.

Netscape has used the modularity of its browser to update its product more easily in response to fast-evolving technology developments on the Internet. For example, it released a large number of working copies of its browser for testing to internal and external users and then incorporated their feedback into many updates before the official release.

Product modularity can change an industry structure. A group of engineers, unhappy with the funds and attention their module is getting from senior management, can walk out and start a company. (For example, the disk drive industry got started this way; at one time there were 114 independent disk drive companies.[11]) Such departures can be prevented by substantially increasing product development resources once a modular architecture has been adopted. But if a company fails to allocate sufficient resources it will not be obtaining the benefit of the modular architecture. A value-maximizing disciplined strategy recognizes that modules tend to take on a life of their own and often move out of the company. Some control must be transferred to the modules, regardless of whether their development is in or out of the company.

How do modules get together? Through alliances, joint ventures, and technology licenses—all the transaction structures prevalent in today's computer industry. Real options tools can support disciplined strategies created around these transaction opportunities.

Using Real Options Tools to Translate Vision into Investment Strategy

In addition to being a lens for seeing strategic alternatives, real options tools can support the process of translating the vision into specific investment programs. Chapter 14 describes how one mortgage bank evaluated whether it should invest in an image processing system. Originally presented by the chief information officer as a stand-alone project, the proposal opened up a larger decision-making process that was supported by the real options approach. Figure 5.2 illustrates how senior management wrestled with the links between the project and their broader vision.

National Mortgage Trust (NMT) was a prominent Canadian mortgage provider that wanted to expand its revenues and profitability. Using traditional tools, NMT identified a promising new strategy: Increase the flow and profitability of mortgages by tailoring them more specifically to homeowner preferences and financial needs and further increase the profitability by packaging the mortgages into securities to be sold in the financial markets. At the time of the analysis, NMT was selling standard mortgages to homeowners and passing them on to another party that transformed them into securities. The new capabilities would allow NMT to break out of its current business practices. The top of Figure 5.2 shows the process that set the vision, identified the de-

Figure 5.2 Translating Vision into Investment Strategy

The real options approach provides a way of thinking that can be used to expand the set of alternatives considered early in the strategy process, and also provides a tool kit to help map strategy concepts into strategic plans. The gray areas in each box represent the additional insights and analysis suggested by the real options approach. The top four boxes in the figure are also shown in Figure 5.1.

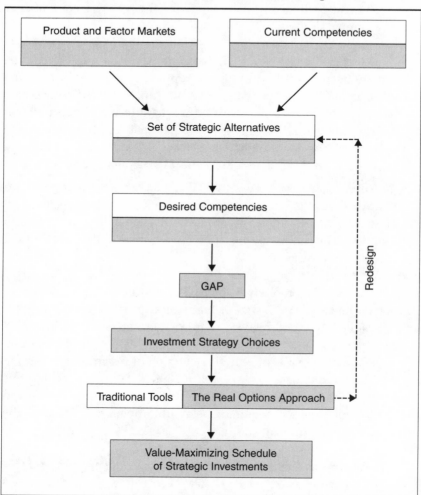

sired capabilities, and analyzed the gap between current and desired capabilities. The specific new capabilities included a more streamlined application process, the ability to process and value tailored mortgages, and the infrastructure and routines to service the variety of mortgages.

Further analysis identified that the gap between current and desired capabilities could be closed by several investment strategies, all including some kind of investment in information technology. Investment in an image processing system was part of most of the investment strategy alternatives. To further detail the size and timing of the investment in this technology, real options tools were used to better articulate the effect of uncertainty and how the technology fit into the larger picture.[12] The real options approach highlighted two key factors missed by conventional thinking:

- *The role of external factors.* NMT faced internal uncertainty: Could the capabilities be acquired in the appropriate time frame? Could the information technology be successfully implemented? But it also faced external uncertainty: Would market growth support the expansion of services? Would interest rates remain at a level to keep the volume of mortgages high? The real options analysis showed how the external environment would affect implementation success.

- *The entire schedule of investment needed to build the capabilities.* A conventional analysis would focus on the information technology alone, but a "drilling down" from desired capabilities to outcomes identified the additional investments required in training and the redesign of routines.

The real options tool kit helped NMT restructure the investment plans and develop a pilot project that would produce meaningful results—results that could be used to make a go/no go decision on full implementation. NMT successfully carried out the pilot program, which included a small-scale implementation of the image processing system. The technology worked well for NMT. However, during this time external factors changed, and the real options approach showed that a strategic shift was required: Delay full implementation until the mortgage demand improved.

This chapter has been a quick tour of a few important applications of the real options approach for corporate strategy. Our bottom line is that the real options way of thinking gives the manager the same probing perspective that doctors bring to their patients: where to look, what the symptoms mean, and what questions to ask. The real options tool kit helps managers implement corporate strategy and identifies when to be flexible in its implementation.

Chapter **6**

Quick Lessons

> Part II of this book outlines the real options solution process and how to "crunch the numbers," and Part III provides a collection of case studies. Before moving on, however, it is useful to summarize the immediate lessons of the real options approach for valuation, analysis, and implementation.

New users of the real options approach often get buried in the details and lose sight of its simple and powerful implications. This chapter brings together some of the insights and new intuitions of the real options approach. The lessons can be applied without building a detailed numerical analysis and can also be used to confirm that an analysis is proceeding in the right direction. They can serve as "rules of thumb" as applications develop and as quick reference points for evaluating new investment opportunities. Many of the lessons are illustrated with examples, including highlights of the case studies in Part III.

Lessons for Valuation

Lesson: A higher level of uncertainty increases the value of the option.

Most managers fear high levels of uncertainty, but the real options approach shows that a higher level of uncertainty increases the value of an option. Uncertainty widens the range of potential outcomes. Contingent decision making limits the loss of a bad outcome, so that greater uncertainty has only the one-sided effect of increasing upside potential.

- Laga Realty owns an operating peach orchard and is evaluating a condo development on their property (Chapter 15). *Should they develop it right away or wait?* Laga Realty has the option to wait to develop. The value of waiting depends largely on uncertainty. The more uncertain the value of developed land, the more value there is in waiting to avoid an unpleasant surprise.

- Portlandia Ale is a start-up microbrewery, chasing a very uncertain market opportunity (Chapter 10). *Does the high level of uncertainty help or hurt Portlandia?* The high level of uncertainty increases the value of the start-up, a real options insight that reverses conventional wisdom. Losses are limited to the small initial investment, and with a high level of uncertainty there is a higher chance of a great payoff.

Lesson: Options create value but may be costly to acquire.

Managers need not use an option and will only do so if it increases the firm's value. Options are not free, however. Capital equipment with built-in options is more expensive. Modular product designs create options but require more up-front investment in the product architecture.

- Redwood Ventures is evaluating whether to invest $10 million in a start-up. The value of the start-up comes from its growth options—opportunities to invest today to obtain the right for further investments (Chapter 11). *Should Redwood Ventures make the investment?* The answer depends on the value of the option. Not all growth options are attractive investment opportunities.

- RamDesign competes in a rapidly evolving marketplace and is considering spending $20 million to reorganize product development so that key modules could be left open until the last minute. *Is the investment worthwhile?* The answer depends on whether the value of the option to wait to finalize products (which will depend on the level of uncertainty in the marketplace) exceeds $20 million.

- Widgets Inc. is evaluating a plant modernization investment, and traditional tools show a large negative value for the investment. Thinking that the option for a staged expansion might turn the negative result into a positive one, the CEO asked his staff to do a more sophisticated real options analysis. *Should this analysis be done?* Only if the economic consequences of uncertainty are large. When there is little uncertainty or not much exposure to uncertainty, there is no need to invest in identifying and valuing the option.

Analysis

Lesson: Start with a simple and transparent framework.

Framing the application is *the* critical step to a good result. The framework should be simple, so everyone can build intuition, and should avoid overmodeling private risk whenever possible. If the relevant risks are captured in traded securities, use them.

- A banker must value a new start-up company, Buy/Sell, which supplies tools for companies to sell products on the Internet. The banker recognizes that the growth options of Buy/Sell depend on several factors: growth of Internet use, growth of Internet commerce, and technical hurdles in completing its products. *Should the valuation framework include all of these sources of uncertainty?* For many purposes, Buy/Sell's growth options can be framed in terms of two risks: its private risk of product development and the market-priced risk of the value of an Internet-driven business opportunity. This bundle of risks can be captured by an index of Internet firms. (Figure A.1 in the appendix shows one such index.)

- Orange County Loans was worried about financing costs, credit risk, and earthquake risk in its local market. It was considering developing a specialized valuation model to make development decisions. *How should financing costs and earthquake risk be treated in the model?* If this model had been built 10 years ago, interest-rate fluctuations would have been a market-priced risk, while credit quality and earthquake risks would have been private risks. Now new financial products—catastrophe bonds and credit derivatives—allow these sources of risk to be market-priced.

Lesson: Identify all the options.

Often managers think of investment decisions as now or never, not considering the option to wait. Sometimes managers evaluate the physical options but not the financial market opportunities to obtain the same flexibility at a cheaper price. Too often managers stop at the first option they find, not recognizing that the real options way of thinking is also about expanding the set of investment alternatives considered.

- New Jersey Refining temporarily shuts down when its gross profit margin falls to a sufficiently low level, incurring sizable shutdown and start-up costs (Chapter 17). Cash flows are necessarily erratic during these periods. *Are there opportunities in the financial markets to insure against the operating cash flow losses?* New Jersey must evaluate whether insurance against losses constructed from financial contracts on the "crack spread" (a measure of a refinery's gross profit margin) is more valuable than a physical shutdown option. When synthetic options are available, it is often cheaper to obtain flexibility through financial contracts than by reconfiguring physical assets.

- Ole Foods is under a tight budget constraint this year but has many valuable investment opportunities. *What should Ole consider when selecting projects for investment this year?* Ole should evaluate the option of waiting another year to start a project, as well as the project's value if it started this year. Some investment opportunities will erode quickly, and others will be preserved. Ole's best strategy is to pick projects so as to maximize the total value of the project portfolios over both years.

Lesson: Think far (into the future) and think wide (across the firm).

Many investment opportunities are rejected because traditional tools—and managers who hunger for certainty—ignore the options for follow-on investments. The real options approach helps managers identify follow-on investment opportunities and their pervasive effects throughout the firm. Options to delay, to temporarily shut down, to abandon, and to rewrite investment plans in midstream can significantly increase value.

- PC Inc. faced a trade-off in its product architecture. It could spend more time and money to create a modular design for its new product, or it could upgrade its current, more integrated design. *Is an investment in modularity always the best choice?* PC Inc. recognized that it would take time for the company and other vendors to organize around delivering upgrades and innovations for the modules, so the payoffs to a redesign might be slow in coming. PC Inc. also recognized that most of the value of modularity came from three key modules. It decided to create just those modules, using a hybrid modular-integrated design to reduce the required investment.

- Mega-Pharm is evaluating a huge investment in a scientific process that will greatly expand the number of compounds it can evaluate.

The payoff to the investment is a larger number of products starting the uncertain process of clinical testing. *How can Mega-Pharm structure the investment to increase its long-term value?* Drug development is an expensive, lengthy, and highly uncertain process. As scientific testing proceeds, Mega-Pharm has many points at which it can exercise the option to abandon a drug project because its value falls below the costs of developing and marketing the drug. The payoff to the large investment can be increased by increasing the number of project reviews and using the abandonment option in a disciplined manner—more drug project starts, more abandonment of marginal and failing projects, and faster transfer of resources to other projects.

- The chief information officer at NMT presented a plan for a $5 million investment in a new imaging system, arguing that it is critical for long-term growth. Senior management worried that the benefits are elusive and uncertain (Chapter 14). *Should this project be dumped?* Before senior management could answer the question, they had to decide on the big picture. What were the vision and the desired capabilities? An analysis showed that the investment in the imaging system was important for achieving the desired capabilities. To increase the value of the investment program, acquisition of the imaging system was staged and a pilot project was undertaken.

Lesson: Look to the financial markets for relevant information.

In some applications the prominent feature of the problem frame is the private risk. Examples include the success or failure of a technology, the scientific risk of drug development, and the geology of oil exploration. Market-priced risk should not be ignored, because decisions are triggered by the interaction of private risk and the market-priced risk.

- Houston Oil was evaluating opportunities to explore for oil in several tracts in Russia. As the engineers reviewed the geological data, they assumed that oil prices would remain constant for the next seven years, the time it would take to complete the planned investments (Chapter 12). *How do oil prices affect the oil exploration decision?* Greater uncertainty about oil prices makes exploration investment more valuable. It increases the payoff of any geological good news, while losses remain fixed at the cost of the exploration investment.

- Great Kids invested heavily in the development of a new video game for children. Their product was a technical marvel. *Will investors flock to Great Kids?* Technical success is only a part of the picture. Investors recognize that entrepreneurial success is a combination of luck (there was a valuable market opportunity) and good technical management (the technology worked on time and on budget).

Lesson: Don't hunger for too much precision.

We live in an uncertain world, but most of our decision-making tools do not fully reflect that uncertainty; the analyses carry an unrealistic degree of certainty. One of the lessons of the real options approach is that strategic investment decisions must be dynamically managed, updated, and revised over time. It is not realistic to pin down the entire investment schedule at any time, only the range of possible outcomes.

Lesson: Don't sweat the details (but do sweat the frame).

Often new users of the real options approach get caught up in the details of numerical methods, the volatility input, and so on. Although these details do impact the results, more often the real options analysis misses its mark because the problem is poorly structured or framed.

Implementation
Lesson: Options must be identified and exercised.

A real options analysis identifies actions managers can take to increase the value of strategic investments. But to capture the value shown on paper, managers must establish an organizational culture that uses options.

- Grace is a product manager for Web Windows, a software company, and her project has been having technical difficulties. *What happens if Grace brings the problem to the attention of senior managers?* Grace will not reveal the news (exactly the information her managers want to know) if the corporate norm is that killing the project will kill her career. Organizations need to be ready to exercise the options they have identified.

Lesson: Watch the trigger.

The real options approach identifies the risk exposure of the investment strategy and the critical value of the underlying tracking asset, the value that triggers a change in the optimal investment strategy. Tools to scan the relevant markets and to make the appropriate response can be pushed down the organization.

- MidAmerica Manufacturing can burn either oil or natural gas to generate electricity (Chapter 16). *How can MidAmerica best use this flexibility?* MidAmerica must monitor the relative prices of oil and gas. When the price of one becomes significantly cheaper than the price of the other, the ratio of prices hits a critical value (determined by a real options analysis), and the corporate intranet automatically sends an urgent e-mail to three key managers so they can switch fuels.

Lesson: It takes a team.

In many companies, the real options approach is introduced by an advocate, an employee who has the vision of the potential improvement in decision making. But to implement the real options approach in your organization, several kinds of people need to be involved: those who can communicate to senior management, those who can develop the quantitative tools, and those who can identify the full set of investment opportunities for the company.

These quick lessons have shown how a review of applications builds an intuition about the effects of uncertainty on investment strategy. The portfolio of applications in Part III will take your intuition up another level.

PART *II*

THE
REAL OPTIONS
SOLUTION
PROCESS

We change our focus in the next few chapters, from the broad implications and power of the real options approach to the "how tos" of option valuation. We show how the arguments behind the option valuation solution shape the process of framing and implementation. A recurring theme throughout Part II is the importance of the application frame. New users often have many questions about the details of option solution methods and create modeling error by focusing on these issues while neglecting the application frame.

Chapter **7**

The Four-Step
Solution Process

This chapter is an overview of the four-step solution process for real options applications, a process that allows users to build up to the "real options way of thinking" and ensures that the right focus is maintained as the application is developed. The chapter is also a road map for new users and a reference point for the case studies in Part III.

While an option in a financial contract is clearly identified, the option in a real options application is sometimes much harder to spot. In the real options approach there is much more need to think through the application frame, making sure that it covers the right issues and achieves the right balance between a simplicity that preserves intuition and richness that delivers realistic and useful results. As a result, implementation of the real options approach requires the integration of a fair amount of detailed material, from the construction of inputs to number crunching. This chapter provides an overview, emphasizing the two steps in the solution process that require important managerial input—framing the application and reviewing the results.

Figure 7.1 summarizes the four-step solution process. Throughout the process, the financial markets are an important point of reference: to better frame the application, for inputs and valuation models, and to provide a benchmark for interpreting the results. Chapters 8 and 9 provide more detail on implementation, including an overview of solution methods, or options calculators as we call them. Chapters 10 through 19 demonstrate the solution process in action.

Figure 7.1 The Solution Process

The four steps of the real options solution process are guided by the financial markets: framing and orienting the application; data and valuation models; reviewing results against financial market benchmarks; and identifying contractual opportunities that might improve the investment design.

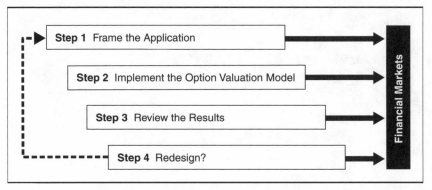

Step 1: Frame the Application

Robert Jarrow, an academic who frequently works on Wall Street, summarizes the framing issue: "The more realistic the model, the more time-consuming it is to compute and estimate, and to understand and use intelligently. People tend to want to use the simplest model for the product and application at hand so that intuition can play a part. If the models become too complex, you lose a lot of the intuition."[1] Our experience is that poorly framed applications are the biggest source of error in real options applications. Figure 7.2 shows the components of Step 1, framing the application.

The Decision

To get started, everyone needs to be "on the same page." Experienced managers will have a strong intuition about the type of decision to be made, when, and by whom, but the analyst who is setting up the application may not. Also, when managers put their heads together to frame a real options application, they often find they have gaps in knowledge, assumptions, and communication.

To quickly identify and solve these problems, begin the process of framing by writing a description of the decision. Clearly state what the contingent decision is, what observable variable triggers the decision, and who has the authority to execute the decision. This statement will be a useful reference point for the solution process.

Figure 7.2 Step 1: Frame the Application

Real options are not specified in a contract, but must be identified through analysis and judgment. Developing a good application frame is the most important step in the real options approach.

- **The Decision**
  Create a word picture: What are the possible decisions, when might they be made, and who is making them?

- **The Uncertainty**
  Identify the form of evolution for each source of uncertainty and lay out any cash flows and/or convenience yields.

- **The Decision Rule**
  Create a simple mathematical expression.

- **Look to the Financial Markets**
  Which sources of uncertainty are private and which are market-priced? Is there an alternate application frame that better uses financial market information?

- **Review for Transparency and Simplicity**
  Who would understand this application frame? Managers who make these kinds of decisions right now? An industry analyst? Your boss?

Some investments have more than one decision; some investments contain more than one option. Real options applications often have a mix of options in a layered or sequential structure. Complex options should be broken apart using the building-block approach for better intuition and easier valuation. Although it is possible to have interactions between options (the payoff of one option depends on the exercise strategy of another), these are not typically the focus of the analysis, and in practice it is better to reframe the application for better tractability and transparency.

The Sources of Uncertainty

There is a difference between financial options and real options regarding the sources of uncertainty. For example, suppose you held a financial option contract on a stock—you had an option to buy 100 shares of Netscape. The contract terms specify the observable underlying asset (Netscape stock). Netscape stock securities are used in the tracking portfolio, resulting in perfect tracking.

Real options are more complex. They often have multiple sources of uncertainty and a mix of private and market-priced risk. The sources of uncertainty that trigger the execution of options may not be observable. For example, one month before its public offering in 1995, what sources of uncertainty would you identify as driving the value of an option to buy 100 shares of Netscape? (Ignore liquidity and transaction costs.) Netscape was one of the first Internet companies to go public, so there were no industry comparables. The Internet was just emerging, and investors were not familiar with its technology and prospects. A portfolio of technology stocks plus a source of private risk to capture

---

A Taxonomy of Options

Here are the kinds of options that often arise in a real options analysis:

- *Operating options* provide flexibility to respond to uncertainty while the asset is being used or operated. Examples include when to switch inputs, when to switch outputs, and when to temporarily shut down a plant. The value of an asset in a real options analysis includes the optimal use of all operating options.

- *Investment and dis-investment options* may significantly change the asset configuration, including decisions about scale (expansion, contraction, or disposal) and choices between type and scale of investment (asset A or asset B). Timing options are also included, such as the option to accelerate or delay investment. Some investments create options by modifying the set of feasible decisions in the future and thus changing possible investment strategies. For example, when platform investments are used in an industry with a short product cycle, investing in one cycle creates an opportunity to invest in the next product cycle.

- *Contractual options* are specific contract terms that change the risk profile faced by asset owners. For example, venture capitalists frequently include contract terms that give them priority in liquidation (down-side protection) and rights to invest alongside follow-on investors (protection against dilution of the up-side potential).

firm-specific effects might be the best approximation to the sources of uncertainty driving Netscape's value.

Establishing the source(s) of uncertainty for a real options application requires a good understanding of the option valuation arguments and modeling judgment. Unlike financial option contracts, sources of uncertainty affecting real options must be identified and framed. Having established the sources, the next task in the solution process is to identify the form of uncertainty.

The Form of Uncertainty

We have been using the cone of uncertainty to depict how uncertainty evolves over time. The more precise concept behind this phrase is a mathematical expression, known as the stochastic process, that describes the evolution of an uncertain variable over time. When the uncertain variable is allowed to evolve continuously, it is modeled as a continuous-time stochastic process, also called a diffusion process. Figure 7.3 shows sample paths arising from two different diffusion processes, log-normal and mean-reverting.

The Black-Merton-Scholes breakthrough used a log-normal diffusion process (also called geometric Brownian motion) to model the sto-

Figure 7.3 Two Forms of Market-Priced Risk
The log-normal process is often used to model the evolution of asset prices because prices are never below zero. Its path can wander over a wide range. The mean-reverting process often arises in commodity-based industries in which there is a strong market force that pulls the path toward a long-run mean.

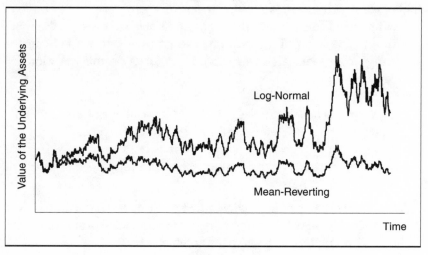

chastic evolution of stock prices. The most salient characteristics of the log-normal process are that stock prices cannot fall below zero (consistent with the limited liability of equity) and that the distribution of outcomes at the final decision date has a long tail to the right (reflecting a small chance of large-value outcomes). The log-normal distribution for stock prices is consistent with the use of the familiar bell-shaped normal distribution for stock returns.[2] As you look out into the future, the possible range of paths for the log-normal diffusion process widens with the length of the time horizon, as in the cone of uncertainty. Mathematically the variance of the stock returns grows with the time horizon; equivalently the volatility of stock returns (measured by the standard deviation) grows with the square root of the length of the time horizon.[3]

The cone of uncertainty can be interpreted as a summary of the mean and the standard deviation of a log-normal process. The fan of the cone widens with the square root of the length of the time horizon, and the tilt of the cone is determined by the expected capital gains return, the expected rate of price appreciation.

The second sample path in Figure 7.3 is the result of a mean-reverting process.[4] Mean-reversion describes the evolution of commodity prices or other assets that experience short-run shocks that move prices away from a long-run level and market forces (such as supply and demand) that push them back. For example, copper prices typically fluctuate about a mean level, one that corresponds to the costs of the least efficient producer with sales in the market. A surge in demand may lift prices, but as new suppliers enter with only slightly higher costs, prices will fall back to near the mean.

Often new users to the real options approach worry about the specification of the form of uncertainty, asking themselves, "Is it mean-reverting or log-normal?" You should not focus on this question for two important reasons:

1. *Logically it may not matter.* Consider a financial option contract on a security whose price followed a mean-reverting process. With dynamic tracking, the value of the option is exactly mimicked by the tracking portfolio, so the form of the uncertainty doesn't enter the option valuation result.

2. *It is likely to be a matter of judgment.* Statistical tests have little power to discriminate between mean-reversion and log-normal specifications, leaving the decision to judgment.[5]

"Electricity Traders Shocked by Black-Scholes"[6]

Thus read the headline in a recent article on the trading of option contracts in the electricity market. Some traders are using the Black-Scholes equation to price electricity option contracts and believe that electricity price dynamics are consistent with the model's assumption that the underlying asset—in this case electricity prices—follows a log-normal diffusion process. Other traders believe that electricity prices are strongly mean-reverting. The article reported that arbitrageurs are betting with their trading activity that the Black-Scholes equation results are in error because of the diffusion assumption and are producing results that are lower than the true value of the electricity option contracts. However, as one industry analyst noted, "model arbitrage" is a high-risk strategy, particularly as markets change and traders update their models.

Private Risk

Private risk frequently enters into a real options application. Examples of private risk include the distribution of the size of an underground oil reservoir, the distribution of the failure rate of a nuclear power plant, and the distribution of the total cost of completing the development of a new product.

In addition, the nature of private risk may vary over time. For example, a nuclear power plant may be periodically inspected, leading to a periodic probability of a forced shutdown. Staircase reductions in private risk arise in learning investments, when each stage of investment reduces the range of possible outcomes; without the investment, there is no reduction in the private risk.

Carefully specifying the nature of private risk and the form and origins of market-priced risk leads to better results. Computationally it is difficult to value options with more than three or four sources of uncertainty, so an iteration back to the word picture may be needed, picking out only those sources of private risk most important for decision making.

Leakage in Asset Value

Real assets often have leakage in value—cash flows and convenience yields that accrue before the option decision date—and these can be uncertain as well. Any leakage in value must be accounted for in the option valuation; adjustments to the option valuation model are discussed in detail in Chapter 9.

The Decision Rule

Having identified the option and the sources of uncertainty that influence its value, we need to get more specific. What does the decision actually depend on? How? The simplest answer is a short mathematical expression, such as: Restart production when variable profits exceed variable costs. When there is one source of uncertainty, it is also straightforward to write down a payoff diagram, an important reference point in the application frame. When there are multiple sources of uncertainty, a separate payoff diagram could be created for each source of uncertainty, but this quickly gets confusing. As our case studies show, you can keep track of all the possible outcomes using some simple diagrams with the decision rule.

Try to make your decision rule as specific as possible—this is when errors in the application frame often get sorted out. For example, is the decision really based on the level of cash flow, or should it be made based on the value of the business opportunity? What must be known to make a decision? What can be ignored for one decision but not for another?

As an example, consider Cute Puffs, a manufacturer of disposable diapers. Cute Puffs planned to outsource production until its disposable diaper sales in China grew large enough to warrant building a plant. Diapers made in-house cost 20 cents each. Meanwhile Cute Puffs was paying 50 cents per diaper to the outside vendor. Cute Puffs had a five-year contract with the vendor, with an option to cancel at any time. The cost of building a plant was $4 million. The decision rule for the investment is to build the plant when:

Value of diaper sales with outsourcing
is less than
Value of diaper sales using in-house production
– $4 million construction cost – the option to wait

Without including the option to wait, Cute Puffs might build the plant too soon, based on a short-lived burst in sales. (We discuss the option to wait in more detail in Chapter 15.)

Look to the Financial Markets

How can the application frame be structured to make best use of financial market information? In the following three examples, the underlying asset captures the key risks affecting option value and is based on the securities priced in the financial markets.

- Jumping Junior, an indoor playland, was expanding operations. Its near-term growth was largely determined by its ability to identify and execute its growth options. The underlying asset is the value of a mature playland business, which could be tracked by a portfolio of playland or amusement companies.

- Quick Call was a high-tech start-up facing a bundle of technical and product market risks for its telecommunication and Internet infrastructure products. PhoneZ held an option to acquire Quick Call during the next two years for $40 million. The underlying asset is the equity of Quick Call and is best tracked by a portfolio of publicly traded companies developing similar products.

- Maple, a venture capital firm, was structuring the terms of its investment in a start-up, Baby Tech. Maple negotiated the right to participate in future rounds of funding and wanted to have objective milestones and performance criteria to evaluate Baby Tech's progress. The real options valuation model included private risk, capturing uncertainty about the remaining development costs, and market-priced risk, capturing uncertainty about the value of the product market opportunity.

Review for Transparency and Simplicity

The real options approach is a way of thinking, and when the application frame becomes too complex, much of the benefit is lost. When the application is hard to understand, no one has the time or patience to work through the implications of the results, to identify fruitful follow-on projects, or to redesign the investment strategy. To avoid losing the full value of the analysis, you should:

- Make sure you can explain the frame to managers who make decisions in the area—it should align and sharpen their intuition.

- Make sure your boss can understand the frame—it should be simple enough to be intuited by busy, experienced senior managers.

- Make sure you can explain the frame to someone with broad experience in your industry but who has no vested interest in the outcome. If you fail this communication test, it's back to the drawing board.

A real options application needs to be simple and transparent for a successful implementation.

Common Errors in Framing Applications

Framing applications is a learned skill. Here are some common errors that we've encountered.

- *Not understanding the exposure to uncertainty.* The payoffs to real options are often more complicated than the payoffs from financial options, particularly because real options are held in combination with straight assets. The first step to any options analysis is a good hard look at the payoff function. Understand how uncertainty affects the firm and its contingent decisions.

- *Using quick-fix solutions to value complex options.* The Black-Scholes equation is a terrific tool for option valuation, and we discuss the range of applications for which it is well suited in Chapter 8. Frequently, however, real options applications are too complicated for Black-Scholes, and managers can be quite misled by these misframed problems.

- *Paying too much attention to private risk and too little attention to bundles of market-priced risk.* Managers new to the real options approach often "overmodel" private risk instead of using a simpler model based on a bundle of private and market risk already valued in a traded security. As with most models, the 80/20 rule applies: 80% of the required realism can be obtained by incorporating 20% of the possible real-world features.

Step 2: Implement the Option Valuation Model

Having laid out the option and its features, the next step is to implement the option valuation model, tailored for the specifics of the application. A summary of the model implementation tasks is given in Figure 7.4.

Establish the Inputs

There are very few inputs into an option valuation model, and in many cases, most of the required data has already been collected for a discounted cash flow analysis. The case studies in Part III provide more detail on the following inputs by application:

- *The current value of the underlying asset.* For an option on a stock, this is just the current stock price. For an option based on a real asset, this sometimes involves a calculation to "size" the securities used to track the underlying asset.

   For example, Soda Falls Links, a private regional Internet service provider, is considering expanding its operations. The underlying asset for this expansion option is the value of Soda Falls post-expansion. Once the expansion is completed, Soda Falls will have about a third the capacity of its direct competitor, Big Premium Connect. Both companies have about the same profit margins per unit of capacity, so Soda Falls estimates that its value after expansion will be about one-third the value of Big Premium, a publicly traded company. The current value of the underlying asset is the discounted value of the post-expansion value, and the market-priced risk of expansion can be tracked by including the appropriate number of shares of Big Premium in the tracking portfolio.

Figure 7.4 Step 2: Implement the Option Valuation Model

The case studies in Chapters 10 through 19 show how to tailor the implementation tasks for each application.

- **Establish the Inputs**
  Calculate the current value of the underlying asset, cash flows or convenience yield, volatility for each source of uncertainty, and obtain data on the risk-free rate of return.

- **Value the Option with an "Option Calculator"**
  Set up an option calculator and obtain numerical results.

- *The leakage in value that accrues between decision points.* This input can be as simple as laying out an explicit schedule of payments (rental income) or cash infusions (monthly overhead) or as complicated as estimating the expected future pattern of convenience yields (the term structure) from futures market data. (See Chapter 9 for further details.)

- *The volatility of the underlying asset (market-priced risk).* This input cannot be observed in the financial markets and must be estimated from either historical data or traded options contracts. For real assets, the most common way to estimate volatility is to make a simple statistical calculation from historical data. (See the appendix for a sample calculation.)

  A second method to estimate volatility uses the price of option contracts on the same underlying asset. For example, five option contracts might be traded on Intel stock with the same maturity but different exercise prices. The prices of these contracts are observed and can be used along with the other option pricing inputs to solve for volatility. This estimate is known as the implied volatility (it is implied from the price of the option and the other inputs) and is viewed as the financial market's forecast of the volatility expected to prevail until the maturity date of the contracts.

- *Private risk.* The current level of this input and the estimate of the range of uncertainty about that value are based on historical data, actuarial information, engineering estimates, and so on. Often organizations have not tracked levels of private risk in the past, but they develop better estimates after a few iterations using the real options approach. The case studies in Part III show that the nature of data available and data desired about private risk varies tremendously across applications.

  For example, Ozark Oil, an oil exploration firm, uses the real options approach to evaluate exploration strategy. Its application frame has one market-priced risk, the price of oil, which is tracked by oil futures contracts, and one private risk, the size of the oil reserve. Before Ozark begins exploration, it purchases geological data to initially estimate of the amount of oil that a tract might produce. Ozark's own records show that in about 4 out of 10 cases, the reserve size estimate was off by more than 50% (bigger or smaller). This provided a confidence interval about the initial reserve size estimate. Field experience also showed that the first round of exploration reduced the confidence intervals by 40% and that the second round reduced it by an additional 20%. (The estimate was also updated.)

- *Risk-free rate of return.* This input is the yield on short-term Treasury instruments. The real options approach differs from traditional valuation tools in that only the short-term rate of return is used, even for long-lived projects. In the real options approach, the risk-free rate is the return to the hedge position over a short time interval.

Value the Option with an "Option Calculator"

There are several solution methods for option valuation, and we call the specific mathematical techniques in each method "option calculators." The next chapter surveys the solution methods and provides detail on two useful option calculators, the binomial option value model and the Black-Scholes equation. Although it is easy to get caught up in the details of the various methods, in practice they should not be the focus of a real options application.

Changes in Volatility

Price fluctuations in commodity markets can be episodic in that the market-clearing price generally fluctuates about one stable level, with an occasional price shock that sends it soaring.[7] In these markets, volatility follows the same path—generally constant at one level with infrequent episodes of high volatility associated with the price shocks. Unexpected changes in volatility can be estimated using a sophisticated econometric model, GARCH, and this has been done in financial markets.[8] Our experience is that the payoffs to most real options are virtually unaffected by unexpected changes in volatility, known as stochastic volatility. Often, including stochastic volatility leads to more error in the real option results, and time is better spent increasing the precision of the valuation estimate through better framing. Financial market players often find that the best approach is to use simple valuation models that can be understood intuitively and adjusting for the possibility of stochastic volatility in some other way. For example, traders widen their bid-ask spreads for those option contracts that might be most sensitive to stochastic volatility.

Forecasting: There's No Free Lunch

Sometimes the real options approach to valuation is introduced by direct analogy to financial options; for example, if you have this nonlinear payoff, use the Black-Scholes formula and these five inputs. Because financial market inputs are directly observable, it would appear that no forecasting is required for a real options valuation. As we have argued, the real options approach is much more powerful than the simple analogy to a financial option. We've also shown that it may require estimates of several inputs: the volatility of the asset, the convenience yield, and private risk. The need for these estimates appears to create an opening for subjective forecasts to reenter valuation.

Forecasting is needed in all valuation models. The options approach highlights the type of forecast needed—one consistent with the risk and return dynamics of asset pricing. When assets are traded on financial markets, the asset price embeds the forecasts of the market players; when a financial or real option is valued using financial market information, it is using the market's forecast. When the underlying source of uncertainty in a real options application is not an asset traded in financial markets, the real options approach suggests how to obtain the forecast in a manner consistent with the market pricing of risk. The tight structure of the option model also quickly highlights discrepancies between market pricing and subjective forecasts. For example, if an estimated convenience yield is out of line with other rates of return in the valuation model, the value of the option is immediately and visibly affected.

Step 3: Review the Results

Once the option calculator has been applied, several types of results might prove useful. A listing is given in Figure 7.5, and illustrative graphs are given in Figure 7.6. Which result is most useful depends on the application. For example, in transactions the focus is on valuation of assets or investment strategies with embedded options. As Figure 7.6(a) shows, it is useful to compare the total value of the asset using the real options approach with the value that would have been

Figure 7.5 Steps 3 and 4: Review and Possibly Redesign

The last two steps in the real options solution process can be used to increase the value of the investment strategy. Initial results should be reviewed against financial market benchmarks and the redesign should consider the cost of achieving the same payoffs through financial contracts.

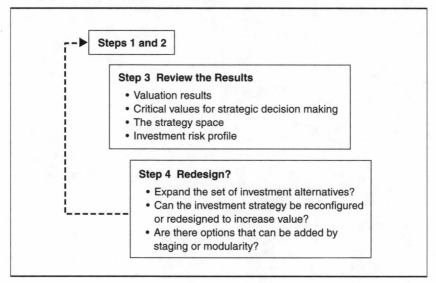

obtained by discounted cash flow. The difference is the value of the embedded options.[9]

The other illustrative results shown in Figure 7.6 are different views of an investment strategy with an option to abandon. Figure 7.6(b) shows the critical values for the investment strategy over time, the threshold level of the underlying asset value at which it is optimal to abandon the asset. A scanning system can be set up to monitor the external environment, triggering action when the critical value is reached.

Figure 7.6(c) shows the strategy space, a plot of the optimal strategy over the likely range of two inputs. This type of output is very useful for decision making because it allows managers to evaluate whether an investment strategy is robust to measurement error, disagreements among managers, and so forth. For example, suppose three engineers had three estimates of the cost to license a new technology. Using the strategy space graph, they can test whether their different estimates would lead to different investment decisions.

Figure 7.6(d) illustrates the investment risk profile and shows that in this case the value in the investment strategy comes from the 60%

Figure 7.6 Illustrative Real Options Results

For many investment decisions, the most important output is not the dollar value of the strategy but the three types of decision-making tools shown. These can be used to manage and design investments and to build consensus around the investment strategy.

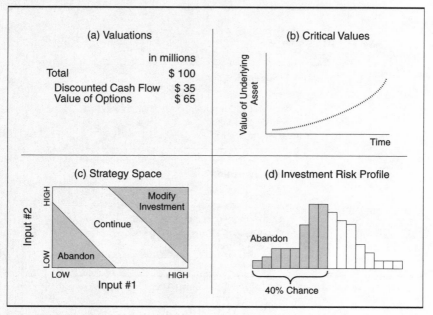

chance that there will be a large payoff. The risk for the strategy is that there is a 40% chance that the investment will be abandoned.

Step 4: Redesign If Necessary

A last question for the review of results is whether the set of investment alternatives should be expanded. Too often there is a tendency to analyze (and overanalyze) a real option to the neglect of cheaper financial market alternatives. Because the real options approach produces valuations that are consistent with financial market valuations, it is possible to make an "apples-to-apples" comparison between the value of an internal option and the value of a financial market counterpart.

Having developed the skeletal framework, crunched the numbers, and reviewed the results, let's step back from the initial framework. Are there ways to create more options by increasing the number of stages or the number of modules? Are there ways to more proactively shape outcomes? Are there alternative investments that deliver the same capabilities? One or two iterations can add tremendous value to investment strategy.

After a few applications, you will almost intuit the solution process outlined in this chapter and its financial market focus. Use this chapter as a map through the type of issues that arise in real options applications. To keep the right balance, refer to it as you tackle the technical details in the next few chapters and the case studies that follow.

Chapter **8**

Calculating Option Values

This chapter is a brief survey of the solution methods available for calculating option values. These methods use mathematical techniques developed in other fields, but their implementation for the option valuation is guided by the no-arbitrage arguments behind the Black-Merton-Scholes breakthrough. While the solution methods differ in approach, in many cases they will give the same option value, if the inputs and application frame are appropriately structured.

*T*here are many ways to calculate the value of an option. The tools used are solution methods and mathematical techniques that are well established in the fields of applied mathematics and engineering. This chapter provides an overview of the computational issues in option valuation, with emphasis on the logic behind each solution method and how financial market discipline is incorporated in the implementation of the techniques for option valuation.

We have not emphasized computational issues in this book for two reasons. First, for many real options applications, if the inputs and application frame are appropriately structured, all methods will give the same result, within the bounds of computational precision. Hence, the choice of solution method should not influence the results. Second, managers can make their largest contribution to the application frame, rather than to the computational detail. Chapter 7 guides managers through the solution process, and this chapter provides a complementary high-level overview of how option values are calculated.

Figure 8.1 summarizes the implementation process and tools for option valuation, linking the focus of this chapter to the four-step solution process of Chapter 7. Step 1, which frames the application at the managerial level described in Chapter 7, is shown at the top. The focus of this chapter is on Step 2. The first task is to establish the mathematical frame, a representation of the stochastic processes, the payoff functions, and decision rules in mathematical terms. Next, the solution method and option calculator are chosen. There are three general solution methods:

- *The pde approach* solves a partial differential equation (the pde) that equates the change in option value with the change in the value of the tracking portfolio.

- *The dynamic programming approach* lays out possible future outcomes and folds back the value of optimal future strategy.

- *The simulation approach* averages the value of the optimal strategy at the decision date for thousands of possible outcomes.

Figure 8.1 Solution Methods and Option Calculators

A number of option calculators are available for each solution method and will provide values consistent with financial market valuations if guided by the real options approach. Step 1 and Step 2 from Figure 7.1 are marked to the left.

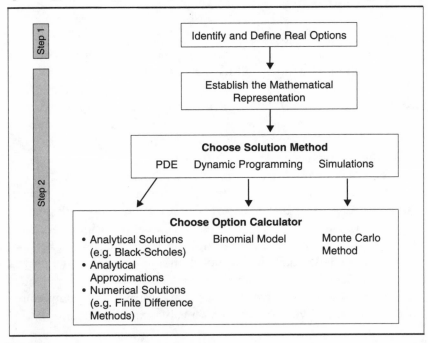

Within each solution method there are many alternative computation techniques to solve the mathematical models. We've called these techniques option calculators. Two of them, the binomial option valuation model and the Black-Scholes equation, are discussed in more detail below because they are fairly easy to use and can be implemented on a spreadsheet. The binomial option valuation model has great flexibility and can be used for a wide range of applications. It is also transparent and allows the user to "peek under the hood" to better understand the basic steps in option valuation and the complications that arise from real assets. The Black-Scholes solution is appropriate for fewer real options applications, but when appropriate it provides a simple solution and a quick answer. We use both option calculators in Chapter 9 and Part III.

Approaches to Mathematical Framing

Solutions to the pde

This approach to valuing the option is based on mathematically expressing the option value and its dynamics by a partial differential equation (pde) and boundary conditions. The pde is a mathematical equation that relates the continuously changing value of the option to observable changes in market securities. Boundary conditions specify the particular option to be valued, its value at known points, and its value at the extremes. As Figure 8.1 shows, several option calculators are used to implement this approach.

In an analytical solution to the pde, the option value is written in one equation as a direct function of the inputs. If available, the analytical solution is the easiest and fastest way to obtain the value of the option. The most famous analytical solution to a pde and set of boundary conditions that define a European call option is the Black-Scholes equation.

Known analytical solutions can be found in many standard references on option valuation such as those listed in the Guide to Literature. The real options user should not expect to obtain an analytical solution for each application; it is really a question of whether an off-the-shelf solution is available. In some cases, a modified pde is solved to obtain an analytical approximation to the option value.

Numerical solutions are used to solve the pde when an analytical solution is not possible and is based on converting the pde into a set of equations that must hold over short time intervals. Computational algorithms are used to search for the option value that solves the equations simultaneously. Finite difference methods are the most widely used numerical solutions to the pde. In this approach, a grid is set up that covers the entire range of values for the underlying asset during the life of the option. The value of the option is obtained for each point in the grid by solving the set of equations.[1]

One advantage of numerical solutions to the pde is that software is widely available and the algorithms are quite fast. A disadvantage is that the computational complexity rapidly increases as more sources of uncertainty are added. Most numerical solutions to the pde can handle just two sources of uncertainty or, in some special cases, three. A second disadvantage is that the decision structure in a numerical solution is opaque, making it harder to trace through the consequences of contingent decision making.

Dynamic Programming

Dynamic programming solves the problem of how to make optimal decisions when the current decision influences future payoffs. This solution method rolls out possible values of the underlying asset during the life of the option and then folds back the value of the optimal decisions in the future. The risk-neutral approach to valuation is used.

Central to dynamic programming is Bellman's Principle, which defines an optimal strategy as follows: Given the choice of the initial strategy, the optimal strategy in the next period is the one that would be chosen if the entire analysis were to begin in the next period. The solution solves the optimal strategy problem in a backward recursive fashion, discounting the future values and cash flows and folding them into the current decision. Solving the one period optimization problem and then moving back ensures that the entire problem is solved optimally.

Consider the classic tree cutting problem: When to cut a tree? Suppose there is uncertainty about lumber prices and hence uncertainty about the value of the cut tree. To use the dynamic programming solution method, lay out the possible future lumber prices and determine the optimal contingent strategy (cut or wait) for each. Fold back the value of future strategies, taking expectations and discounting. In each period there will be a threshold value for the price of lumber—above this price, cut the tree. With each fold back, the threshold value will increase because there is value in waiting for higher lumber prices.

Dynamic programming is a useful solution method for option valuation because it handles various real asset and real options features transparently. Intermediate values and decisions are visible, which allows the user to build a stronger intuition about sources of option value. Dynamic programming can handle complex decision structures (including constraints), complex relationships between the value of the option and the value of the underlying asset, and complicated forms of leakage, such as those that vary with time and the value of the underlying asset. These advantages are present in the binomial option valuation model, an option calculator that uses the dynamic programming approach.

Simulation Models

Simulation models roll out thousands of possible paths of evolution of the underlying asset from the present to the final decision date in the option. In the commonly used Monte Carlo simulation method, the optimal investment strategy at the end of each path is determined and the payoff calculated. The current value of the option is found by averaging the payoffs and then discounting the average back to the present.

The Monte Carlo simulation method can handle many aspects of real-world applications, including complicated decision rules and complex relationships between the option value and the underlying asset. Adding a new source of uncertainty to a simulation analysis is computationally less burdensome than in the other numerical methods.

Simulation models also can solve path-dependent options, in which the value of the option depends not only on the value of the underlying asset but also on the particular path followed by the underlying asset. An example is the path-dependent option to switch from your current fuel contract to one based on the average of daily fuel prices during the past three months. Simulation models are not well suited for American options, nested options, or sequences of options because each possible decision starts a new path.[2]

Using the Real Options Approach to Discipline the Mathematical Analysis

All the solution methods described above require forecasting the future or knowing the entire distribution of future values, and the characterization of uncertainty can lead to subjectivity. When the solution methods are used in the physical sciences, these values are estimated from empirical data or inferred from the physical properties of the system under study. In economic applications a discount rate is needed to form the pde or discount asset values in the dynamic programming and simulation models.

For example, as we mentioned in Chapter 3, researchers before Black, Merton, and Scholes expressed the value of an option in terms of a pde and its boundary conditions. However, these mathematical formulations need the risk-adjusted return of the option as a model parameter.

The Black-Merton-Scholes breakthrough recognized the opportunity for replication and based the pde on the Law of One Price. They obtained the pde by setting up a riskless hedge position consisting of the tracking portfolio and the option and equating the rate of return of the hedge position to the risk-free rate of interest. Because the resulting option value does not depend on the required rate of return on the stock or any other factor whose value is determined by risk preferences, it is clear that the option valuation can be done without regard to risk preferences. This insight led to the risk-neutral approach to valuation—in which it is assumed that all investors are risk neutral so that

---

The Risk-Neutral Approach to Option Valuation

The risk-neutral approach to valuation, introduced by Cox, Ross, and Rubinstein in 1976, is based on the same arguments that underlie the option valuation model. The authors recognized that because the hedge position—the combination of the option and the tracking portfolio—earns a risk-free rate of return, it would have the same value under any preferences for risk. As the value of the underlying asset fluctuates, dynamic tracking updates the composition of the tracking portfolio to maintain a risk-free hedge position. The return to the hedge position and the composition of the tracking portfolio are the same for all sorts of investors, risk-averse, risk-loving, or risk-neutral (indifferent to risk). The value of the tracking portfolio and the option are independent of risk preferences. Hence, for valuation purposes, Cox, Ross, and Rubinstein could assume that everyone is risk neutral, eliminating the need to estimate any sort of risk premium. Use of this argument does not mean that the valuation results are correct only if investors are indifferent to risk. The value of an option is the same in the "risk-neutral world" and our everyday world, the "risk-averse world."

computations can be done most easily. Operationally, the risk-neutral approach allows us to replace the required risk-adjusted rate of return with the risk-free rate of interest in the solution methods above. The risk-neutral approach to valuation is one of the ways in which the solution methods originally developed in other fields are adapted to the discipline of the financial markets.

The Binomial Option Valuation Model
Binomial Representation of Uncertainty

The binomial option valuation model is based on a simple representation of the evolution of the value of the underlying asset. In each time period the underlying asset can take only one of two possible values. As Figure 8.2 shows, the up or down movements lay out the possible paths.

In the most widely used version, the multiplicative binomial model of uncertainty, the asset has an initial value, A, and within a short time period either moves up to Au or down to Ad. In the next period, the possible asset values are Au^2, Aud, or Ad^2. Figure 8.2(a) shows the binomial tree and how it results in a distribution of outcomes on the final date. Each bar on the distribution is placed at a single outcome,

Figure 8.2 The Binomial Representation of Uncertainty
(a) In each short time interval the value of the asset A increases by u or decreases by d. Future asset values are calculated in the binomial tree. (b) At the final date, the distribution of possible asset values can be flipped over to its more familiar horizontal form.

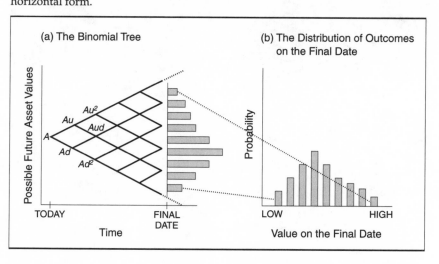

and as Figure 8.2(b) shows, the height of the bar is the frequency of obtaining that outcome over all possible paths in the binomial tree.

The binomial representation of uncertainty is very flexible. Figure 8.3 shows that as the interval of time between changes in value grows shorter, the final distribution of outcomes becomes smoother. When the underlying asset changes value once per year, as shown in Figure 8.3(a), only three outcomes are possible at the end of two years. At four changes per year, there are nine outcomes at the end of two years, as in Figure 8.3(b). A very smooth representation of the final distribution is possible with weekly periods, as in Figure 8.3(c).

Figure 8.3 Shortening the Time Interval

This figure shows that the distribution of outcomes becomes smoother as the number of price changes per year increases. A very smooth representation of the distribution of asset values in two years is obtained with weekly price changes.

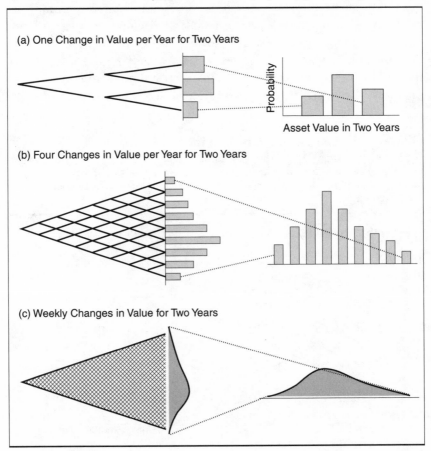

The specific parameter values are chosen so that the resulting final distribution corresponds to the empirical reality. For example, when the risk-neutral approach is applied to the binomial model, the expected return to the underlying asset is the risk-free rate of interest, r, but its volatility, σ, will be the same as that observed in the real economy. With continuous compounding, the expected return during each period is[3]

$$\frac{p\,Au + (1-p)\,Ad}{A} = e^r$$

The probability, p, weights the outcomes to obtain the risk-free rate of return and is called the risk-neutral probability.

Similarly, equating the variance of the return from the binomial model to that of the observed normal distribution gives:

$$pu^2 + (1-p)\,d^2 - [pu + (1-p)\,d]^2 = \sigma^2$$

One solution to the above equations that assumes the underlying asset has symmetric up and down movements (i.e., $u = 1/d$) is given by[4]

$$u = e^\sigma; d = e^{-\sigma}$$
$$p = (e^r - d) / (u - d)$$

An Example of Option Valuation with the Binomial Method

This example is motivated by several recent acquisitions that have run into last minute snags because the target company experienced a significant drop in stock price between the date of the handshake agreement and the formal close of the acquisition.[5] To avoid this problem, a contract clause guaranteeing a price floor can be added to the acquisition offer and the binomial model used to determine the value of the guarantee.

Suppose that Walt Inc. agrees to purchase SunMedia, the publicly traded cable TV subsidiary of M-Systems, at a price of $55 million. Historically SunMedia's line of business has been extremely volatile with rapid changes in technology and frequent competitor moves. Walt Inc. wants some protection against a drop in SunMedia's stock price during the six months preceding the formal acquisition. They negotiate that if SunMedia's stock value is less than $50 million in six months, M-Systems will compensate Walt by paying the difference between $50 million and the prevailing market price. This would limit Walt Inc.'s losses over the next six months.

The payoffs to this contract are shown in Figure 8.4. If in six months SunMedia's equity value is greater than $50 million, Walt Inc. just gets the original deal and the guarantee expires worthless. If in six months SunMedia is worth less than $50 million, the value of the acquisition is maintained by issuing new stock to Walt. M-Systems shareholders will lose $5 million or more off the $55 million purchase price. Figure 8.4(b) shows that the contract payoffs to M-Systems are composed of the $55 million acquisition price less a put option (a guarantee to cover some of the possible losses to Walt Inc.).

What is the value of the acquisition to M-Systems shareholders including the guarantee they've sold? What is the likelihood that

Figure 8.4 Payoffs to the SunMedia Acquisition Contract

Walt Inc. has agreed to purchase SunMedia for $55 million, with the condition that if the value of SunMedia is below $50 million when the acquisition is completed in six months, M-Systems will issue Walt Inc. additional shares to restore the drop in value of its purchase. (a) The contract gives Walt Inc. a call option with an exercise price of $50 million. (b) M-Systems provides the guarantee through a put option, with an exercise price of $50 million.

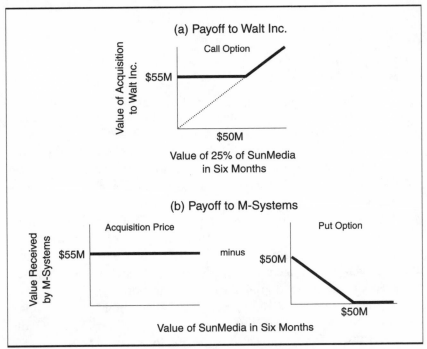

the value of SunMedia is below $50 million at the end of six months? M-Systems's contract can be analyzed using a binomial model. The underlying asset is SunMedia's equity, which has a current value of $45 million. The monthly volatility of SunMedia, calculated from historical stock price data or implied volatility from options traded on SunMedia, is 13%, and the guarantee has six months' time to expiration. The risk-free rate of return is 5% annually, or 0.42% monthly.

Rolling Forward

Figure 8.5 shows the rollout of the binomial tree for the value of SunMedia. To keep the figure simple, one stock price change per month is shown, but an actual application should use more frequent price changes to obtain a richer set of outcomes. Upward movements in the tree are along the row, and downward movements are along the diagonal. The tree shows that, in six months, the value of SunMedia might range from $20.6 million to $98.1 million. Each endpoint is not very likely, but it is quite different from the current value of $45 million.

Figure 8.5 The Rollout of the SunMedia Acquisition Contract

This layout illustrates how the binomial valuation model can be set up for calculations in a spreadsheet. The binomial tree is tilted down so that a horizontal movement is an increase in value and a diagonal movement is a decrease in value.

Data Inputs	Calculated Inputs
T = 6 months	$u = e^\sigma$ = 1.14
σ = 13% per month	$d = 1/u$ = 0.88
A = $45.0 million	

Time (months)

	1	2	3	4	5	6
A	**Au**	**Auu**				
45.0	51.2	58.4	66.4	75.7	86.2	98.1
	39.5	45.0 **Aud**	51.2	58.4	66.4	75.7
	Ad	34.7	39.5	45.0	51.2	58.4
		Add	30.5	34.7	39.5	45.0
				26.8	30.5	34.7
					23.5	26.8
						20.6

Stock Price

Establishing the Decision Rule

At the end of six months, Walt Inc. will buy SunMedia for $55 million. The value of what Walt Inc. receives will be $\max[S_6, \$50]$, where S_6 is the value of SunMedia in six months. The value of the guarantee to Walt is $\max[\$50 - S_6, 0]$. The guarantee is applied on only one date, at the end of six months, so the decision rule is imposed on only the final column of the binomial tree, time T.

Folding Back the Values

The final step in the binomial option valuation is to bring back future values to the present. In Figure 8.6, begin at the bottom right node at time $T - 1$. The value at time $T - 1$ of the optimal decisions at time T is

$$[23.25p + 29.37(1 - p)]e^{-r} = 26.30$$

The remainder of the tree is filled in the same manner, resulting in a current value of SunMedia's guarantee of $8.20 million. This guarantee is paid by M-Systems shareholders, so the value of the sale to them is $55 million less $8.20 million, or $46.8 million.[6]

Calculating Risk-Neutral and Actual Probabilities

What is the chance that the value of SunMedia will be greater than $45 million at the end of six months? The answer raises an important distinction between the risk-neutral probabilities in option valuation in the binomial model and the actual (observable) probabilities. Table 8.1 compares the risk-neutral and observable probabilities for outcomes in six months at time T. The actual probability of an upward movement, q, is based on the risk-adjusted discount rate r:

$$q = (e^R - d) / (u - d)$$

(A risk-adjusted discount rate is greater than the risk-free rate by a risk premium, an additional return that compensates investors for the additional risk.) For a risk-adjusted discount rate of 15%, the actual probability of an upward movement is 51%. Using the observable probabilities, the calculations show that there is a 37.4% chance that the acquisition price will be greater than $45 million at date T. Note the analysis of observed probabilities requires an estimate of the risk-adjusted discount rate, while the valuation analysis did not.

Figure 8.6 The Fold Back of the SunMedia Acquisition Contract

The fold back of values begins in the final period. At each node the optimal strategy is chosen, and the value of the optimal strategy is folded back to the previous period using the risk-free discount rate and the risk-neutral probabilities, p.

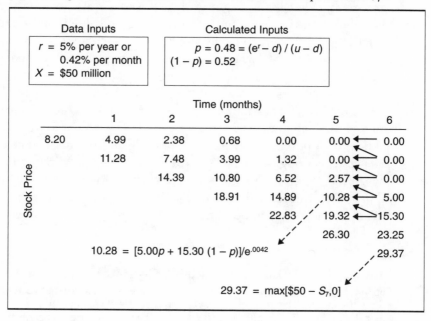

Table 8.1 What Is the Probability That SunMedia Will Be Acquired?

The answer of 37.4% is calculated from the observable probabilities using the risk-adjusted rate of return. The risk-neutral probabilities, never observed, are part of the risk-neutral approach to valuation.

		Price of SunMedia at Time T	Observable Probability (%)	Risk-Neutral Probability (%)
Observable Probability		98.1	1.9	1.3
Prob (up)	51%	75.7	10.6	8.2
Prob (down)	49%	58.4	24.9	21.9
		45.0	31.2	31.1
Risk-Neutral Probability		34.7	21.9	25.0
Prob (up)	48%	26.8	8.2	10.7
Prob (down)	52%	20.6	1.3	1.9

Sum = 37.4% (for observable probabilities 1.9, 10.6, 24.9)

Using the Binomial Model for American Options

Now suppose that Walt Inc. wants the option to use its guarantee at the end of any month between the handshake and the formal agreement. What is the value of the revised acquisition contract to M-Systems? The binomial model can be used to value this contract as well, but now the decision rule is imposed at each node. Each month, Walt Inc. will evaluate whether to exercise the guarantee immediately or wait; Walt's new guarantee is an American option.

The results are shown in Table 8.2. The decision rule in the final column remains unchanged. In the column for $T-1$, Walt Inc.'s decision is whether to obtain the guaranteed value of $50 million or to wait, so the value of the option is the maximum of the gain from immediate exercise versus waiting. Because Walt can wait, the value of the option in any period reflects Walt Inc.'s optimal use of the contract in future periods. The result is that the value of the guarantee is a bit higher, $8.4 million, because the contract increases the number of Walt's decision-

Table 8.2 Fold Back of the Revised SunMedia Acquisition Contract
The fold back of values change when Walt Inc. wants to use its guarantee at the end of any month. The decision rule at the final date is unchanged, but the decision rules at the end of months one through five become American in style and are modified to compare the value of continuing to hold the option with the value of immediately invoking the guarantee.

Data Inputs	Calculated Inputs
r = 5% per year or 0.42% per month X = $50 million	p = 0.48 $1-p$ = 0.52

			Month			
	1	2	3	4	5	6
8.41	5.09	2.41	0.68	0.00	0.00	0.00
	11.58	7.64	4.05	1.32	0.00	0.00
		15.37	11.06	**6.63**	2.57	0.00
			19.53	**15.30**	**10.49**	5.00
				23.25	**19.53**	15.30
					26.51	23.25
						29.37

$$10.49 = \max[\$50 - S_t, (5p + 15.30(1-p)/e^{0.0042})]$$

making opportunities. The value of the revised acquisition contract to MediaSystems's shareholders falls to $46.4 million.

The value of the acquisition does not increase significantly because Walt Inc. only uses the guarantee at a few nodes, those shaded in Table 8.2. Early in the six-month period, waiting is the best strategy; later in the period, Walt Inc. will exercise the guarantee early only if SunMedia's stock price is very low.

The Black-Scholes Equation

The Black-Scholes solution is easy to use; five inputs and one equation are all that are needed to compute the value of the option.[7] The Black-Scholes equation for a call option, the definition of the variables, and an interpretation of the equation are shown in Figure 8.7.[8] Interpreting the Black-Scholes equation in terms of risk-neutral probabilities highlights the connection between dynamic tracking and the risk-neutral option valuation approach.

In option valuation models, the change in the value of the option due to a small change in the value of the underlying asset is known as delta, Δ. When the option value is displayed in terms of the underlying

Figure 8.7 The Black-Scholes Equation for a Call Option

The Black-Scholes equation for a call option (the option to buy) and an interpretation using risk-neutral probabilities.

The Equation

$$V = N(d_1)\, A - N(d_2)\, X\, e^{-rT}$$

Definitions

V = Current value of call option
A = Current value of underlying asset
X = Cost of investment
r = Risk-free rate of return
T = Time to expiration
σ = Volatility of the underlying asset
$N(d_1)$ and $N(d_2)$ are the value of the normal distribution at d_1 and d_2
$d_1 = [\ln(A/X) + (r + 0.5\,\sigma^2)\,T] / \sigma\sqrt{T}$
$d_2 = d_1 - \sigma\sqrt{T}$

An Interpretation

Risk-Neutral Probability of $A > X$ at Expiration

$$V = N(d_1)\, A - N(d_2)\, X\, e^{-rT}$$

Expected Value of A if $A > X$ at Expiration (expectations taken using risk-neutral probabilities)

Present Value of Cost of Investment

asset value, as in Figure 8.8, delta is the slope of the option value function at the current value of the underlying asset. For the European call option shown in the figure, delta equals $N(d_1)$; for a European put option, delta equals $N(d_1) - 1$. Delta is an important metric for dynamic tracking because it quantifies the required sensitivity of the tracking portfolio and thus the number and type of securities needed to update the tracking portfolio.

An Example of Option Valuation Using the Black-Scholes Model

Mega-Pharm wants to fill a gap in its product line and has proposed to Bio/Line that it invest $35 million today for rights to a certain product and for the right to buy Bio/Line for $200 million in three years. Bio/Line is a publicly traded company, with 12 million shares outstanding and a current price of $16 per share, for a total company value of $192 million. Is the Mega-Pharm offer attractive?

The option to acquire is fairly straightforward and the Black-Scholes solution can be used. The inputs are $A = \$192$, $X = \$200$, $T = 3$ years, $\sigma = 30\%$ per year, and $r = 5\%$. The volatility is estimated from a six-year history of weekly stock prices. Given these inputs, the Black-Scholes equation is used and the result is that the value of the option to buy Bio/Line in three years is $48 million. It appears that Mega-Pharm's proposed payment to Bio/Line is too low.

Figure 8.8 The Delta of an Option

Delta measures the sensitivity of the value of the option to fluctuations in the value of the underlying asset, and is the slope of the option value function at the current value of the underlying asset. In the Black-Scholes equation for a call option, delta is equal to the term $N(d_1)$.

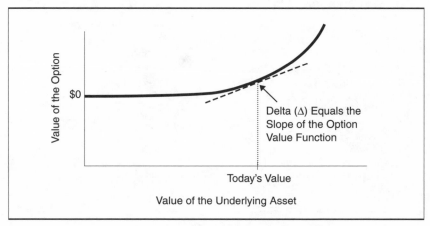

Partial Differential Equations and Analytical Solutions

Partial differential equations, commonly known as "p-d-e-s," are at the heart of option valuation. A partial differential equation for the value of an option describes the conditions that the underlying asset value and the value of the option must satisfy over time with respect to each of the input variables.

For financial options, the derivation of the key pdes began with careful definition of the nature of uncertainty about stock prices. These were modeled as continuously changing. The study of continuous stochastic variables is not confined to the stock markets but is also important in the physical sciences. (This is why rocket scientists find employment on Wall Street!)

Option valuation requires the pde (an equation describing the changes in option values to changes in the underlying asset value) and a set of boundary conditions (equations that reflect the decision rule and determine the extreme values that the option value might take on). If the pde is simple enough, it may be possible to use mathematical methods (algebra, calculus, or probability theory) to obtain the exact value of the option; this is called an analytic or closed-form solution.

For example, for any underlying asset A that follows a log normal process, the value of the option V must satisfy the pde formulated by Black and Scholes:

$$\frac{\partial V}{\partial t} + r \, \frac{\partial V}{\partial A} \, A + \tfrac{1}{2} \, \frac{\partial^2 V}{\partial A^2} \, \sigma^2 A^2 = rV$$

To obtain the current value of the option, the pde must be "tied down" at some boundary points. For example, one of the boundary conditions for a European call is that the value of the option on the final decision date, T, equals $\max[A_T - X, 0]$. (A_T is the value of the underlying asset on date T.) The Black-Scholes equation is the analytical solution to the Black-Scholes pde and the above boundary conditions.

The Elegant and Practical Logic of the Black-Merton-Scholes Breakthrough[10]

Here is a four-step description of their breakthrough approach to option valuation. The four steps set up the pde that is solved by the Black-Scholes equation.

1. *Establish the payoff at time T to the contingent investment decision.*

2. *Establish a tracking portfolio for the option.* The tracking portfolio consists of a mix of risk-free securities and the underlying asset. It has the same current value of the future payoffs as the option and the same change in value as the option for a change in the value of the underlying asset for a short time interval.

3. *Combine the tracking portfolio and the option to form a hedge position.*

4. *Update the hedge position frequently.* The updates change the fraction of holdings in the underlying asset so that the tracking portfolio and the option continue to have the same sensitivity to the underlying asset over a short time interval. This is known as dynamic tracking. As time passes and the value of the underlying asset fluctuates, the sensitivity of the option to the underlying asset value changes, requiring an update in the hedge position. The hedge position is self-financing in that the only investment required was the original investment—all updates are funded out of sales of securities in the portfolio.

The option value is defined by the dynamic relationship between the composition of the hedge position and the risk-free rate of return. Mathematically this dynamic relationship is specified by a partial differential equation. The pde defines the evolution of the option value in terms of the value of the underlying asset, the risk-free rate of interest, the volatility of the underlying asset, and the time to the exercise date of the option.

Since this is a European call option, its delta can be calculated as $N(d_1)$ and is equal to 0.68. Mega-Pharm could mimic the option to acquire by buying 0.68×12 million shares of Bio/Line and updating its holdings over time based on changes in delta.

Using the Black-Scholes Equation in Real Options Applications

Several extensions to the Black-Scholes equation have relaxed some of the assumptions in the original solution and have accounted for the specific features of the underlying asset in various financial options. Extensions that are particularly relevant for real assets include cases where the underlying asset has leakages and its value follows a log-normal diffusion process with random jumps.[9]

Sometimes it is possible to frame a more complex problem so that the Black-Scholes equation can be used. A switching option that exchanges one underlying asset for another is a good example. This type of option can be handled by the Black-Scholes equation by reinterpreting the underlying asset as the ratio of the two asset values.

Choosing the Option Calculator

In most real options applications, the option valuation problem can be solved by several option calculators. Here's a quick guide for choosing the solution method.

- *Use an analytical solution, if one is available.* Analytical solutions will be the easiest and fastest solution method. Most real options applications, however, have features such as multiple sources of uncertainty, sequences of decisions, and so on, that make them too complex for an analytical solution.

- *Choose an option calculator based on ease of use, transparency, and ability to reuse code.* Often, after several real options applications, a user becomes familiar with one option calculator and will choose it for most new analyses. A large fraction of the computer program that implements the option calculator must be tailored to the specifics of the application, so using a familiar option calculator becomes a way to shorten time to implementation.

An exception to these guidelines are path-dependent options, in which the current value of the option depends on its history or path. While the standard solution method for path-dependent options is a simulation model, this is an area of active research in academia and on Wall Street.

Implementation of an option valuation model can feel complex. A good check on the implementation is to review the application frame. Can it be simplified? In sum, we return to a theme of this book: Don't sweat the option calculator details, do sweat the application frame.

Choice of solution method is largely a matter of preference and, with repeated use, habit. Analytical solutions and the binomial model are two option calculators that are easy to implement on a spreadsheet. Managerial time and effort are best used to guide the mathematical formulation of the solution method with the real options way of thinking.

Chapter 9

Adjusting for Leakage in Value

Many real assets experience leakage in value, in the form of explicit cash flows and/or an implicit convenience yield. These features change how the value of the underlying real asset evolves and hence affect the value of the option and the timing of the optimal investment decision. An adjustment to the option valuation model is required.

*T*his chapter focuses on a feature of real assets that must be accounted for in a real options valuation model: leakage in value arising from cash flows or a convenience yield that accrues between decision points. Leakage arises because only the holder of the underlying asset obtains the cash flow and/or convenience yield from the underlying asset. To holders of a contract on the underlying asset—such as an option—it appears that there is "leakage" in the return of the underlying asset. Sources of leakage include: explicit positive cash flows (dividends, rental, interest, license, royalty income), explicit negative cash flows (storage costs, taxes, licensing/royalty fees, insurance costs, loss from perishable damage), and implicit benefits (convenience yields). Unless an adjustment to the option valuation model is made for the leakage of the underlying asset, the option will not be correctly valued. Figure 9.1 summarizes the problem and the required adjustment.

Figure 9.1(a) shows that in the original option valuation model only the realized capital gains return of the underlying real asset determines the change in the value of the option. Without adjustment, the capital gains return enters into the option valuation model as the entire return—although it is not—and tracking error is introduced. Figure

Figure 9.1 Adjusting the Option Valuation Model for Leakages

(a) The original option valuation model imperfectly tracks assets with leakages by treating the capital gains return as the total return. (b) The adjusted option valuation model perfectly tracks assets with leakage by treating the capital gains return as part of the total return. In this illustration it is assumed that there is no private and basis risk.

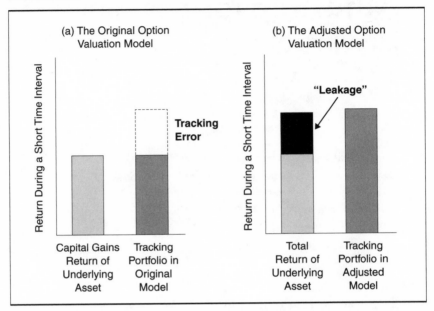

9.1(b) shows how tracking error is eliminated by adjusting the option valuation model to recognize that the total return to the underlying asset has two components.

This chapter shows how to make the required adjustment to the option valuation model for several forms of cash flows and convenience yields and how to estimate the convenience yield from futures prices. We also summarize the economic story behind convenience yields—how they are determined by industry economics, costs of storage, and expectations about the future.

Real Assets with Cash Flows

Eventually all real assets generate or take in cash flows. Examples of options that require an adjustment for cash flows generated include an option to expand an office park that generates rental income, an option to shut down a product line that generates current cash outflow, and an option to acquire a company that pays dividends. Examples of options that require adjustment for negative cash flows include license royalties that must be paid regardless of whether the product is launched, overhead for R&D that is not contingent on any project, and insurance and other continuing fees.[1]

Real Assets with Convenience Yields

Convenience value arises from the ability to store a commodity and to sell it at will in the spot market. Owners of commodities obtain benefits that are not obtained by owning a contract on the commodity. The rate at which convenience value accrues is known as the convenience yield and is expressed as a percentage of the value of the underlying asset. For example, suppose an earthquake disrupts the major oil pipelines in California. The spot price of oil soars, and the oil stored at the refinery experiences an increase in convenience value. Other sources of convenience value include the ability to smooth production and to better coordinate production and sales. Convenience value is the reason firms hold inventory, even when the capital gains return is low or negative.[2]

Convenience value can also be specific to the geographic location of the inventory. For example, there is a convenience value for the delivery of electricity to Nebraska on a hot summer day that is not captured by the price movements generated by trades in the spot market in New Jersey.

The convenience yield is not directly observable, but it can be inferred from the relationship between spot and futures prices. (The futures price is the price specified in the futures contract at which the commodity will be delivered.) The basic argument is that the Law of One Price should hold for the spot and futures prices of a commodity; the two should differ by an amount that prevents arbitrage. If the futures price is too high, an arbitrageur can buy the commodity at the spot price, hold it until the maturity of the futures contract, and sell it at the specified date at a profit. If the futures price is too low, no one will want to hold inventory. Arbitrageurs will sell the commodity short (if possible) and buy the futures contract so the short position can be unwound at a profit. Hence the difference between the spot and futures prices is determined by the rate of interest (to account for the time value of money), storage and other costs of carrying the inventory, and the return to holding inventory. The return to holding the commodity net of storage costs is the convenience yield.

The size of a convenience yield reflects expectations about the

Short Selling

The opportunity to sell borrowed financial securities, short selling, is an important feature of financial markets. A term that summarizes a series of actions, short selling is done as follows: borrow the security, sell the security now, at some time in the future buy the security (hopefully at a lower price), and repay the loan. A short seller will profit from falling prices and suffer losses from rising prices.

Short selling adds discipline to asset valuation because it allows the price to be determined by two groups of investors: those who expect the price to increase (buy and hold the stock) and those who expect the price to fall (short sell the stock). With short selling, the asset price contains the value of all possible future price changes.

Short selling is also important for the valuation of derivative contracts. For example, if you own an option, the option is priced as if the tracking portfolio is sold short to create the hedge position and to earn a risk-free rate of return. This result is key because it permits valuation without regard to risk preferences.

Short selling of commodities is done through the futures market and rarely done through physical inventory. For example, suppose 1 million barrels of heating oil were sold short in November, for delivery in April. If the winter were unusually cold with temporary local shortages, the short seller would profit. But because the realized profits would depend on the specifics of each transaction, the lender of the oil would have difficulty determining the convenience yield. Futures contracts, however, can be held (an obligation to buy the commodity in the future) or sold (an obligation to sell the commodity in the future.) Consequently they can be used to accomplish the no-arbitrage feature of short sales.

Short selling also can be accomplished by other derivative contracts, such as options or swaps, which create an opportunity for a no-arbitrage valuation. For example, an option to expand a semiconductor manufacturing facility is framed with the price of chips as the underlying asset. The tracking portfolio would be constructed from option contracts on the price of chips and risk-free securities.

future. If inventories are high and there is little chance of shortage, the convenience yield will be low. If market participants anticipate shortages the convenience yield will be high. The convenience yield will fluctuate with revisions in expectations, causing the spot and futures price to fluctuate as well. For example, an unanticipated cold spell in late spring will simultaneously cause a sharp spike in the price of gas and a spike in the convenience yield.

Adjusting the Option Valuation Model for Leakage in the Underlying Asset

The rationale for the adjustment to the option valuation model can easily be seen in the case of a one-time cash payout. On the payout date, the value of the real asset will fall by the amount of the payout. This causes the value of the option to fall. An adjustment is required to the tracking portfolio so that it realizes the same fall in value. The information required is the amount of the cash payout and the payout date.

Now consider a continuous cash payout of 4% of the value of the underlying asset each year. In a risk-neutral world, the capital gains return to the underlying asset is now 4% below the annual risk-free rate. The result is that the underlying asset is expected to grow more slowly. The reduced expected value of the underlying asset lowers the value of a call option and increases the value of a put option. An adjustment is required to the tracking portfolio so that it tracks the option, given the change in the evolution of the underlying asset.

Including the adjustment for real asset leakage in the option valuation model requires a trade-off between precision in valuation and model complexity. For example, if the treatment of the convenience yield is simplified, there may be "capacity" for other asset features in the option valuation model. Or frequent cash flows might be approximated by a continuous constant rate, simplifying option calculations. As with other framing issues, there is a danger of overmodeling introducing modeling error in the quest for precision in details.

Single Cash Payment

Georgia Properties, a developer, holds an option to buy a commercial property in six weeks at $82 million. The property generates $2.5 million per month in lease income. Ownership of the property has been transformed into a traded financial instrument by a real estate investment trust (REIT). The price of the property, $80 million, is observed in the financial markets, and the volatility, 25% per year, can be estimated from historical REIT price data.

At the end of four weeks, there will be a single payment to the REIT from rental income. Georgia Properties does not benefit from this payment and suffers a capital loss on its option because the value of the REIT falls once the payment is made.

Georgia Properties holds a European option (they can only exercise at the end of six weeks), so the only effect of the payment is on the distribution of possible REIT prices in six weeks' time. The European feature of the option allows a simple adjustment for the payment in the option valuation model: take it out up front. As Figure 9.2 indicates, for a European option, reducing the mean of the final distribution by the future value of the cash payment is an equivalent adjustment. This shifts the distribution down. Discounting is done at the risk-free rate, using the risk-neutral approach to valuing the option.

The inputs to the option valuation model are $A = \$80$ million $- PV(\$2.49$ million$) = \$77.51$ million; $X = \$82$ million; $T = 6/52$ years; $r = 5\%$ per year; $\sigma = 25\%$ per year. The Black-Scholes formula can be used to value this European option, and its value is $1.14 million. (If the cash payment had not been considered, the option value would have been mistakenly calculated as $2.04 million, a $900,000 error.)

Now let's modify the example. Suppose Georgia Properties could exercise its option anytime during the next six weeks. This change in

Figure 9.2 Adjusting the Option Valuation Model for a Single Cash Payout

A single cash payment by the REIT causes the tree to shift down. The option valuation model is adjusted by subtracting the present value of the payment ($2.49M) from the current value of the underlying asset (the REIT). For a European option, an alternate adjustment is to subtract the future value of the lease payment ($2.51M) from the values in the final distribution.

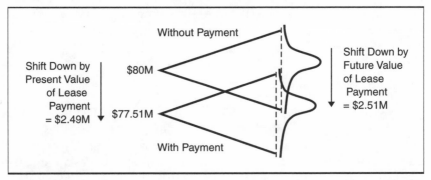

Figure 9.3 Adjusting the Option Valuation Model for a Single Cash
              Payout When the Option Is American

The timing of the cash payout must be recognized for an American-style option. In
this binomial example, the REIT makes a cash payment at the end of four weeks.
The tree does not recombine because the rates of return from the end of week 4 to
the end of week 6 are different for each value of the REIT.

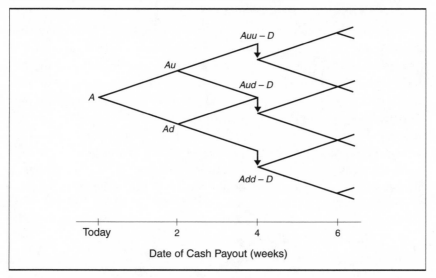

terms requires an understanding of how the income payment will
affect the REIT price over time, because the decision to acquire will be
reviewed periodically during the six weeks. This American type of
option cannot be valued by the Black-Scholes equation but is easily
handled in the binomial option valuation model.[3] The transparency of
the binomial model also illustrates how the new option term is handled.

Note the one-time rental income payment as D. Figure 9.3 shows
that the price of the REIT is shifted down in the binomial tree by D. (To
keep the figure simple, we have shown the REIT price moving every
two weeks, but later we will use weekly prices to obtain a more precise
option valuation.) This breaks up the nice latticing of the standard binomial tree because the rate of return after the payment date will depend on the value of the underlying asset. For example, the return on
an upward movement before the payment date is u, and after the payment date the returns on an upward movement are $[Auu - D]/Au$, $(Aud
- D)/Au$, $(Adu - D)/Ad$, and $(Add - D)/Ad$. The result is many more
endpoints at six weeks and a corresponding increase in the number of
computations to be done to value the option.

The inputs to the binomial model for weekly evolution in the REIT prices are A = $80 million, X = $82 million, T = 6/52 years, r = 5% per year, σ = 25% per year, and D = $2.5 million. The value of the option is $1.66 million. (If the dividend payment had been omitted from the option valuation, the option value would have been $1.06 million.)

Schedule of Cash Payments

A schedule of cash payments, such as the monthly payroll required to keep a factory idle, can be handled in the option valuation model in a similar manner. For a European option, the current value of the underlying asset is decreased by the present value of the schedule of payments, and the Black-Scholes equation is used to value the option. For an American option, the binomial option valuation model or another numerical technique is required. The complexity of the calculations increases substantially with a schedule of payments because each cash payment breaks the lattice (or tree) in the next period. As the number of time steps increases, the number of decision points to keep track of becomes quite large.[4]

Constant Rate of Leakage

It is very convenient in option valuation models to treat cash flows or convenience yields as a constant percentage of the value of the underlying asset. For example, an asset might earn a 4% capital gains return and a 2% convenience yield each year. Some real assets may have a schedule of payouts that closely approximates the constant rate, and for commodities, a constant average convenience yield is easily estimated from futures data. Use of the constant rate significantly reduces the computational burden.

Let δ denote the constant rate of payment. Under the risk-neutral approach to option valuation, the underlying asset will have a total return of r and a capital gains return of $(r - \delta)$. In the binomial option valuation model, the following equation must hold each period:

$$Ae^{(r-\delta)} = p\,Au + (1-p)Ad$$

(The up and down movements in the underlying asset must average out to the continuously compounded capital gains return over time.) The terms in the equation can be rearranged:

$$p = \frac{(e^{(r-\delta)} - d)}{(u - d)}$$

Now the risk-neutral probability p is reduced to account for the smaller capital gains return.

The Black-Scholes equation also changes:

$$V = Ae^{-\delta T} N(d_1) - X e^{-rT} N(d_2)$$

and $r - \delta$ replaces r in the calculation of d_1 and d_2. The future investment costs are still discounted at the risk-free rate, the value of the underlying asset is adjusted downward to reflect the "leakage" in value from the payouts, and the adjustments to d_1 and d_2 change the expected capital gains return on the underlying asset from r to $r - \delta$.

Let's look at an example to bring these concepts together. Telcom Inc. sells switches for the cellular market and believes that the current value of their U.S. market is $100 million, with 25% annual volatility of returns. Telcom expects that the business's annual cash flow will be 22% of value during the next five years. Because the value of the switch business is decaying rapidly, Telcom is considering abandoning the U.S. market and moving its assets to a foreign market. They estimate the value of the switch business in the foreign market to be $75 million. How valuable is the option to abandon the U.S. operation at a floor price of $75 million? How low should the current value be before exercising the abandonment option?

To answer these questions, we used the binomial option valuation model for an American option on an underlying asset with a constant payout rate. The option valuation model inputs are A = $100 million, X = $75 million, T = 5 years, r = 5% per year, σ = 25% per year, and δ = 22% per year. A binomial model with 50 time steps was constructed. The annual variables were adjusted to 10 periods a year by multiplying by 0.10. The parameter values used were $u = e^{.25 * \sqrt{.1}} = 1.08$, $d = 1/u = 0.92$, $p = (e^{.1\,(.05 - .22)} - 0.92) / (1.08 - 0.92) = 0.37$. If there was no cash flow out of the business, δ would equal zero and p would equal 0.52.

The value of the abandonment option is worth $27 million, so the total value of the U.S. market is $127 million. The option to move the switch business to a foreign country establishes a floor to the value of the uncertain U.S. operations, and the ability to react to uncertainty creates the high option value. A second result is the critical value, the value of the U.S. market that would trigger abandonment, which is $15.2 million. Its low value reflects the enormous uncertainty. Telcom will not abandon the U.S. market too soon, despite the size of the foreign market.

Leakage That Changes with Time or the Value of the Underlying Asset

In some commodities markets, convenience yields have seasonal patterns. For example, most agricultural commodities will have a high convenience yield just prior to harvest, when it is most likely that shortages will occur. Gasoline convenience yields are highest in the summer, when demand is high; for the same reason, the convenience yield of home heating oil is highest in the winter. Figure 9.4 shows that heating oil and gasoline have a seasonal pattern of convenience yields, but gold does not. The plotted values are calculated from futures market data.

The Black-Scholes equation cannot be used to value options when there is a seasonal or time-varying pattern to the convenience yield. A time-varying pattern can be accommodated in the binomial options valuation model by calculating separate values of p for each node, based on the changing values of δ. The lattice of the binomial tree will remain intact, because the rate of return to the underlying asset is independent of its value.

The binomial model can also be extended to the case when the convenience yield changes with the value of the underlying asset. We

Figure 9.4 A Seasonal Pattern of Convenience Yields

The interaction of changing demand, levels of inventory and capacity utilization causes a seasonal pattern to the convenience yields for heating oil and gasoline. Gold, however, does not exhibit seasonal convenience returns. These convenience yields were estimated from futures market data (see Table 9.1).

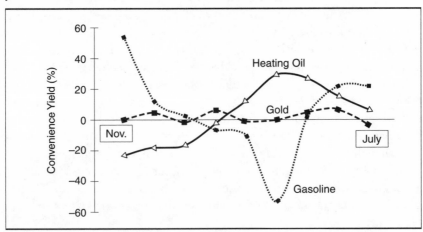

Mean-Reversion in Commodity Markets

In some commodities markets, the spot price fluctuates in the short run but is driven toward a long-term stable value by market forces. For example, many in the petroleum industry believe that the long-term value of oil per barrel is roughly $20 (in constant dollars) and expect that as the price drifts away from this level, market forces will drive it back. These price patterns are known as mean-reverting.

The size of the convenience yield reflects the convenience value of the commodity to the marginal holder, the one with the highest storage cost and lowest benefit from access to inventory. When the spot price changes, players enter and exit the market, and the marginal holder changes. The long-term stable value for the commodity price is determined by the costs of storage and other physical features. Often most of the fluctuation in commodity prices can be explained by fluctuations in the convenience yield, and data from futures contracts can be used to estimate whether the convenience yield itself is mean-reverting.[5] In practice, it is difficult to identify the source of mean-reversion.[6]

demonstrate this extension in Chapter 16. In this case there will be different values of δ and p at each value of the underlying asset on the tree.

Calculating the Convenience Yield from Futures Prices

A futures contract specifies the terms of a future delivery, such as a contract written in September 1997 for delivery in March 1998 of one ton of corn at $1.25 per bushel. To prevent arbitrage, when storage is available, the difference between the spot and futures prices is determined by the rate of interest (to account for the time value of money), storage costs, and the convenience yield. When storage is available, the value of the futures contract can be perfectly tracked by a portfolio of the commodity and risk-free securities, so the risk-neutral approach to valuation can be used to value a futures contract.

Valuing Options on Commodities That Can't Be Perfectly Stored

Futures contracts can play a large role in the valuation of real options in commodity-based markets because futures prices are highly correlated with spot prices. Some commodities, however, are perishable (wheat), some have constraints on storage (natural gas), and some have very limited storage (electricity.) The ability to store the commodity is a large determinant of the correlation between spot and futures prices. Imperfect storage causes imperfect tracking and moves the source of uncertainty from market-priced risk to private risk.

When a commodity can be perfectly stored, a no-arbitrage condition is established because a physical strategy (hold and sell the commodity) can be perfectly replicated by a financial strategy (buy a futures contract). The no-arbitrage condition sets up a dynamic relationship between the spot and futures prices, and they are jointly determined by market forces.

For perishable commodities, the futures price (the expected price of the commodity at a specified date in the future) cannot exceed the spot price by more than the costs of storage. If it did, arbitrage opportunity would be created because someone could buy the commodity, hold it, and then sell it at the specified date for a profit. There is no corresponding lower bound to the futures price for perishable commodities, so the correlation between the spot and futures prices is weakened.

When a commodity can't be stored or has limited storage, the physical arbitrage strategy cannot be undertaken, and there is no specific relationship between spot and futures prices. Electricity, for example, has very limited storage—in the form of water behind the dam and local storage of natural gas. Electricity futures contracts specify delivery for a fairly long period, 16 business days. In this case, the futures price is not highly correlated with the underlying asset, which is electricity delivered at a specific time and place.

With a constant δ, the expected capital gains return to a futures contract is $(r - δ)$, where δ is net of storage costs. The relationship between the futures price and the spot price is

$$\text{Futures price} = \text{Spot price} \times e^{(r - δ)T}$$

where T is the time to maturity of the futures contract. Because the futures price, the spot price, and the risk-free rate of return are observable, the convenience yield (net of storage costs) can be calculated using this equation. The economic interpretation of the result is that the estimated convenience yield is the one obtained by the party in the market with the highest storage costs.[7]

Table 9.1 illustrates the calculation of the convenience yield from futures market data. On September 15, 1997, the futures price for a March 1998 delivery of heating oil was $0.5575 per gallon. The spot price on the same day was $0.5250 per gallon. Setting $T = 0.5$ years and using a 5.22% risk-free return, the calculated convenience yield from September 1997 to March 1998 is −9.2%. The net yield is negative because most storage facilities are full in the autumn, and the cost of the

Table 9.1 Calculating Heating Oil Convenience Yields from Futures Contracts

The convenience yield is calculated from futures data using the following inputs: the spot price, S; the futures price, F; the length of time to contract maturity, T; and the risk-free rate of return, r. The equations used are given in the text. Convenience yields are typically expressed as annualized rates.

Date Contract Matures	Risk-Free Return (% per year)	Futures Price ($ per gallon)	Average Annualized Convenience Yield (Net of Storage)
Spot Price, September 1997		0.5250	
Nov 1997	4.98%	0.5375	−23.26%
Dec 1997	5.04%	0.5480	−20.69%
Jan 1998	5.10%	0.5580	−19.28%
Feb 1998	5.16%	0.5610	−14.74%
Mar 1998	5.22%	0.5575	−9.20%
Apr 1998	5.28%	0.5460	−2.56%
May 1998	5.34%	0.5360	1.79%
Jun 1998	5.40%	0.5315	3.55%
Jul 1998	5.46%	0.5310	3.94%

remaining storage is high. The cost of storage exceeds the benefits of inventory. This result has been annualized and can be directly used in option valuation models.

When δ varies over time and with the value of the underlying asset, the relationship between the futures price and the spot price is more complex. The futures price for delivery at time T, F_T, depends on the spot price at the time the contract was entered, S_0, the risk-free rate of return, and the current convenience yield, S_t. The equation is

$$F_T = S_0 \exp[r - \delta(S_t,t)]T$$

When δ itself is stochastic, determining the value of the convenience yield and how it changes over time becomes more complicated. An assumption must be made regarding the form of the evolution of δ and whether it is a market-priced or private risk. These issues are beyond the scope of this book; the Guide to Literature includes recent papers on this topic.

The tools of this chapter extend the real options approach to accommodate the returns to real assets that affect option valuation. Omitting these adjustments can cause significant misvaluation of the option and can lead to misguided investment decisions. The case studies in Part III provide additional examples.

Part *III*

A Portfolio
of Applications

Part III is a series of 10 case studies that apply the real options approach to valuation and decision making. Each case isolates a central issue of importance across many industries and abstracts other points that would be relevant in an actual application. Good real options results require a bit of tailoring to the application specifics—developing inputs, checking for leakage in value, and so on—which tends to cloud other insights that are valuable in different applications. Consequently these case studies are stylized examples that keep the framing focused on the central issue. In actual use, more detail would be required. For additional information, see our Web site: www.real-options.com.

Chapter *10*

Valuing a Start-up

Portlandia Ale was two guys and a dream. The company was started by two brewers who wanted to develop their own products. The company needed $4 million to begin product development and manufacturing and another $12 million in two years for the market launch. The entrepreneurs were very optimistic about their business opportunity, despite considerable uncertainty about the value of the market opportunity they were chasing. In other words, Portlandia Ale was a typical start-up. How much was it worth?

Figure 10.1 shows Portlandia's simple start-up plan. The company needed $4 million to get started and an additional $12 million to launch the product. Prospective investors were worried about the marketplace. Once distribution and sales began, Portlandia would earn the same margins as other microbrewers and would be expected to be able to sustain its future growth from profits. The microbrewery segment of the beer market was becoming increasingly crowded, however, and sales migrated across products. Portlandia knew that it would need to continue to develop new products as an established microbrewery, but that the value of a first product introduction was uncertain.

The brewers had tried to value the company using a discounted cash flow analysis, but the result had been a negative value. As they searched for financing, the brewers had shown prospective investors a business plan with a single very optimistic forecast for future sales that everyone knew did not accurately reflect the risks of the start-up. Portlandia's value came largely from its growth option: Today's $4 million investment creates the opportunity to make the $12 million investment in two years to become an established microbrewer.

143

Figure 10.1   Portlandia Ale's Business Plan

Portlandia's business plan calls for the microbrewer to raise $4M in initial funding and $12M in follow-on funding 2 years later. The follow-on investment will be made only if the market value of an established brewer exceeds the required investment.

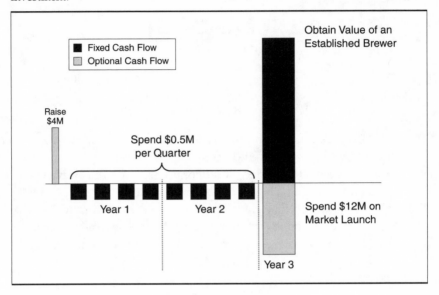

Parallels to Other Applications

Many growth opportunities derive their value from future contingent investment decisions and are nearly impossible to value with discounted cash flow and other conventional tools. This case study shows how the value of a start-up is derived from growth options. Although the firm in this case is private, the results obtained by the real options approach are aligned with financial market valuations of established firms in the industry.

Many projects and investment opportunities are similar to a start-up venture, and this simple model of a growth option covers a wide range of applications, including corporate R&D, "intraprenurial" ventures, and platform projects. The real options approach shows that using realistic inputs, investments that embed growth options will have higher expected returns, conditional on survival, than the underlying asset. This helps to explain differences in performance across firms in the same industry.

The Questions

What is the value of Portlandia Ale that correctly reflects its growth option? What company-specific and financial market information is used in this valuation?

The Application Frame

If all goes well, in two years Portlandia will have a viable business with a complete product line moving through its distributor. The company will have arrived as an established microbrewer with a business model similar to that of other microbrewers. Discounted cash flow, or use of comparables such as P/E ratios, can be used to value the firm as an established microbrewer because the value is largely based on cash flow.

Before establishing itself, Portlandia has a growth option. The option's exercise is triggered by the value of the firm as an established microbrewer, which is calculated as follows:

- Forecast Portlandia's sales level in two years, as an established business. The brewers expected that this would be $6 million per year.

- Calculate the average of the current market value–to–sales ratio for established publicly traded microbrewers whose current sales are in the same range. (Make sure not to select firms with valuable growth options, but rather ones that are representative of the business model of the industry for established firms.) The average market value-to-sales ratio of three of these firms as of March 1997 was 3.66.

- The current value of Portlandia's market opportunity, the value of being an established firm, is $22 million ($6 million × 3.66). This is the initial value of the underlying asset in the growth option.

The average stock price volatility of three established microbrewers is estimated to be 40%. It is expected that the microbrewer's value will fluctuate in value with financial market revisions of the market-to-sales ratio or from revisions in Portlandia's sales forecast that arise from industrywide factors, such as a change in alcoholic beverage taxes or increased bottling costs from recycling restrictions.[1]

The real options analysis recognizes the uncertainty about the value of an established microbrewer, and it also recognizes that the second investment opportunity limits some of the downside risk because it is contingent on a strong value of the market opportunity. The option to invest in two years is analogous to a European call option on the value of an established microbrewery. The Black-Scholes equation can be used to get a first-cut valuation.

The Results

For comparison, we first calculate the value of Portlandia Ale using the discounted cash flow method. The analysis assumes that Portlandia will follow a fixed strategy of expanding into a full-fledged microbrewer regardless of market conditions in two years. This results in a –$0.08 million valuation. A risk-adjusted discount rate for the microbrewer of 21% is used.[2]

A simple real options analysis includes the contingent nature of the launch decision in two years. Portlandia and its investors will commit $12 million required for launch only if the value of Portlandia as an established brewery at that time exceeds $12 million. Although the forecast in the discounted cash flow analysis was for a $22 million valuation, this is only a forecast. The actual realization may be substantially higher or lower.

The Black-Scholes equation is used to value the growth option (see Figure 8.7). The input parameters are $A = \$14.46$ million (the present value of $22 million), $X = \$12$ million, $\sigma = 40\%$ per year, $r = 5\%$, and $T = 2$. The result is $4.96 million, the value of the option to invest $12 million in two years' time. Hence, the value of the firm is $1.33 million after accounting for the present value of the $4 million required during the next two years ($1.33M = \$4.96 – PV (\$4) – \$0.89$).

Portlandia's management and investors have even more flexibility in their investment decisions. During the first two years, they can decide at the beginning of each quarter whether to invest another $0.5 million to keep the project (with all the subsequent investment options) alive or to abandon it. The value of the firm, including this American-style option, can be obtained with the binomial option valuation model. Under these assumptions, the value of Portlandia increases to $1.74 million.

The contribution of the growth option to Portlandia's value can be seen by comparing the value of the company obtained from the real options approach and the value obtained from the discounted cash flow analysis. The difference, $2.63 million, arises from uncertainty about the value of the market opportunity and from Portlandia's contingent

P/E Ratios—Valuation Using Comparables

P/E ratios are the valuation tool favored by financial analysts on Wall Street. The P/E ratio, defined as stock price to earnings per share, is a quick summary of how much investors are willing to pay per dollar of current earnings. For a quick analysis, analysts use P/E ratios from companies comparable to the one they want to value. (Value equals earnings times the comparable company P/E ratio. Either forecasted or current earnings are used.)

The long-term stock market average P/E ratio is 13, but individual company P/E ratios vary significantly, even in the same industry. Stock prices embed growth options, and firms differ by their portfolio of growth options and their ability to execute to realize the value of these options. Also, the amount of debt issued by the firm affects its P/E ratio. Earnings are net of interest expense, so a firm with substantial debt obligations will have lower earnings and a higher P/E ratio, all else being equal.

Both P/E ratios and dynamic tracking are objective financial market information, not subjective estimates. It is hard to argue with a price determined by a set of investors who are willing to pay real dollars. However, the use of P/E ratio for valuation is based on a static selection of the comparable firms, whereas dynamic tracking defines a comparable firm as one with the same sensitivity to the same underlying asset—a much more precise basis of comparison.

Start-ups often have no earnings or earnings so small as to make a P/E ratio–based valuation appear arbitrary. Consequently, it is customary to value them using a price-to-sales ratio.

decision in two years. Not only does the real options analysis produce a more attractive valuation, it also better communicates the risks.

The real options results can also be used to calculate the minimum growth rate that Portlandia must realize if the second investment is to be made. At the end of two years, Portlandia will invest only if its value as an established brewer is greater than or equal to $12 million. ($12 million is the critical value.) Examination of the binomial tree shows that if the value of the established market was $12 million or higher,

Portlandia's investors would realize a 66% return over the two-year period.

This very simple analysis has captured the essence of the contingent decisions in start-up opportunities and has established the value of a private firm from financial market values. No detailed forecasts of cash flows were used in the valuation, although pro forma forecasts will have other uses in assessing the business opportunity.

This case study valued a growth option with a single, market-priced source of uncertainty. The next case study incorporates private risk, which is present in most real options applications.

Chapter *11*

Investing in a Start-up

Redwood Ventures, a venture capital fund, is evaluating the business plan of Lighthouse Services, a start-up company providing Web page design tools in the exploding Internet market. Lighthouse is asking for a $10-million investment. Venture capitalists have a few rules of thumb that they often use to evaluate prospective deals: Their investment should be doubled in the next round of financing; the size of the market opportunity must be large enough to justify the investment and the risk; and there must be an exit opportunity—a way for the venture capital fund to liquidate its holdings—within six years. Redwood uses an in-house real options tool to evaluate whether start-up business plans meet the required terms.

*L*ighthouse Services sent a very simple business plan to Redwood Ventures:

- Invest $10 million now.

- Other investors will put in $10 million in two years.

- Yet more investors will put in $20 million in three years, and Lighthouse will be an established firm selling an easy-to-use tool kit for Web page design.

- Investors can liquidate their holdings at a profit when the firm goes public around that time.

After evaluating the plan and meeting the management team, Redwood Ventures was seriously considering investing in Lighthouse. However, the partners at Redwood saw two major sources of uncertainty: the value of the business after the three rounds of investment

149

Figure 11.1 The Investment Opportunity at Lighthouse Services

Initially, Lighthouse Services faces risk from private and market-priced sources, but by the third year the firm faces only market-priced risk. Much of the firm's value comes from the opportunities to respond to unfolding events at the end of the second and third years. In this figure a binomial market outcome is shown for simplicity; in fact, there is a distribution of outcomes.

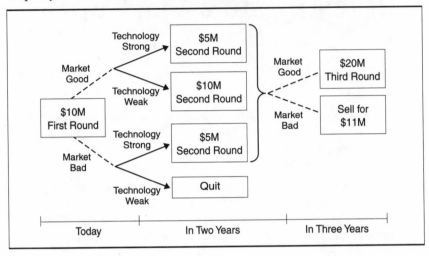

and the chance of technology success. The business plan was based on a discounted cash flow analysis, assuming that all stages of investment were made. Figure 11.1 shows the types of outcomes that everyone expected.

During the first two years, Lighthouse has private and market-priced risk. The private risk is whether the Web page tool kit could be completed at the end of two years and within the budgeted $10 million. The market-priced risk is the value of being in the Web page tool-kit business. During the third year, Lighthouse has only market-priced risk, because the technology risk is fully resolved in the first two years. The distribution of possible outcomes for the market-priced risk widens with time.

At the end of the second year, Lighthouse would need additional funding from outside investors: a $5 million investment if the technology was successfully completed and $10 million if the technology was weak. If the value of the market opportunity decreased and the technology was weak, everyone expected that the business would fold, but that decision was contingent on the value of the market opportunity in two years. At the end of three years, Lighthouse would need its last round of financing. If the business opportunity had a sufficiently high value, a final $20 million investment would be required. Otherwise,

Redwood believed that Lighthouse would be sold without further investment. As a first guess, they put the value for this outcome at $11 million and planned to test whether the results were sensitive to this input.

Redwood and Lighthouse began negotiating the terms of the first $10 million investment. Discussions quickly centered around one term of the deal: What share of the equity of the firm would Redwood receive for their $10 million investment? This hinges on the value of Lighthouse after the $10 million investment is committed, V_0. (In the language of venture capitalists, V_0 is the "post-money valuation.") The value of the entrepreneur's share is smaller than V_0 minus $10 million, because the venture capitalists want to claim a bit extra equity to ensure that they obtain a 100% return in the next round of funding at the end of year 2.

The real options framework can be used to figure out the expected value of Lighthouse in year 2 and work back from this to compute the current share of the firm required to attain this rate of return.

The Questions

What is the value of Lighthouse Services? What share of the firm should Redwood receive for its $10 million investment? How should the terms of the venture capital investment be structured?

Parallels to Other Applications

Often good investment opportunities for real assets are contracts written on growth options. Venture capital investments are typical of this situation—the business opportunity is risky, but contract terms can be used to modify the risk profile of the investment. To help them navigate these murky waters, experienced investors have developed rules of thumb—proven yet simple decision criteria that are effective in characterizing investment opportunities. The real options approach provides a transparent and quantifiable framework that integrates the valuation of the growth opportunities, the contract terms, and the rules of thumb.

The framework here can be used for corporate venture capital investments; comparison of acquisitions, joint venture, and licensing opportunities; and so on.

The Application Frame

This application has two decision points, two sources of uncertainty for the first two years, and one source of uncertainty in the last year. This stylization captures the early-stage technology risk and the importance of business risk, particularly when the technology platform is complete.

In the model, private risk is treated very simply: There is a 50% chance that the technology is completed in two years and a 50% chance that it remains incomplete. Although the model could be made more "realistic" by directly modeling the factors that determine success, such as costs to complete the product, time to market, quality of marketing efforts, and so on, the importance of including more detail depends on the decisions to be made. Would the value of the firm or the terms of the investment change significantly if costs were high but quality of marketing was good compared to the case when costs were low and marketing was poor? If so, model these two private risks separately; otherwise, the simple characterization is appropriate.

Lighthouse will be selling to a retail segment of the Internet market and once fully established will have profit margins and selling expenses that are similar to those of a software publisher. To estimate the value of their market, we multiplied the total segment sales by the average market-to-sales ratio of several software publishers.[1] Lighthouse's expected share of this value is their forecasted sales divided by total segment sales. The volatility of this segment is estimated from the average stock price volatility of the software publishers. The current assessment is that the value of Lighthouse's business opportunity in three years is $130 million, which will be obtained if both stages of investment are completed.

The next step is to add the contract terms. For simplicity, only Redwood's share of equity is analyzed, but the application can be expanded to handle many other standard terms. Redwood Ventures wants a 100% rate of return on its $10 million investment if Lighthouse continues. Let y be Redwood's share of the equity and W be the expected value of Lighthouse just before the second round of financing, including the value of its growth option. The rule of thumb can be written as

$$yW \,/\, \$10 \text{ million} = 200\% \quad \text{or} \quad y = \frac{\$20 \text{ million}}{W}$$

We used a simple binomial model to get illustrative results.

The Results

The real options approach shows that Lighthouse's current value is $38.5 million. This valuation includes a range of outcomes, including the possibility of becoming the next Yahoo! Clearly there is only a remote chance of this event; based on historical start-up success rates and Internet volatility, there are many more outcomes with moderate returns.

The $38.5 million company valuation includes the $10 million investment. At face value, Redwood's share of the firm might be calculated as $10 / $38.5 = 26%. However, Redwood wants to ensure that if a second round of financing is done, the value of the $10 million investment must increase by 100%. The real options model was used to value the firm at each outcome. The constraint requires increasing Redwood's share of the firm to 47%. By taking a larger share, Redwood will obtain its 100% return even when Lighthouse does not grow in value by 100%. In sum, the venture capitalists invest $10 million today in return for equity valued at $17.86 million and the entrepreneur has 53% of the company, equity valued at $20.14 million.

The real options framework can be "reverse-engineered" to address the size of the market opportunity rule of thumb that is used by venture capitalists.[2] Private risk reduces the sensitivity of the value of the firm to the size of the market opportunity because good news about market outcomes may be coupled with bad news about the private risk. This suggests that the rule of thumb requiring a large size of market is a good screening device; investment selections will tend to stay out of the zone of indeterminacy (good technology outcome, bad market outcome) and in the range where the firm will have substantial value.

Finally, notice the role of luck in the success of a start-up. The private risk can resolve favorably, but the value of the market opportunity can turn sour. Venture capitalists seem to recognize that failures of start-ups may not be entirely the fault of the entrepreneur. In fact, Silicon Valley has another rule of thumb: The successful entrepreneur has had two failed start-ups.

This case study has shown how two sources of uncertainty interact to change the risk profile of an investment. The real options approach provides a way to address the issues that concern managers and investors in a start-up venture: valuation and terms of investments, the role of luck, and how to structure an investment to achieve the venture capitalists' financial performance objectives.

Chapter **12**

Exploring for Oil*

> Houston Oil had leased a large tract of land on the Alaskan North
> Slope and was evaluating alternate exploration strategies. Seismic
> investments would provide additional information about the
> amount of oil in the ground, and drilling would add information
> about the amount of oil and resolve whether the oil could be pro-
> duced. Should Houston begin exploration? Which exploration in-
> vestment strategy should they use?

*H*ouston Oil knew the risks of oil exploration:

- Six to fifteen years needed to bring an unexplored tract into production

- The millions of dollars required for exploration and development

- The small chance, 10%, that exploration efforts would ultimately
  lead to oil produced from the tract

Many exploration efforts were halted because the estimates of
the amount of oil in the ground and/or the geological features of the
oil reservoir implied that development costs would exceed production profits or because the price of oil fell too low to justify more
expenditures.

Oil exploration activities determine whether oil and gas are present and produce data to better estimate the size of the field. Development activities provide data to improve the estimate and build the

*This case study is part of a larger ongoing real options initiative at Anadarko Petroleum
Corp. and reflects the joint work of Scott Albertson, Martha Amram, Ron Bain, Michael
Cochran, Steve Rutherford, and Ron Simenauer.

infrastructure required for production. Most of the uncertainty about the size of the field is resolved before production begins.

Exploration and development are learning investments, a sequence of options that resolve uncertainty about the amount of oil that can be recovered from a tract. Although all options require the purchase of an opportunity to make a contingent decision, learning investments also require the holder to purchase information for decision making and to invest to keep the option alive.

The oil learning investment works as follows. The first investment creates the option to continue exploration or to move on into development. The information generated is about the amount of oil in the ground, the reserve size, and about the chance of success (COS), the physical possibility of pulling the oil out of the ground.[1] Uncertainty about the reserve size can be reduced by probing the geology with seismic waves or by drilling wells; uncertainty about the COS can be resolved with drilling. The value of the follow-on options depends on the updated geological uncertainty and the level and nature of oil price uncertainty.

Exploration decisions based on geology alone are incomplete. The value of the oil in the ground is driven by market-priced risk, oil prices. Traditional decision analysis models of oil exploration have tied geological information to one particular oil price or oil price forecast. Real options models ensure that the financial market pricing of the risk-return trade-offs is incorporated into oil exploration decisions.

Figure 12.1 shows how uncertainty about reserve size is reduced with exploration efforts. Before the first stage of exploration, estimates of the size of the reserve and uncertainty about the reserve size are obtained from other sources, such as commercially available maps or government surveys. During the first stage of exploration, the new data are analyzed and a new estimate of the size of the reserve is announced, one that can be made with additional confidence because the range of uncertainty has narrowed. The exploration efforts might increase or decrease the estimate of the reserve size. The question now is: Given the newly revised estimate, is it worthwhile to continue exploration? Figure 12.1 shows how reserve size uncertainty is reduced with four stages of exploration.

The choice between seismic and drilling investments is based on the value of the tract under each strategy, accounting for cost of exploration, updates in reserve size uncertainty, resolution of the COS (resolved with drilling, unchanged with seismic), and future exploration options. Figure 12.2 shows a sample sequence of possible oil exploration investments. The five possible decisions at the beginning of each

Figure 12.1 Learning from a Sequence of Oil Exploration Investments

Activities that generate otherwise unavailable information are learning investments. Oil exploration investments update the estimates and reduce uncertainty
about the reserve size and/or the chance of success. The option to continue exploration will be exercised if the revised estimates are sufficiently good, given the reduced uncertainty about their value.

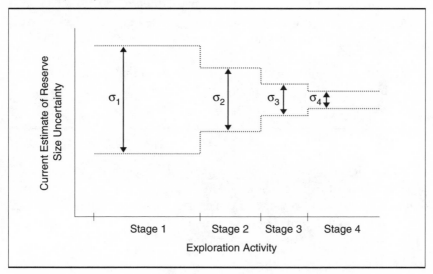

Figure 12.2 Illustrative Oil Exploration Decision Structure

Although oil exploration is a frequently cited application of the real options
approach, there is considerable variation in actual implementation. For the decision
structure shown, the real options outputs are the value of the reserve before exploration (accounting for the options depicted) and the optimal initial exploration
strategy.

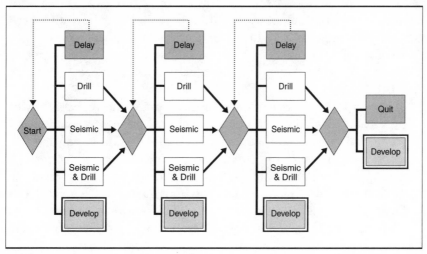

Parallels to Other Applications

Oil exploration is a clear example of a common real options application, one that involves learning investments and how much managers are willing to pay to reduce private risk. Oil prices are a market-priced risk evolving over time without investment and will influence the value of private risk information. This is one of the important links between internal decision making and financial market discipline. Examples of learning investments abound and include product development, R&D, and mining.

---

phase are delay, develop immediately, explore using seismic, explore using drilling, or explore using seismic and drilling. Delay is the optimal strategy when at current oil prices it is not worthwhile to invest. It is unlikely the tract would be abandoned before the end of the lease because of the chance of an increase in oil prices.

The Questions

Should the tract be explored? Which exploration strategy should be used?

The Application Frame

The oil exploration decision is made by valuing the tract under each initial exploration strategy (and all contingent follow-on strategies). The strategy that provides the highest-valued tract is chosen. The value of the tract depends on three sources of uncertainty—oil prices, reserve size, and COS—and is the value of a sequence of investment options.

The current spot price of oil is reported daily, and the volatility of oil prices is estimated as the volatility implied by option contracts on oil. The convenience yield was estimated from oil futures contracts. A common assumption in oil geology is that the distribution of reserve sizes is log-normal, and as mentioned earlier, an initial estimate of the range of uncertainty is available at the time the tract is acquired. The initial level and the standard deviation of the COS are based on historical experience in the region and experience with specific geological features. The market-priced risk is easily tracked, and the private risks are uncorrelated with any traded asset and can be accounted for by taking expectations over their range of values and discounting at the risk-free rate.

Because exploration is a learning investment, another set of inputs is needed, the reduction in uncertainty from each stage of exploration. A "learning ratio" for reserve size and one for COS can be defined as the standard deviation after the exploration investment divided by the standard deviation before the exploration investment.[2] The learning ratio is always less than one, differs by type of investment, and decreases with the stage of investment. The learning ratio for the COS with drilling equals zero, because drilling fully resolves the COS uncertainty.

This application has one source of market-priced risk, two sources of private risk, and a long sequence of options, making dynamic programming the most straightforward solution approach. At the end of the lease, the tract is either developed or abandoned. Moving back one stage, the optimal last-stage exploration decision is conditional on the optimal decision at the end of the lease. Continuing the fold back, the value of the tract under the first-stage strategy can be found.

The Results

The first result is the value of the tract under each first-stage strategy. (The subsequent investments are contingent on the first-stage results and are not yet known.) When the optimal strategy is delay, the same analysis is repeated after one year's time, with updated oil prices and a shorter time to the expiration of the lease. Immediate development will be the optimal strategy when the payoff to producing oil is so high that managers are willing to risk abandoning the tract after a sizable development expenditure.

Figure 12.3 shows the optimal first-stage exploration investment strategy as a function of the current estimate of reserve size and of current oil prices, holding the other inputs constant. This type of sensitivity analysis can be produced for any input combination and can be quite useful for decision making by committee. It might be that the group has two opinions about the value of one input, and that the disagreement is of no consequence because both input values lead to the same investment strategy.

Figure 12.3 also shows two types of waiting. In the lower left, the optimal strategy is to wait to explore because oil prices and the

Figure 12.3 Sample Strategy Space for Oil Exploration Investment
The strategy space diagram can be used to build consensus around investment strategy. In this example, holding other inputs constant, seismic is the optimal first-stage exploration strategy over a wide range of reserve size estimates.

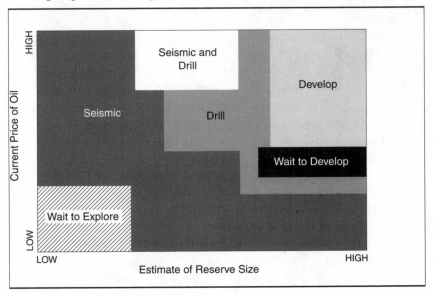

estimate of reserve size are low. In the upper right, the optimal strategy is to wait to develop because the estimated reserve size is high, but oil prices are a bit too low to justify development. This figure captures an important feature of the oil industry: an increase in oil prices brings tracts out of delay mode and into exploration, creating demand for oil services (the companies that do the exploration and development work). This raises the cost of further exploration development, reducing the value of the exploration options.

The final result is about the value of information. For oil exploration, the value of information is how much the oil company would be willing to pay to further resolve reserve size or COS uncertainty. The real options approach shows that the value of resolving uncertainty depends on the following:

- *The future:* future contingent exploration decisions, the magnitude of development costs, the range of evolution of market-priced risk, and so on

- *Current values:* the current oil price and the current estimate of the reserve size

- *The type of uncertainty:* mean-reverting, log-normal, and so on

For example, when development costs are high, the value of resolving the COS uncertainty is high, and seismic investments are not terribly valuable because they don't supply the critical piece of information. Using the real options approach, the value of information is aligned with financial market valuations.

This case study has highlighted the value of information, how much a firm would be willing to pay to resolve private risk. Although we did not emphasize this point, the framework also shows that there is a role for oil price fluctuations in exploration decisions. The next application, drug development, has a similar structure, but pharmaceutical industry practice differs from oil industry practice in that fluctuations in the value of the market opportunity have a much smaller impact on learning investments.

Chapter *13*

Developing a Drug

Recent academic research only confirmed what Mega-Pharm already knew: that the NPV of an investment in drug development was nearly zero.[1] It now costs over $300 million to develop and take a drug through the FDA approval process and nearly $500 million to market it. Drug sales vary widely; a blockbuster like Prozac could earn billions, but many drugs have life-cycle revenues of only $100 million.[2] Drug development and marketing go through well-established phases, and Mega-Pharm wondered how they could use the real options approach to better manage the process.

*D*eveloping and marketing a drug is a very expensive and lengthy process. Figure 13.1 shows a typical profile of annual expenditures over the life cycle of a drug.

For the first 14 years, a successful drug passes through various phases of preclinical and clinical testing, culminating in a filing with the Food and Drug Administration (FDA) and approval. After year 14, the drug is sold and the profile of marketing expenditures roughly follows that of sales.[3] There is considerable uncertainty about the drug's value throughout the process.

Mega-Pharm has a number of decision points during this lengthy life cycle in which it could decide to stop development or marketing efforts. If development is halted, the drug can be abandoned, licensed to another company, or sold. Drug development efforts resolve two private risks:

• Does the drug work and can it be profitably produced?

• Is the size of the market for this drug large enough to warrant further expenditures?

163

Figure 13.1 Basic Profile of Drug Development and Marketing Costs

Drug development can be seen as a sequence of options. The options that arise just before the peaks in spending are particularly valuable because they prevent regret. Data sources: Myers and Howe (1997) and *The Economist* (1998).

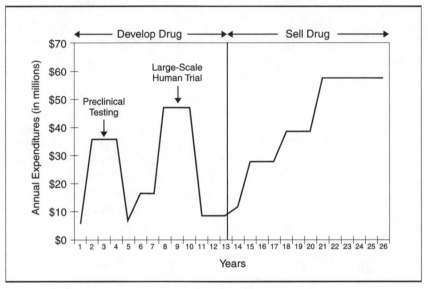

Development efforts sometimes reveal that the drug won't work on certain diseases as expected, reducing the potential sales, while early-stage marketing efforts resolve the size of the market uncertainty. At the time of the marketing launch, it is expected that the drug's sales will increase until it comes off patent protection and then slowly decrease over time. What is not known is the magnitude of peak sales, which depends on competitive entry, changes in distribution channels, and so on.

The market-priced risk for drug development is about the value of the market. This will be determined by factors influencing the entire industry, including insurance company practices, employer inclusion of pharmaceutical costs in health plans, provisions for pharmaceutical payments in government programs, and so on.

Recently Mega-Pharm had been bringing marketing managers and scientists together in an attempt to better manage the drug development process. Quantitative analyses of the drug life cycle were available in the form of NPV calculations with scenarios.

Parallels to Other Applications

Drug development is very expensive and highly uncertain, appearing to make it a terrific candidate for the real options approach to investment decision making. Drug development can be viewed as a learning investment, in which R&D investments reduce the uncertainty about the remaining costs to complete the development of the drug, and initial marketing efforts resolve uncertainty about the size of the drug's market. While market-priced risk evolves during the years of drug development, its level of uncertainty is relatively small compared to the private risk uncertainty. The real options approach to drug development relies more on evaluation of the consequences of private risk through stochastic dynamic programming than on the valuation of options by relationships that must hold to prevent arbitrage.

Real options applications that contain learning investments can be placed on a continuum, one that characterizes the relative importance of private risk to market-priced risk to option valuation. Market-priced risk is relatively important in oil exploration applications and disciplines oil exploration strategies and transacted values of reserves. Private risk is relatively important in drug development, and while the real options approach provides needed discipline for transactions to license early-stage drug projects and for joint ventures, financial market discipline has a smaller effect on transaction values.

The Questions

What are the roles of private risk and market-priced risk in drug development decisions and valuation? What are the implications of the large amount of private risk for the application frame and the solution method?

The Application Frame

The drug development and marketing process can be modeled as a sequence of learning investments and abandonment options. In each period, Mega-Pharm decides whether to spend a predetermined amount for further development or marketing or to abandon the drug. The reward for continuing is the next option. Each option contains the opportunity to make a similar decision in future periods and the possible profits late in the life cycle.

The application can be framed in terms of the following sources of uncertainty[4]:

- *Industrywide index of value.* This is a market-priced risk that captures the effects on project value from changes in regulation, changes in drug delivery by HMOs, and so on. This risk can be tracked by a stock index of drug companies, which will capture their common revisions in valuation and diversify away their firm-specific revisions (such as those arising from announcements about a particular drug or joint partner).

- *Size of market for the drug that finishes development.* This is a private risk and one that is resolved by drug development and marketing efforts. An estimate of future sales can be built up using well-established models that count the number of potential patients, disease days, quantity of drug per day, and so on. The value of the market opportunity for the drug that finishes development is the joint outcome of private and market-priced risks; the value of the market for the drug is equal to the size of the market (in units of sales) multiplied by the value of the market (dollars per unit sold). Uncertainty about the size of the market is resolved with marketing expenditures.[5]

- *Remaining life-cycle costs of the drug.* The initial value of this private risk is simply the present value of future drug development and marketing expenditures. As expenditures are made, bad news will increase the remaining costs, so this variable becomes a way to model scientific or technical risk.[6] The remaining costs can be avoided by abandoning the drug. As with the value of the market, uncertainty about the remaining life-cycle costs can be modeled as resolving with expenditures.

- *Probability of passing regulatory tests.* Based on historical experience, an estimate can be made of the probability of passing each phase of FDA tests. The cumulative probability of surviving all clinical trials and gaining FDA approval is around 12%.[7] In this application frame, these estimates are not revised during drug development.[8]

The outcome of the drug development and marketing process depends largely on the resolution of the three sources of private risk. The largest expenditures arise during marketing, and options to avoid these expenditures for a marginally profitable drug—one whose private risk resolved less than satisfactorily—can be quite valuable. Pilot marketing programs and tests of selected markets are valuable options because of the information they generate. Similarly, investments to resolve uncertainty will be most valuable just before a large expenditure, such as just before the large expenditures for preclinical testing and large-scale human trials.

The application frames for both drug development and oil exploration demonstrate the value of a sequence of learning options, but industry-specific features change the role of market-priced risk. In oil exploration, the value of exploration activities is strongly influenced by the price of oil, because oil price volatility is fairly large in magnitude and because of the option to temporarily cap a producing oil field to wait for higher oil prices. This late-stage option creates an opportunity to reverse strategies and makes current exploration decisions more sensitive to the price of oil. In contrast, the decision to stop selling a drug is irreversible. The critical value for this decision will be lower than for a reversible decision. The drug development decision is also affected by the structure of expected expenditures—a riskier later-stage investment increases the value of the option to develop a drug and makes it more likely that the drug will continue to be developed over a range of market values.

The Results

This application frame can be used to obtain a number of results for each phase of the drug life cycle. Figure 13.2 shows an illustrative set of results. Figure 13.2(a) shows that as managers use the option to abandon, the number of drugs in development falls by phase of investment. Figure 13.2(b) shows the value of a surviving drug by phase. The value of the drug increases as it passes the FDA hurdles and as uncertainty about the remaining costs and size of the market is resolved. The value of early-phase drugs is higher using a real options analysis rather than conventional tools. Figure 13.2(c) shows how the level of uncertainty about surviving drug projects decreases by phase, until all private risk is eliminated and the project uncertainty is equal to the volatility of the market-priced risk.

Figure 13.2 Illustrative Results for Drug Development

Three types of real options results are shown. The results are common to learning investments that contain valuable options to abandon.

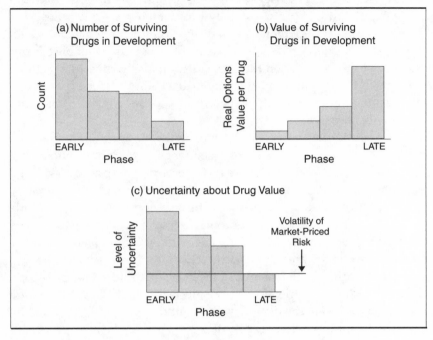

Although a discounted cash flow analysis might show that developing a drug is a zero-NPV investment, consideration of all the options during the drug's life cycle shows that the correct valuation can be much higher. For example, for the particular application frame and inputs used in one study, it was found that a drug that had a zero NPV with discounted cash flow had a value of $14.6 million using the real options approach.[9] Using the real options approach to manage a portfolio of drugs causes more drugs to start the development process and more drugs to be abandoned, a result consistent with trends in industry practice.[10] Also, realized returns to a successful drug will be quite high because they are the result of successfully executing options, while the returns across the drug portfolio should be significantly lower.

This case study has shown how industry-specific features will influence real options results. The last few cases have focused on a project-level analysis, and our next case study moves up to the next level, showing how to value the elusive company-wide contingent benefits of an infrastructure investment.

Chapter *14*

Investing
in Infrastructure*

The chief information officer (CIO) of National Mortgage Trust (NMT) had been arguing with senior management for $5 million for a new document imaging system. Other managers worried about the assumptions in his analysis that supported the investment—an increase in the number of mortgages processed and a reduction in processing costs. What if the mortgage market did not grow as expected? The result was a divided team.

NMT is a small but aggressive financial institution specializing in mortgage lending. NMT currently offers several fixed or variable interest rate plans but wants to migrate from this limited menu to offering customized mortgages sold directly to the homeowner. For example, NMT hopes to market over the Internet, with customers sending in applications electronically. The CIO's view is that the imaging system would help to serve this objective by moving NMT to a paperless office environment.

Mortgage lending requires dealing with several outside customers: prospective homeowners (and the real estate agents who guide them) who apply for loans; banks and other financial institutions who assume the mortgages; and actual homeowners as they require services. NMT believed that it could become a larger and more profitable enterprise by offering better service and more customization to both homeowners and financial institutions.

---

*This chapter is based on case study prepared by E. Balasubramanian, John Henderson, Nalin Kulatilaka, Robert Materna, John Storck, and Janet Wilson.

Figure 14.1   From Strategic Vision to Information Technology
               Investment at NMT

The strategic vision is translated into tangible business goals and then into desired
competencies. Comparison of desired and current competencies surfaces the
competency gap, which is closed by physical and organizational investments. For
NMT, the image processing system was the key information technology investment required to obtain the desired competencies.

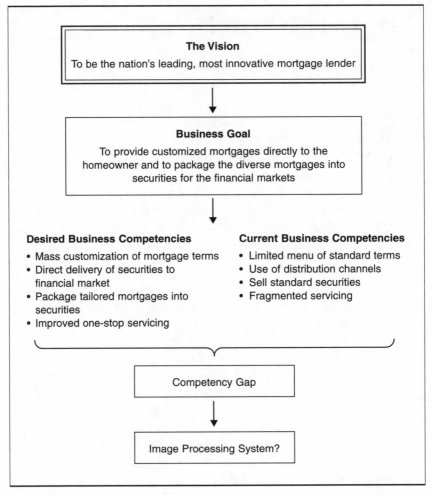

After the larger vision was in place, senior management broke
down the vision into the set of desired competencies shown in Figure
14.1. Also shown is the set of current competencies. The gap between
the two sets brought to the surface the need to acquire a paperless office competency, which takes more than an investment in a document

imaging system. Acquisition of the competency would require investments in other information technology systems and changes in the way work is organized around that technology. The document imaging system, however, was at the center of change.

Although the CIO had originally requested the system as a stand-alone project, he and other senior management now saw the document imaging system as a platform investment for the other projects. Everyone recognized that the full value of the document imaging system would be obtained only if other investments—training, reworking of office procedures, and so on—were made as well. In addition, senior management reworked the capital request and divided the investment into three stages, with an option to abandon at the end of each stage:

Stage 1: Implement the document imaging system in a few locations for new mortgages.

Stage 2: Use the system for all new data in all offices and redesign workflows.

Stage 3: Implement direct delivery of mortgages to financial markets.

The imaging investment was part of a broader investment program to develop strategic business competencies. Each stage of investment was a package, and a decision to invest would be made only if mortgage market activity reached a critical level.

The Questions

Should NMT invest in the document imaging system? What do the benefits of this investment depend on? How can the imaging project be structured to best integrate it with the overall business strategy?

The Application Frame

As the senior management team reviewed the CIO's budget request, they were bothered by his assumptions that the technology would be successfully implemented. In addition to concerns about an implementation stumble, they viewed the demand for new mortgages as highly uncertain and driven by the level of interest rates and health of the economy. In addition, a proposed change in regulations might narrow NMT's "spreads," the difference between their rev-

---

Parallels to Other Applications

Infrastructure investments are hard to value because their benefits are elusive, spread across the company, and contingent upon
follow-on investments. The real options approach can be used to
take a broad look at the alignment of the investment with corporate strategy. For instance, a telecommunications firm that buys
the right to use a portion of the radio frequency can realize its
value only after building a radio network and offering various
services. The decisions to build the network (itself done in stages)
and offer services would be contingent on the degree of success of
the preceding stages and the attractiveness of the realized market
for the services.

---

enues (mortgage interest rates) and costs (costs of funds and processing expenditures.)

Figure 14.2 shows the decision to invest in the image processing
system and subsequent possible events of Stage 1. The technology implementation either is successful and delivers the competency C_S or
fails and delivers the competency C_F. The competency outcomes are
defined in terms of three performance measures that affect cash flow:
market share, fixed costs, and variable costs. A portfolio of mortgage
company stock returns tracks the level of mortgage activity. Further
analysis showed that overall mortgage activity and NMT's profits were
only weakly related, so the use of this proxy introduces some tracking
error. But using such a market-based measure results in fewer errors
than would be introduced by overmodeling private risk. Total revenue
from mortgages is assumed to have a log-normal distribution, and an
estimate of volatility, 35%, was obtained from historical data on the
mortgage market. A simple binomial representation of mortgage demand is shown in Figure 14.2 for illustrative purposes.

The remaining inputs are as follows. Initial cash flows were calculated from annual revenues of $200 million at current levels of mort-
gage demand, fixed costs equal to 20% of revenue, and variable costs
equal to 70% of revenue. Market share was 10%. Changes in competencies and mortgage demand affect the levels of these inputs to cash flow.
It was assumed that the probability of implementation failure in Stage
1 was 10%, the probability of implementation failure in Stage 2 was
20%, and that success of Stage 2 was independent of the results of Stage

Figure 14.2 Fold Out of NMT's Stage 1 Investment

The figure lays out how the information technology investment translates into competencies, and how the cash flows are determined by a combination of market and competency outcomes. Competency outcomes are linked to specific performance outcomes for variable costs, fixed costs, and market share.

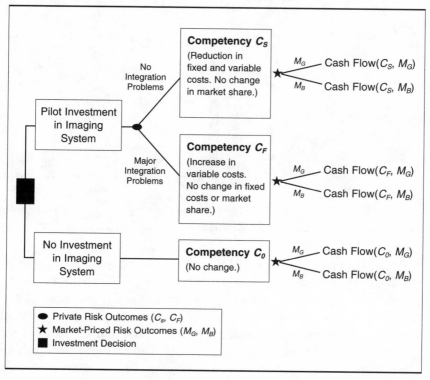

1. Specifically, the failure was most likely to come from the imaging technology in Stage 1; other organizational and coordination difficulties would occur in Stages 2 and 3. The cost of Stage 1 is $500,000, and the cost of Stage 2 is $5 million.

The Results

The real options analysis changed the Standard NPV results dramatically. The value of the project in the CIO's proposal was $500,000 (revised by senior management to a loss of $380,000), and the real options project value was $2.1 million. The optimal Stage 1 investment strategy with Standard NPV is abandon; the optimal Stage 1 investment strategy with real options is proceed with a pilot project. The real options approach to the imaging investment creates more value, yet is more incremental.

Figure 14.3 Investment Risk Profile of the Imaging Project

The risk profile of an investment shows the distribution of possible values at the project's conclusion. For NMT, the one-shot rollout has many final values below $0. The distribution for the value of the three-stage rollout is shifted to the right and has a large chance of a positive outcome.

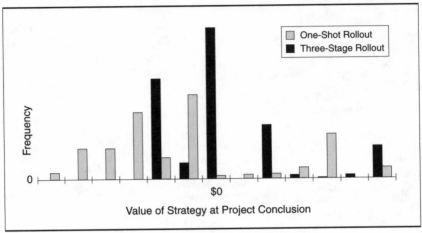

The risk profile of the imaging project is another useful output of the real options analysis and is shown in Figure 14.3. The figure plots the frequency count for the value of the project at its conclusion of the three-stage project described earlier and for a one-shot project in which the staging options are ignored. The results show that the risk profile for the three-stage project has many outcomes with positive value, while the one-shot project has greater exposure to losses. Staging clearly reduces risk. Also, staging made the project more palatable to senior managers who weren't comfortable giving the CIO carte blanche but wanted milestones and contingent approval of future budgets.

The real options analysis highlighted the potential learning of a pilot project, and it was successfully completed. The demand for mortgages fell, however, as interest rates rose, and NMT decided to delay Stage 2 until market conditions improved.

This case study has shown how the real options approach valued an infrastructure investment by a combination of "thinking wide," tracing through the impact of infrastructure on business competencies, and "thinking far," linking the value of the investment to external as well as internal factors. The next case study evaluates the option to delay, the option actually used by NMT.

Chapter *15*

Valuing Vacant Land

The city of Metropolis has been expanding for years, coming out to the peach orchards. Laga Realty, a developer, owned two orchards: one was overgrown long ago, but the other continues to produce a harvest, generating profits of $10,000 per year. It was estimated that, at current values, the properties can be developed immediately for a net profit. Should the property be developed immediately or should development be postponed?

*F*orty years ago, the valley surrounding Metropolis had been filled with fruit orchards. Now technology companies that need room to expand drive the local economy. Laga Realty owns two 40-acre orchards: one has been overgrown for 10 years and is no longer harvested; the other generates $10,000 per year from its harvest.

Immediate development would cost $2 million, and the developed property would be worth $2.2 million. However, as the technology sector of the economy experiences boom and bust cycles, so does the value of developed property. These fluctuations are well tracked by several regional real estate investment trusts (REITs), portfolios of real estate properties that have shares listed on a stock exchange.[1]

The Questions

Should the properties be developed immediately or should the developer wait? What is the effect of the harvest on the development timing decision?

Parallels to Other Applications

Managers often intuitively use the option to wait, comparing the value of an investment today with the uncertain value of the same investment later. Investing in either period could have positive value. The problem is to choose the strategy with the highest value. This leads to a decision rule to invest now if:

Value of Immediate Investment *less* Cost of Investment
is greater than
Value of Option to Wait

or

Standard NPV *is greater than* Value of Option to Wait

The option to wait has many applications, including waiting to expand a product line, waiting to enter a new market, waiting to destroy an old hotel and build a new one, and so on. Abandonment options can also be viewed as options to wait: abandon today for an immediate salvage value or wait and abandon later for an uncertain salvage value. The common factors across the applications are uncertainty about the underlying asset and irreversibility—the option to wait avoids unpleasant surprises.

The Application Frame

Current development is somewhat attractive, but there is tremendous uncertainty about the value of the developed property. The developer is worried that the market for developed property will fall, making it impossible for him to recoup the development expenditure. In other words, investing today might lead to regret tomorrow.

However, the investment opportunity does not disappear by waiting. There is clearly some value to the option to "wait and see before investing." By investing today, the developer not only gives up the $2 million, but also kills a valuable option. The prudent investment decision must compare the value of developing today to the value of waiting and developing at later points in time. If postponed, however, the cost of development will rise with the local construction inflation index. The decision today requires looking into the uncertain future and then working backward in time.

Figure 15.1 is a simple characterization of how the option to wait is valued. Begin in the far future at time T, a date further in the future than the true time horizon to ensure that the arbitrary starting point does affect the valuations.[2] At time T, decide whether or not to immediately develop the land. Then move back in time to $T - 1$: Should you develop the land immediately or wait and possibly develop at time T? The value of the land at time $T - 1$ includes the value of the option to wait and depends on the current value of developed property. The fold back continues to the present, and the value of the land includes the option to develop it at any future date.

Figure 15.1 Solution Method for the Option to Wait

The solution begins at time T, far in the future, and folds back to today, time t. In each period, the optimal strategy is found by comparing the value of immediate development ($V - C$) with the value of waiting to develop (*option to wait to develop* $- M$).

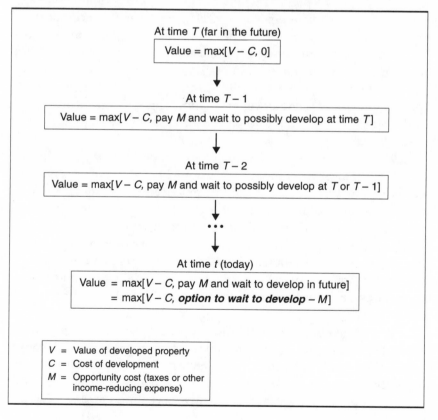

The value of the developed property can be tracked, for instance, by the value of several regional REITs, which are also used to obtain an initial estimate of the value of the developed parcel as 40 times the share price of the REIT. The volatility of the developed property, 50%, was estimated from several regional REITs.

The Results

At current values for developed properties, both properties should be held without development. The value of the postponement option for the idle land is $1.8 million. Hence, immediate investment costs the developer $2 million in development expenditure plus the $1.8 million postponement option that is killed. A second result showed that the developed property value must be nearly twice the initial investment to justify immediate investment.

Figure 15.2 shows the value of the postponement option plotted against possible values of developed property. The optimal exercise of the option is at the point of tangency between the option to wait and the value of immediate development. Higher levels of uncertainty increases the option value and pushes this point of tangency to the right.

As intuition would suggest, the harvest revenues will further delay development because killing the option to wait forgoes the profits from the peach harvest. The effect will be tempered by the carrying costs (property taxes) of the undeveloped land. (This situation is analogous to the effect of operating idle parcels of land in city centers such as parking lots.)

Cash flows accruing to the developed property create the opposite incentives to those accruing to undeveloped land. Because postponing development also postpones the commencement of rental income, rents act as an incentive to invest early, thus lowering the threshold value needed to justify immediate investment.

The developer can increase the value of development by staging the investment, for example, by starting development and then halting it if the economy sours. A staged investment allows for mid-course corrections and decreases the value of waiting, leading to earlier development.

Let's add a few other wrinkles. Suppose development restrictions are introduced, reducing the uncertainty about the value of developed land.[3] What would happen to the peach orchards? The reduction in uncertainty reduces the value of waiting and increases the incentive to exercise the option. In Figure 15.2, the two curved lines representing the

Figure 15.2 Value of the Option to Wait

The option to postpone the development of idle land increases with the value of the developed property. The value of the option to wait to develop largely depends on the volatility of the value of developed property and the opportunity cost of waiting. The optimal time to develop is when the option to wait is just tangent to the value of immediate development.

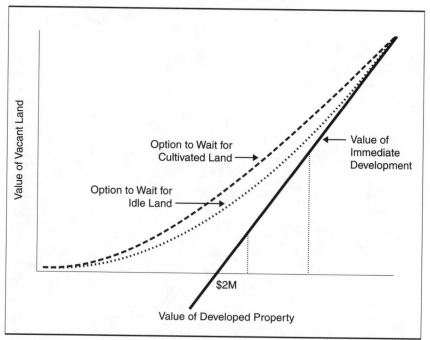

value of the option to wait would shift down, and the points of tangency would move to the left. This change alone might be enough to trigger immediate development. The value of waiting is driven by uncertainty. Other realistic wrinkles include rental income that fluctuates with the value of developed property—which tends to accelerate investment when the value is high and delay investment when the value is low—and the uncertain interest rate on construction loans. This is an additional, independent source of uncertainty and will increase the value of the option to wait, shifting up the curves in Figure 15.2, and hence raising the trigger point of development.

This case study has shown how to value the option to wait, an option that can be "killed" only once. In contrast, the value of the option to switch, the subject of the next case study, depends on its reversibility, the option to switch back.

Chapter 16

Buying Flexibility

MidAmerica Manufacturing is choosing between three industrial boilers to generate steam. The first boiler burns natural gas, the second burns No. 2 fuel oil, and the third can switch between the two inputs. The price of the third boiler is $2,000 more than the first boiler and $5,000 more than the second, a premium for the built-in flexibility. Which boiler should MidAmerica buy?

*T*o compare the industrial boilers, MidAmerica Manufacturing put the fuel costs on an efficiency-adjusted basis. An efficiency-adjusted price is the spot price multiplied by a factor that accounts for the thermal efficiency of the boiler. The efficiency-adjusted prices quoted below are for the particular boilers in question; different models and makes will have adjustments of a different magnitude.

Here are some more details on the boilers MidAmerica is evaluating:

- *Natural gas.* This boiler costs $63,500 and its efficiency-adjusted price of fuel is 1469 P_{GAS}

- *No. 2 fuel oil.* The cost of this boiler is $66,600, and its efficiency-adjusted price of fuel is 1408 P_{OIL}

- *Dual-fuel.* This boiler costs $68,700. It has the same thermal efficiencies as the single-fuel boilers

MidAmerica also gathered historical data on fuel prices. The recent history of the ratio of the efficiency-adjusted prices for the boilers under evaluation is given in Figure 16.1. When the price ratio equals 1.04 (1469/1408), the efficiency-adjusted prices are equal. The figure shows that the price ratio crosses this level quite frequently, and it

Figure 16.1 Recent History of the Price Ratio

The price of natural gas equals the price of No. 2 fuel oil, on an efficiency-adjusted basis, when the price ratio equals 1.04. The option to switch fuel inputs is more valuable if the efficiency-adjusted price ratio frequently crosses the point of equality.

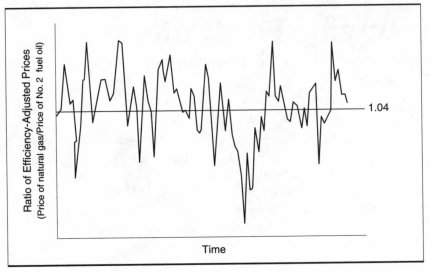

appears that the ratio is mean-reverting. There is an economic story behind this feature. Because the two fuels are substitutes for each other, the efficiency-adjusted price of gas will tend to converge to the efficiency-adjusted price of oil in the long run. The long-run mean is at the point where the cost of fuel is the same for the marginal purchasers of oil and gas.

After examining this price history, MidAmerica wondered how often they would actually switch fuels. If it cost nothing to switch, the cost-minimizing decision rule is switch to the cheaper fuel at any time. With switching costs (S), the cost-minimizing strategy depends on the current fuel being used. If gas is currently being used, there is a cost to switch to oil fuel. If gas is currently being used, the cost for the next month is:

$$C_{GAS} = \min(1.04P_{GAS}, P_{OIL} + S)$$

Similarly, if fuel oil is currently being used the cost for the next month is:

$$C_{OIL} = \min(1.04P_{GAS} + S, P_{OIL})$$

The subscripts on the cost C indicate which fuel is currently being used.

Parallels to Other Applications

Managers are often faced with decisions requiring the valuation of flexibility. Flexibility can be purchased through special features in capital equipment, or it can be obtained by investing in training, routines, or flexible contracts. Flexibility in capital equipment is common and includes flexible manufacturing systems, options to change the product mix in oil refineries, and the opportunity to temporarily shut down and restart equipment. Flexibility also includes options to switch production across locations, depending on local labor conditions, demand, and currency fluctuations. Some contracts contain flexibility, such as a contract to deliver natural gas or electricity each month, whichever is cheaper.

In many cases, the need for flexibility is largely predictable, but with some uncertainty. For example, some electricity-generating equipment is used just during hours of peak demand, certain times of day, and certain seasons. It is purchased for the predictable need for flexibility, but the exact price at which each hour of generated electricity will be sold is still uncertain, and in fact, the realized price may be so low that no power will be generated. Predictable flexibility can be handled by a discounted cash flow analysis, but the uncertain component requires a real options analysis.

The Questions

What is the value of the flexibility of the dual-fuel boiler? How should the flexible boiler be operated? What is the role of the switching costs?

The Application Frame

The method to value the dual-fuel boiler is very similar to that used to value the option to wait in Chapter 15 and is shown in Figure 16.2. Valuation starts at time T, at the end of the physical life of the boiler. All three boilers were expected to have a 10-year life. The currently lower-priced fuel, heating oil, is selected as the initial fuel; if the time horizon is sufficiently long (if T is far enough away from the present), the valuation results will not be sensitive to the initial fuel choice.[1] The initial monthly profits are calculated at time T as revenues,

Figure 16.2   Solution Method for the Option to Switch Fuels

As the flow of this figure shows, the option to switch has the feature that the options available and the cost of switching depend on the fuel currently being used and the fuel expected to be used in the next period. Dynamic programming folds back the possible price paths of two fuels, the expected fuel choices and the current fuel choice. In this illustration, it is assumed that gas is used at time T in the far future. Time subscripts have been omitted.

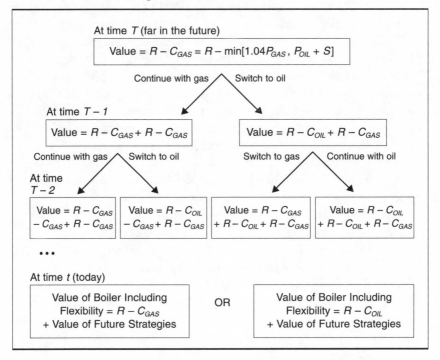

R, minus costs, C_{OIL}. (To keep Figure 16.2 simple, we have suppressed the time subscripts.) The next month, $T - 1$, the optimal fuel is chosen based on current fuel prices and, because of switching costs, is based on which fuel was used at T.

In the same manner, the valuation continues to fold back. At $T - 2$, four values of the dual-fuel boiler are possible, based on the optimal fuel (given current prices) and the strategies that would be optimal in the subsequent periods. Because these strategies include switching, the value of the boiler obtained by folding back includes the value of flexibility. As the figure shows, the current value of the boiler depends on the current fuel choice and future strategies. This valuation model can be solved using a stochastic dynamic programming solution method.

The application has two sources of uncertainty, the price of oil and the price of gas, but the solution is easier if the analysis is framed in terms of a single source of uncertainty, the ratio of efficiency-adjusted fuel prices. The contingent operating decisions depend on this single source of uncertainty. Let Q denote the ratio of the fuel prices, $Q = 1.04$ P_{GAS} / P_{OIL}. For example, the cost function, given that oil was used last month, is:

$$C_{OIL} = \min(1.04Q + S, 1)$$

The decision rule does not change, but now we need only a single estimate of volatility, that of the ratio of the efficiency-adjusted fuel prices.

The recent history of the price ratio shown in Figure 16.1 suggests that the price ratio is mean-reverting, and this assumption was made in estimating the volatility. A regression analysis was done to estimate how quickly the price ratio moves to the mean after accounting for the expected price trend. Volatility was calculated as the deviation from that trend. Thus, the volatility estimate depends on the assumption of mean-reversion and the empirical estimates of the speed of mean-reversion.[2] The estimated volatility is used to roll out a tree showing the range of possible values for the price ratio, and then the dynamic program described in Figure 16.2 was used to fold back the valuation.

Mean-reverting prices can arise from a mean-reverting convenience yield or from mean-reversion in the risk premium, the additional returns required by investors for bearing risk. A mean-reverting convenience yield requires an adjustment to the tracking portfolio; a mean-reverting risk premium is already captured in the fuel prices. In some cases, the source of mean-reversion can be identified with empirical tests of the price data; in other cases, the source is imposed by assumption.

The Results

MidAmerica is willing to pay the extra cost of the dual-fuel boiler if its flexibility adds value. Table 16.1 summarizes the valuation results for the three boilers. For consistency, the value of a single-fuel boiler was obtained by setting the switching cost S to such a large number that switching was never the optimal strategy. (The real options valuation method gives the same answer as discounted cash flow when the option is "hardwired" out of the valuation.)

As Table 16.1 shows, MidAmerica actually did two separate calculations. The first was based on 10 years of fuel prices ending in 1977, and the second on 10 years of fuel prices ending in 1997. MidAmerica estimates showed that the volatility of the price ratio, after accounting for mean-reversion, was higher in the 1970s than in the 1990s.

Table 16.1 The Declining Value of Fuel-Switching Flexibility

In 1977, the dual-fuel boiler was the optimal investment, after accounting for all fuel-switching options. During the subsequent 20 years many firms and utilities purchased dual-fuel boilers, reducing the volatility of relative fuel prices. In this example, the natural gas boiler emerged as the optimal investment in 1997.

Type of Boiler	Purchase Price (constant dollars)	Value to MidAmerica at Current Fuel Prices	NPV
1977 Results			
Natural gas	$63,500	$65,000	$2,500
No. 2 fuel oil	$66,600	$62,000	*approx.* $0
Dual-fuel	$68,700	$98,000	$26,000
1997 Results			
Natural gas	$63,500	$68,000	$3,000
No. 2 fuel oil	$66,600	$62,000	*approx.* $0
Dual-fuel	$68,700	$69,500	$800

The dual-fuel boiler was the best choice in 1977. The value of its flexibility to MidAmerica exceeded the purchase price premium. By 1997, however, the value of the dual-fuel boiler flexibility had decreased dramatically, and the single-fuel natural gas boiler was the best choice. Why?

During the 20-year interval, many industrial manufacturers and utilities added dual-fuel boilers, increasing the speed of mean-reversion and reducing the volatility of the price ratio. As these companies switched between fuels, decreasing demand for one and raising demand for the other, their actions caused the spot price of gas to rapidly converge toward the spot price of fuel oil. The long-run forces reflecting the efficiency of the least-efficient dual-fuel boiler in the market and its switching costs. In recent years financial contracts have been introduced that synthetically create a dual-fuel boiler at a lower switching cost than many boilers in place, further reducing the volatility of relative fuel prices.

This case study has shown how to value flexibility. Electric utilities face the same flexibility choices for generation capacity, but at a scale 10 times larger than shown here. When important capital equipment has built-in input flexibility, it can actually change the dynamics of commodity markets. The next case study illustrates an additional force at work: Financial market contracts can also be used to obtain flexibility, further disciplining the optimal operating decision.

Chapter 17

Combining Real
and Financial Flexibility

New Jersey Refining had been watching the new financial products available on the crack spread, the gross profit margin for oil refiners. Currently it operated its plant using a dynamic programming algorithm, temporarily shutting down whenever the crack spread was too low, after accounting for shutdown and start-up costs. New Jersey Refining thought that its competitors were using the new financial contracts to avoid temporary shutdowns and wondered whether it should adopt this approach as well.

New Jersey Refining was a typical oil refiner, using a process called "cracking" to break down crude oil into a mix of refined products, including gasoline, heating oil, kerosene, jet fuels, solvents, and so on.[1] The crack ratio summarizes the refining process. New Jersey Refining's ratio is 5:3:2, meaning that five barrels of crude oil yield three barrels of gasoline and two barrels of heating oil. Crude oil is about 85% of the total operating cost, while gasoline and heating oil are about 80% of New Jersey Refining's revenues, so the crack ratio is an approximate indicator of its gross margin.

There had been times in the past when New Jersey Refining had temporarily shut down, incurring substantial costs. These included the fuel costs of warming up the refinery furnace and distillation tower and from "wear and tear" on the equipment. In addition, while shut down, New Jersey had ongoing maintenance and safety costs. Despite

---

This chapter is based on research done by Nalin Kulatilaka and Changku Yi at Boston University.

these costs, sometimes the crack spread was so low that shutdown was the best strategy.

Managers at New Jersey Refining had noticed that futures and options contracts were trading on several exchanges based on the 5:3:2 crack ratio and wondered if these contracts could be used to smooth cash flow. The contracts had a constructed underlying asset, the crack spread, which is a weighted average of the appropriate spot prices. Typically there were two months between the date a refiner purchased the crude oil and the date it sold its output, and the constructed underlying asset included this timing difference in spot market prices.

In addition, a number of investment bankers and commodity brokers had approached New Jersey Refining about creating options and futures contracts tailored to its own gross profit margin. The crack spread in the traded contracts imperfectly tracked New Jersey's gross margin because New Jersey's sale of output lagged its oil purchases by only one month. Although a tailored contract would eliminate the basis risk of a traded contract, it would also have a higher cost, because it would include a fee to the investment bank for designing and providing the contract.

The Questions

How can financial market information help New Jersey Refining determine its optimal operating strategy, including the optimal rule for temporary shutdown? Can New Jersey Refining use the traded crack spread contracts to smooth cash flows, or should it buy contracts from the investment bankers?

The Application Frame

Under its current operating strategy, based on a dynamic programming model, New Jersey Refining shuts down when its gross margin falls below a critical value and restarts operations when the gross margin rises above a second critical value. Using a real options analysis, the refinery uses financial market information—the convenience yield and the volatility of crack spreads—to discipline its operating strategy, changing the critical values for shutdown and restarting operations. The real options analysis does not require any forecasts of future crack spreads, another difference with standard dynamic programming. The application frame for the shutdown option is similar to the frame for the switching option discussed in Chapter 16, because a shutdown op-

---

Parallels to Other Applications

What if a new competitor came along with lower costs of delivering product? In some product markets, financial contracts are available that mimic operating options. The presence of financial options expands the opportunities to acquire flexibility and undertake risk management. The list of financial contracts available to track gross profit margin is growing, and it includes:

- *The crack spread in oil refining,* the difference between the weighted average of prices for refinery outputs and the price of crude oil

- *The crush spread in soybean processing,* the difference between the price of crushed soybean oil and raw soybeans

- *The spark spread in electricity generation,* the difference between the price of electricity and the price of gas adjusted for a standard thermal efficiency

---

tion is really an option to switch between two modes, refining and shutdown.

The shutdown decision rule depends on the current refinery status (shutdown or operating), the shutdown cost, d; the start-up cost, s; the maintenance costs during shutdown, f; and the crack spread, k. For example, if the refinery is currently operating, it should continue operating for the next period only if:

$$\text{Value when in operation} + k$$
$$+ \text{Value of option to shut down in the future}$$
$$\textit{is greater than or equal to}$$
$$\text{Value when shutdown} - f - d$$
$$+ \text{Value of option to start up in the future}$$

Each side of the inequality captures current cash flow (k or $-f-d$) and the future value of the refinery under the operating mode. The decision rule for a refinery that is currently shut down is similar. The real options analysis is required to correctly value the options.

The value of the shutdown and start-up options depends on the cost of each action (*d* and *s*), the current crack spread (*k*), the volatility of the crack spread, and the convenience yield on the crack spread. The parameters *s*, *d*, and *f* depend on the technology, organizational structure, and contractual arrangements of New Jersey Refining. The crack spread parameters are obtained from spot and futures market data.

The Results

Figure 17.1 shows the optimal shutdown and start-up rules, the output of a real options analysis. The figure shows an area of inertia, known as a hysteresis band. The band ranges between $2.75 per-barrel crack spread (the critical value for shutdown) and $4.25 per-barrel crack spread (the critical value for start-up). Inside the hysteresis band the refinery has negative cash flow; the refinery will continue operating, although it is incurring losses and will remain closed although it could be earning profits. The refinery incurs these short-run losses because the costs of switching operating modes make the strategy

Figure 17.1   Critical Values for the Refinery's Shutdown Option
The refinery's operating strategy for a particular path of the crack spread is shown. When the crack spread falls below the critical value for shutdown, the refinery pays $*d* to temporarily close and then $*f* per month while idle. The spread must exceed the critical value for start-up before the refinery is willing to pay $*s* to reopen. In this band of inertia or hysteresis the refinery remains in operation although it would generate negative cash flow and stays idle although operations would generate positive cash flow.

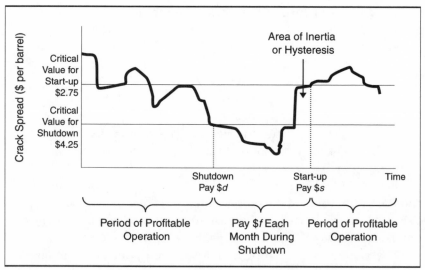

optimal in the long run. Note that the critical values of crack spread at which the refinery should be shut down and started up do not depend on a private forecast of crack spreads; the critical values depend on objective information, the cost parameters and market information about the crack spread.[2]

In addition to the critical values, the real options analysis produces another output, the risk profile of future cash flows that would result from using these operating rules. This profile may not be acceptable to New Jersey Refining. For example, senior management may feel that the company is too exposed to oil price fluctuations and would prefer to smooth cash flows. Financial hedges based on the crack spread can then be used to modify this risk profile. Because these financial contracts are based on the cost structure of the marginal producer in the industry, they benchmark New Jersey's performance over a range of outcomes and provide a reference point on the cost of modifying the risk profile.

Does the existence of financial contracts change the actual operating strategy of the refinery? It may if the market-priced insurance against crack spread fluctuations is cheaper than the cost of shutting down the refinery. In this case, New Jersey Refining would never shut down. Instead it would purchase insurance to compensate for the losses incurred by continued operations below the critical shutdown level of the crack spread. Cheap insurance can change the operating strategy. Note that even if New Jersey Refining does not buy the crack spread hedge, it should use the price information to improve its operating strategy.

Note that for a new entrant, the financial options become an entry barrier—don't enter unless your physical operating options are more valuable than the financial options. Industry capacity expansion will take place through an increase in superefficient physical capacity and the expansion of virtual refineries through contracts.

Financial contracts are useful for shedding commodity price risk but may introduce other risks, including:

- *Counterparty risk.* Generally, tailored contracts are available through investment banks, which are the only source of pricing information as well. Credit risk can also be a concern when other companies are the counterparties.

- *Legal risk.* Specialized unproven contracts may have ambiguous terms of sale or undisclosed risks—matters that sometimes incur legal costs to resolve.

- *Basis risk.* The refinery's gross margin can differ in composition from the market-traded crack spread.

- *Liquidity and execution risk.* Some contracts are illiquid and/or have high transaction costs. These costs must be paid whether the owner of the physical asset or the bank runs the tracking portfolio (although the bank is likely to have cheaper transaction costs).

This case study has demonstrated the power of using the synthetic flexibility of financial assets in the operation of a real asset, a strategy that has important implications for competition in the marketplace. The firms in the previous case studies have been "pricetakers"; the next case study shows how the applications involving "pricemakers" are treated in the real options approach.

Chapter *18*

Investing to Preempt Competitors

GoodTech was nearing the end of product development for its latest electronic product, a personal digital assistant (PDA). GoodTech usually introduced its new products once a year in October, just before the big Christmas selling season. The size of the market for PDAs was very uncertain, and the PDA product introduction would be very expensive. Senior management at GoodTech was divided over which strategy to take: hold back the product one year and wait to see how this season developed or introduce the product this year, using it to set industry standards on PDA features.

*E*veryone knew that the market for PDAs was very uncertain. Other companies had introduced products, but these had been more consumer novelties than products ready for the large-scale consumer market that GoodTech usually sold into. This season it might be different.

GoodTech's product management team has a dilemma. If GoodTech launches its PDA this year, other competitors will be discouraged from entering the market; if competitors did enter, GoodTech would be well positioned against them. If the market for PDAs turns out to be weak, however, GoodTech will not be able to recoup its investment, even with a strong market position. If GoodTech waits, it will not have an advantage over potential competitors, but it will be saved from the regret of making an investment in a weak market.

Parallels to Other Applications

GoodTech faces a trade-off common to many new markets: Uncertainty increases the value of waiting, but early investment may actually change the payoffs to investment. Certainly many companies believe that this sort of trade-off is at the heart of their market. Drug companies believe that early entry locks up market share. Technology companies believe early entry sets standards. Internet companies believe early entry is needed to be at the center of an increasing returns spiral. There are also numerous examples of this type of thinking in recent corporate spending. Western consumer goods companies have rapidly acquired most brand names in Eastern Europe, though uncertainty over these markets is still enormous. Pharmaceutical firms routinely purchase the rights to new compounds developed by biotech companies well before their commercial viability is established. Cable companies have been committing large amounts to the media industry at a stage when uncertainty over future regulation, technology, and consumer tastes is still large. This case study shows what must be behind the "gold rush" mentality to justify giving up the option to wait. As strategy guru Gary Hamel summarizes: "We live in a discontinuous world. . . . Who will capture the new wealth? . . . In an increasingly nonlinear world, only nonlinear strategies will create substantial new wealth."[1]

The Question

Should GoodTech retain the waiting-to-invest option or should they take the plunge in order to gain competitive advantage?

The Application Frame

Framing an application in which today's investment changes the rules of the market or tilts a market outcome toward one competitor requires blending insights from game-theoretic models of strategic market interactions with real options models of investment in uncertain markets.[2] This is quite hard to do in a way that provides a general way of thinking about the trade-offs. Often the results are specific to features of the model used.

This case study has a second difference from the others in this book. In the other case studies, the firms use strategic investments to shelter themselves from adverse outcomes while capitalizing on the good outcomes. Here the firm also uses strategic investments to change the market structure itself, enhancing upside benefits. Increasing returns investments are currently being generated in many similar new markets.

For GoodTech, product introduction expenses include advertising, branding, and development of distribution channels. GoodTech's early sales would attract other companies to write programs, design accessories, and create plug-in components, such as talking address book software, cellular phone adapters, and personalized carrying cases for the basic GoodTech PDA. This would establish the GoodTech PDA as the industry standard.[3]

GoodTech's preemptive investment opportunity can be viewed as the purchase of a "strategic growth option." This option not only allows GoodTech to capture the upside of a potentially good market but also has the strategic effect of influencing competitor behavior. One way to model the benefits of the growth option is as the capture of a greater market share. Investment creates capabilities to possibly take advantage of future growth opportunities. The competitive value of these capabilities may deter potential new entrants and restrict the output of those who do enter. This stylization captures the benefits and risks of a preemptive investment in a simple, tangible way, and is entirely consistent with the richer story of the real world.

Figure 18.1 summarizes how the strategy choice can be modeled as the choice between two options—the option to wait and the growth option—that are triggered by the same underlying asset, the value of the PDA market. The payoff to the growth option is very sensitive to the underlying asset because early entry results in larger market share and higher profits. The option to wait has a flatter payoff and allows GoodTech to avoid investment altogether if the value of the PDA market is unattractive.

Now turn to the uncertainty. The option to enter is triggered by the value of a newly emerging market. The players in a new market are often large, diversified companies (the ones that can more easily finance platform investments). What data might we draw on to understand the volatility of a new market? Much of the early industry experience is buried in the data of large companies, and traded companies that would serve as "pure plays" (companies facing the risks of just one industry) are unlikely to be available. The traded securities that

Figure 18.1   Invest Immediately or Wait?

In this example the payoff to immediate entry has a steeper slope than the payoff to the option to wait because the firm influences the market structure, creating greater up side exposure. By investing early the firm buys a growth option with a very steep payoff.

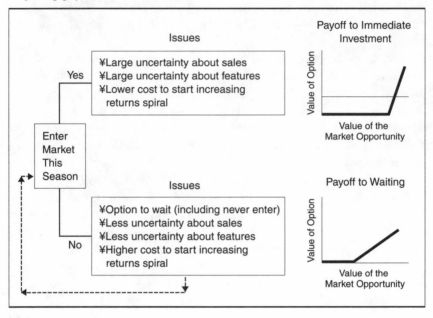

provide the best tracking are likely to be recent IPOs selling into new markets, but significant tracking error will remain.

The Results

Figure 18.2 summarizes an important result. Figure 18.2(a) shows the waiting and growth options for a market with low uncertainty, and Figure 18.2(b) shows the two options for a market with high uncertainty. The investment threshold is defined by the intersection of the two curves. The firm should commit the investment and acquire the strategic growth option only if the expected value of the market is higher than the threshold.

The best strategy will be determined by the relative values of three variables: the cost to enter (lower now, higher later); the impact of the investment on the market structure, which determines the slope of the payoff function (steeper now, flatter later); and the level of uncertainty (higher now, flatter later). In many applications, the growth option is more sensitive to uncertainty than the option to wait, making preemp-

Figure 18.2 Greater Uncertainty Makes Entry More Likely

The firm enters the market at the investment threshold, when the value of immediate investment equals the value of waiting. (b) shows that as volatility increases, the increase in the value of the preemptive growth option (and hence the value of immediate investment) is larger than the increase in the option to wait. An increase in uncertainty moves the investment threshold to the left, making entry more likely.

tion the best strategy in markets with high levels of uncertainty.[4] This is shown in Figure 18.2(b). (A note of caution: Think through whether this result can be generalized to your application or if your market has some strategic interaction not captured in the model just described.)

In some industries, winning the time-to-market game changes the industry rules, and the preemptive model of this chapter will capture the right trade-offs. James Morgan, CEO of Applied Materials, recounts one success story: "In 1997 we lost money for two quarters so that we could introduce our . . . architecture six months ahead of schedule. But we broke even for the year, and now we own the architecture of choice."[5]

In other industries, time-to-market pressures are different from the "price-making" investments of this chapter. If market arrival time does not confer any special market power, "rushing to the market" consumes investment resources but does not increase profits to the firm. It just takes additional money to get to the starting gate.

In some cases there is trade-off between preemptive investment and the option to wait, but at high levels of uncertainty preemptive investment is likely to be the dominant strategy. The next case study looks at another kind of opportunity to shape outcomes: setting the terms of technology license contracts.

Chapter *19*

Writing a License

Bonzyme is a "virtual" biotech firm, one constructed by licensing arrangements. It has contracts with academic researchers, supplying part of their funding in exchange for rights to discoveries. It contracts with firms specializing in running clinical trials to get the drugs through testing. In the late stages of clinical tests, Bonzyme gets its payoff: BG Pharma, a large pharmaceutical company, may acquire a license from Bonzyme giving BG Pharma the rights to market the drug. Bonzyme must negotiate a license knowing that the terms of the contract give options to BG Pharma and that they may even influence BG Pharma's decisions regarding the launch and marketing of the drug.

*M*ost managers recognize that licenses are hard to value with traditional valuation tools because future sales are uncertain. One common solution is to establish payments as royalty rate, sharing the risk of the uncertain market between the two parties of the license. If the license changes how the real options are exercised, the license valuation can be complex. Licenses also have explicit options written into them; the license may contain options regarding an asset that itself has many implicit real options.

Bonzyme owns a drug that contains the option to launch and a series of options to abandon. When it grants BG Pharma a license, Bonzyme may transfer the options, it may influence the exercise of these options with the payment terms, or it may effectively destroy these options with onerous cancellation penalties. To negotiate the license, Bonzyme must know how to value the alternative contract terms. A real options model must be used to account for how the terms of the license affect BG Pharma's optimal exercise strategy for the drug's options.

Parallels to Other Applications

In the new economy, you don't have to buy a firm to get its technology. Some firms have competitive capabilities in the production of intellectual capital, and other, often larger firms, have complementary capabilities in turning the intellectual capital into a product. In the biotech industry, drug companies offer financial assistance during the lengthy development process, distribution channels, and large marketing budgets. In the semiconductor industry, some companies specialize in aggregating and integrating blocks of code from others and then combining the blocks into "a system on a chip." Many high-tech firms started with a technology developed at a university, including Open Market, Silicon Graphics, Yahoo!, and Lycos.

The Questions

How do the terms of a license affect BG Pharma's decisions to launch the drug? How can the license, with its contractual options, be valued?

The Application Frame

Although actual licensing terms can be more detailed and complex, the basic arguments for how to structure a license are captured by tracing through the effects of two different forms of payment, an annuity of fixed payments over time that are triggered by the market launch and a royalty rate (royalties are computed as a percentage of sales). In practice, a license may have both terms. To keep our arguments clear, we model BG Pharma as having a single market launch option.

Let's consider the effect of each form of payment on BG Pharma's launch decision. First, to consider the most simple case, think of the annuity as a perpetuity, a schedule of fixed payments lasting forever. Let the value of this perpetuity be equal to L. The value of the market opportunity to BG Pharma has fallen by the amount L; its option to launch has an underlying asset equal to the value of the market opportunity minus L. Equivalently, the cost of the launch to BG Pharma is increased by L. This is shown in Figure 19.1.

Figure 19.1 A License Changes the Payoff to Market Launch

The option to launch is modified by a license granting Bonzyme a perpetual annuity of fixed payments upon launch. The present value of the payments equals L, and can be treated as a cost of launch in the option analysis.

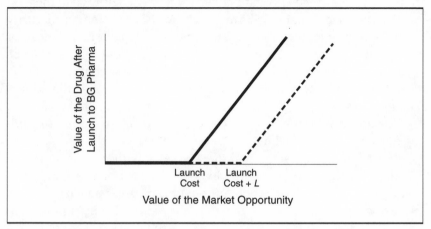

If BG Pharma had developed the drug in-house (or if the license required the fixed payments regardless of the launch), the development costs would be considered sunk costs and would not affect the launch decision. This is the payoff with the solid line in Figure 19.1. When the fixed payments to Bonzyme are included in the option valuation, the launch occurs only at a higher value of the market, shown by the dotted line. The fixed payment terms will delay the launch, all else being equal.

To show the effect of a fixed payment in its most simple form, we assumed that the payments were made in perpetuity. In practice, they are likely to be made for a limited time. As time goes by, less is owed to Bonzyme, and the difference between the two payoff functions in Figure 19.1 will shrink. BG Pharma holds an American-style option to launch; thus, the effect of the fixed payments on the option solution method is complex. (See Figure 9.3.)

Now consider the case when the payment is a royalty on sales. At each date a launch decision is evaluated, the present value of expected royalties, L^*, can be computed from the sales forecast. A sales forecast will be needed because the launch decision will depend on the value of the market opportunity. In most firms, there is not a constant relationship between expected sales and value of the market opportunity—expected sales must be computed outside the real options framework.

As before, the expected payment can be added to the launch costs for valuation of the option to launch.

The effect of the license terms on the option to launch will depend on the specifics of the application, including the magnitude of the payment terms, the remaining term of the license, the time to maturity of the option to launch, whether the option to launch is American or European, and the level of market uncertainty. These factors must be taken into account in the design and evaluation of the contract. The dynamic programming solution method can be used to value the license. The foldback will simultaneously value the real options, the effect of the license terms on these options, and the value of the license (including any options specified in the license contract).

In Chapter 13, we suggested that the value of the market opportunity for a drug could be tracked by a stock index of pharmaceutical companies. This index does not represent the present value of life-cycle profits of the drug but more generally the value of being in the business. It is appropriate for tracking the underlying asset of the option to launch. (It may not be appropriate, however, for tracking the value of the remaining market opportunity when the drug goes off-patent.)

The Results

Three broad-ranging results emerge from this case. First, license valuation requires that the contractual terms be simultaneously valued with the real options contained in the asset. The real options approach can consistently value the internal real options of BG Pharma and the value of the license to Bonzyme.

Second, the value of a license depends on the magnitude of uncertainty in the product market. How BG Pharma exercises its real options will influence the value of the license, and exercise decisions depend on uncertainty. Even when the license is a one-time up-front fee, license terms will affect the real options, and the effect of the modified real options must be included in the license value.

Third, terms of the license affect the way the licensee, in this case, BG Pharma, develops the market for the drug. For example, a fixed fee per unit sold would create an incentive for BG Pharma to discontinue selling the drug if prices fall sufficiently low, thus truncating the stream of license fees received by Bonzyme. BG Pharma can credibly threaten to discontinue sales, and it might demand new negotiations to lower the licensing fee. It might be possible to prevent this outcome by imposing a penalty for renegotiations in the original contract, but it is not possible to completely contract against all perverse outcomes. Depending on the terms, the license may be subject to the "holdup problem," the threat of negotiations for new terms at a particularly disadvantageous moment. The holdup problem occurs when one party holds all the decision rights. The interplay between issues of incomplete contracting and valuation is crucial in the design of licensing contracts and is an area of current academic research.

This chapter has shown how the structure of license terms can affect the value of the business opportunity. Licenses are an increasingly important way of transferring and combining assets and an area where real options converges with "financial engineering"—the design of contingent contracts.

PART **IV**

CONCLUSION

The final chapter is a guide to the questions that define the real options way of thinking. We hope this chapter helps you to achieve the right balance in your applications, to start on answers without crunching a number, and to use the real options way of thinking to shape investments, business strategy, and possibly your industry. As a recent article states, "To keep up, you need the right answers. To get ahead, you need the right questions."[1]

Chapter 20

Changing the Questions We Ask

The previous chapters have demonstrated the power and breadth of the real options approach and have shown that it is a disciplined way of thinking about the consequences of uncertainty. It changes what questions you ask when making strategic investment decisions. This chapter presents 10 questions as a summary—a guide through the real options approach.

*T*he purpose of this chapter is to get you started using the real options approach. We provide 10 questions that summarize the real options way of thinking. Checking an application against the questions will give you immediate answers, without your crunching a number. Checking quantitative results against the questions will give you ideas of how the investment strategy can be reshaped for further increases in value.

Despite a 25-year history, the real options way of thinking is in its infancy. This chapter summarizes where we are in 1998. Current information can be found at our Web site, which also contains news about recent research, a community forum, and links to academics and practitioners in this area. See www.real-options.com.

Strategic Application Frame, Tools, and Results

What are the key decisions to be made?

It's the first meeting on a large investment project. The group around the table spans a number of functions and meets occasionally. What is the key decision to be made? What are the subsequent decisions? There are as many different answers as there are people in the room. Often, managers do not come to the first meeting with the same perceptions. Tracing through the initial and subsequent decisions is the first step in framing the application.

What sources of uncertainty would cause the decision to change?

Managers can think of a hundred sources of uncertainty that affect their jobs and corporate investment decisions. (They often get confused between the two.) A successful real options application is framed with relatively few (one to four) sources of uncertainty, so it is critical to start the short list based on those sources of uncertainty that will most significantly change investment strategy.

How can financial market information be used?

Analysts enjoy analysis and consequently tend to build structural models of multiple sources of uncertainty, cash flows, and option valuation. Sometimes this is needed, but in many cases, after the skeleton frame is established, it is useful to turn back to the financial markets and ask: Is there any asset out there that bundles together the uncertainty I've just described?

What is the risk profile of the investment and how does it change the firm's exposure to private and market-priced risk?

Organizations must live with the decisions they make, and some high-valued investment strategies are simply too risky for certain organizations. Examples include a high expected return but a great deal of year-to-year variation, an unacceptable chance of a particularly bad outcome, and a large amount of uncertainty about whether the next milestone will be met. Think through how private risk affects the bottom line. Is the firm positioned to profitably bear this risk? Can it be transferred or mitigated at some cost? Before proceeding with an investment strategy it is important to review the risk profile, and to match it with the company's comparative advantage for bearing this risk.

Can the option be obtained more cheaply in the financial markets?

For example, a synthetic oil refinery may be cheaper to buy than a physical refinery (see Chapter 17). In general, because of the sophistication and efficiency of financial market capabilities to price and the "slice and dice" risk, operating and investment options are often more costly than their financial contract counterparts. Given the rapid pace of innovation in financial products, it always pays to ask: "Can I achieve the same objective more cheaply in the financial markets?"

Is this valuation result credible?

Each real options result should be given a credibility check. Where does value come from? Is the monetary size of this option reasonable? Are there any critical assumptions that should be checked out further? For example, the growth options described in Chapters 10 and 11 are not simple multiples of cash flow. A reversed analysis—one that lays out the required outcomes for success—may flush out any buried optimism.

Review and Redesign

Can the value and risk profile be improved by a redesign?

In some cases, real options are contracts written on real assets. Contract terms can be negotiated, so it is worthwhile to look at how the risk profile is modified by each contractual term. In other cases, real options are created by the design of the investment process or product architecture. Reviewing the initial results often identifies refinements that increase option value. A note of caution: Often analysts focus unduly on the details of the numerical calculations, creating a last-minute rush to finish. Consequently the analyst skips the review and redesign step, giving up a large potential increase in the value of the investment. A good review and redesign process requires an iterative and collaborative effort among designers, analysts, and managers.

Implementation and Realization

Who controls the decision rights to the option?

Previous questions have identified the option, but who owns it? Who will make the decision? This issue cuts across firms and markets. For example, Sun Microsystems created a modular software language, Java, giving product development options to other firms. Now Sun must herd them like ducks, without direct control of their options. Inside a firm, decision rights and option creation may also be separated. Perhaps one manager does not see all the relevant contingencies and another manager, who does see what is going on, doesn't have decision-making authority. In these firms, the organization won't be able to capture the value of the option.

What changes in the firm's processes are needed to manage real options?

The capabilities and value created by many investments reach far across the organization and deep into the future. In many cases, this question identifies the additional investments needed to realize the desired capabilities and the milestones that trigger future investments. Decisions can't be hands-off—made by the capital allocators, handed over to project managers, and revisited only for performance evaluation. Decisions must be hands-on, made by someone with authority close to the markets.

What changes in the organization are needed to capture the option value?

Some managers will read this book but won't be able to capture the value of the real options approach in their organization. In general, to capture the value of real options, organizations must be more flexible, take more risks, start a lot more projects, and kill a lot of projects. Which of these things must happen to capture option value in your organization? Sometimes these changes are hard, and real options thinking is the catalyst for change.

We wish you well on your real options journey. Our Web site, www.real-options.com, may provide useful details and updates that will assist you in the application of the real options approach. We hope that this book and the Web site are the catalyst for creating a community of those who have used and those who want to use the real options approach for better strategic decision making in an uncertain world.

Appendix

A Quick Introduction to Discounted Cash Flow and the Estimation of Volatility

This appendix gives two examples to help you get started on discounted cash flow analysis and the estimation of volatility. See Guide to Literature for references and further reading.

Example of Discounted Cash Flow (Standard NPV)

Suppose you are offered an opportunity to invest in a start-up company that will make and sell a "mouse house," a desktop home for a computer mouse that is designed to be attractive to children. Up-front design and production costs require an immediate investment of $10 million, and the entrepreneur forecasts the project's cash flows at $1 million per year for the first three years, beginning one year from now. These cash flows are shown in Table A.1.

If you had the first cash flow today, you could invest it elsewhere and, for the same degree of risk, earn 15%. In one year, the value of the investment would be $1.15 million ($1 million × 15% + $1 million). Using the same logic, you would pay only $0.87 million ($1 million ÷ 1.15) today to obtain $1 million one year from now. In the language of finance, $0.87 million is the present value of $1 million; it is the first year's cash flow discounted to today's dollars. The second $1 million is discounted twice ($1 million ÷ 1.15^2 = $0.76 million), because the cash is available only two years from now. The discounted cash flows are shown in the second line of Table A.1. The sum of the discounted cash

211

Table A.1 A Discounted Cash Flow Analysis of the Mouse House

In a standard discounted cash flow analysis, the cash flows are forecasted over the time horizon (in this example years 1–3), a value of the business after the time horizon (year 4 and beyond) is established and all are discounted back to the present.

in millions Item	Now	1 Year	2 Years	3 Years
Cash flows	–$10	$1	$1	$1
Discounted cash flows	–$10	$0.87	$0.76	$0.66

Sum of discounted cash flows	–$7.72
Value of business, year 4 and beyond	$8.54
Total value of business	**$0.82**

flows—a *negative* value—is given in the lower box. So far, this project does not seem like a great investment opportunity.

Of course, the entrepreneur assures you that the business won't die after three years. You could try to forecast cash flows out even further or put some dollar value on those cash flows without a forecast. A common way to value the future business opportunity is to multiply the final projected cash flow by today's P/E ratio for firms in the same type of business.[1] Note that earnings are not precisely cash flows (earnings include non-cash accounting adjustments), so using P/E ratio to value business opportunities provides only an approximate valuation. Historically, the P/E ratio for novelty manufacturing has averaged 13, so the value of the mouse house business from year 4 far into the future can be calculated as $13 million ($1 million × 13). The value of this future business in today's dollars is $8.54 million. The total project value, then, is $820,000 (–$7.72 million + $8.54 million).

Because $831,000 already includes discounting (it is net of the return that could be earned elsewhere for the same risk), the $831,000 is pure profit, a cash flow above a competitive return to the investment.

Example of the Estimation of Volatility

This example shows how to estimate the volatility of the underlying asset from historical data. To illustrate, we calculate the volatility of an index of Internet companies, the ISDEX.[2] Figure A.1 graphs the value of the ISDEX from January 1, 1997, through February 9, 1998. The bundle of private and Internet market risks are captured in the volatility of a single Internet stock, but private risks are diversified out of the portfolio of stocks that make up the ISDEX index .

Figure A.1 Internet Index (ISDEX)

The 1997 history of the ISDEX is shown. The index equaled 100 on January 2, 1997 and experienced significant fluctuations during the year, falling to a low of 69 in April and reaching a high of 120 in October. The ISDEX is an index of 35 Internet stocks reported by Internet World. Copyright 1998 Meckerlermedia Corp. Internet Stock Report. Used by permission.

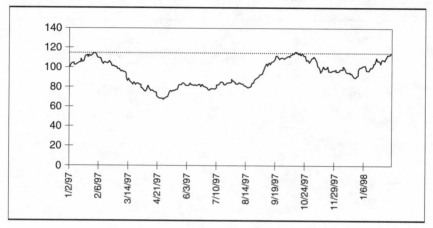

Volatility is calculated from the returns of an index or stock price; for consistency with assumptions and conventions in option calculators, the continuously compounded return to the underlying asset should be used. A sample calculation for the daily volatility for January 1998 is shown in Table A.2. The continuously compounded return is calculated as:

$$u_t = \ln(A_t / A_{t-1})$$

where u_t is the return between $t-1$ and t, and A_t is the asset value at time t. Volatility is then calculated by the usual formula for the standard deviation:

$$\sigma = \sqrt{\frac{1}{(n-1)} \sum (u_t - \bar{u})^2}$$

The number of data points (n) used for a volatility estimate is a matter of judgment. The estimate will be more precise with more data points, but the true volatility may slowly change over time, so the distant past might not be a good prediction of the future. At a minimum, the historical time period should be as long as the time to maturity of the option. This will capture the infrequent but large movements in the

Table A.2 Estimating Volatility from Historical Data

This table shows how to calculate the monthly and annual volatility of the ISDEX. The second column lists the daily close, and the third column is the ratio of the current price (A_t) to the prior day price (A_{t-1}). The fourth column lists the natural log of the price ratio. The monthly standard deviation is calculated from the values in the fourth column. The annual volatility is calculated from the monthly volatility as follows: 7.97% = 2.30% × √12.

Date	Close	Price Ratio $[(A_t / A_{t-1})]$	Daily Return [ln (Price Ratio)]
1/2/98	100		
1/5/98	101	1.010	0.995%
1/6/98	102	1.010	0.985%
1/7/98	102	1.000	0.000%
1/8/98	102	1.000	0.000%
1/9/98	97	0.951	−5.026%
1/10/98	97	1.000	0.000%
1/12/98	97	1.000	0.000%
1/13/98	100	1.031	3.046%
1/14/98	100	1.000	0.000%
1/15/98	102	1.020	1.980%
1/16/98	104	1.020	1.942%
1/19/98	104	1.000	0.000%
1/21/98	110	1.058	5.609%
1/22/98	107	0.973	−2.765%
1/23/98	107	1.000	0.000%
1/26/98	105	0.981	−1.887%
1/27/98	104	0.990	−0.957%
1/28/98	108	1.038	3.774%
1/29/98	108	1.000	0.000%
1/30/98	107	0.991	−0.930%
Monthly volatility			**2.30%**
Annual volatility			**7.97%**

underlying asset—an important consideration because an option obtains a large part of its value from these outcomes.

Volatility is measured per period, such as per week or per month, and there may be occasions when an estimate must be converted to a different frequency. For example, suppose the underlying asset had only monthly data available, but decisions were to be made weekly. The monthly volatility estimate can be translated to a weekly estimate by dividing the monthly estimate by the square root of the additional periods, in this case, the number of weeks per month. A 20% monthly volatility would then translate into a 9.4% weekly volatility. This type of adjustment can be made inside the option calculator or during input preparation.[3]

Guide to Literature

The literature on the real options approach is growing quickly, particularly for applications. We expect this only to accelerate as more firms recognize the potential for improved management of strategic investments. Our Web site, www.real-options.com, has up-to-date resources, additional references, and pointers to other Web sites of interest.

Chapter 1

Some short, general introductions to the real options approach can be found in Dixit and Pindyck (1995), Mason and Merton (1985), Chapter 2 of Dixit and Pindyck (1994), and Chapters 20 and 21 of Brealey and Myers (1996). Myers (1984), Kulatilaka and Marcus (1992), and Ross (1995) show why standard discounted cash flow tools fail to capture the contingent nature of investment decisions. Commentaries on the limitations of conventional tools aimed at a general management audience include Hayes and Garvin (1982) and Baldwin and Clark (1992). Bodie and Merton (1998) reviews the financial market developments that are changing the structure of many industries. An introduction to some of the strategic implications of the real options approach is Kogut and Kulatilaka (1997).

Chapter 2

The contingent nature of investments and their impact on valuation are addressed in many finance textbooks. Strong books at the MBA level include Brealey and Myers (1996) and Grinblatt and Titman (1998). Two good books for the college level are Bodie and Merton (1998) and Brealey, Myers, and Marcus (1998). All these also provide a solid introduction to financial option contracts.

There are a number of more detailed studies along the lines of our stylized examples. Morck, Schwartz, and Stengeland (1989) uses the real options approach to value forestry resources. Moel and Tufano (1998) finds that shutdown behavior of gold mines is consistent with the real options approach. Kester (1984) is an early article on growth options. Luerhman (1992, 1995) is a good first case study, applying the real options approach to the valuation of movie sequels.

Chapter 3

Two books by Bernstein, (1992) and (1996), are good histories of the development of the option valuation model. The Nobel Prize Lectures of Merton (1997) and Scholes (1997) also describe the collaboration of the two Laureates and Fischer Black. Hull has two books with very clear treatments of the option valuation model. Hull (1998) is aimed at the college market, and Hull (1997) is aimed at a graduate audience. Grinblatt and Titman (1998) has a smooth transition between the valuation of financial options and real options, using the language of dynamic tracking throughout their textbook. Smithson, Smith, and Wilford (1995), Luenberger (1997), and Luehrman (1998) are also very accessible introductions to option valuation.

The academic papers containing the breakthrough work on financial option valuation are Black and Scholes (1973) and Merton (1973). The contribution of these papers is well stated by the Nobel Prize committee. See www.nobel.se. An important paper by Cox and Ross (1976) introduced the risk-neutral approach to valuation, and Cox, Ross, and Rubinstein (1979) is the standard reference for the binomial implementation of the risk-neutral approach.

Clemson (1990) is a very readable introduction to decision analysis. Law and Kelton (1991) is a standard reference on simulation analysis. Chapter 11 of Grinblatt and Titman (1998) contains a good treatment of how P/E ratios are used in practice.

Berger, Ofek, and Swary (1996) provides empirical results on how the financial markets value the option to abandon.

Thermo-Electron is a company that has sought out financial market discipline by spinning out its divisions. There are 22 "Thermo pups," as the divisions are known, each with 51% of shares retained by the parent company and 49% held by the public. For more information, see www.thermo.com.

Chapter 4

The building-block approach is well covered in Smithson, Smith, and Wilford (1995). Merton's Nobel Prize speech (1997) provides an analytical framework for tracking error, and the topic is presented at a more introductory level in Grinblatt and Titman (1998). An introduction to basis risk and convenience yields in the energy markets is given in Risk (1995) and (1997). Bodie and Merton (1998) has a good discussion on the quality of information produced by a futures market when the underlying asset is perishable. The effect of the nonstorability of electricity on its futures market is discussed by Johnson and Sogomonian (1997) and Deng, Johnson, and Sogomonian (1998).

Tufano (1996a), (1996b), and (1998a) are excellent papers on financial innovation and the use of proprietary contracts for risk management. The Nobel Prize speeches of Merton (1997) and Scholes (1997) and the two books by Bernstein, (1992) and (1996), chronicle the rapid growth of the financial markets. The first two chapters of Mason, Merton, Perold, and Tufano (1995) review market developments in light of modern finance theory. Overviews of the many futures markets are in Hull (1997) and Edwards and Ma (1992).

Material on the market for pollution trading allowances can be found at the EPA Web site, www.epa.gov/ardpublc/acidrain/allsys.html. Reinhardt (1992, 1993) and Chapter 12 of Dixit and Pindyck (1994) are real options analyses of investments in pollution reduction technology.

Kulatilaka and Marcus (1994) develop a model to value employee stock options taking into account the restrictions on trading and the resulting lack of employee wealth diversification. Rubinstein (1995) examines the relative importance of the various parameters in the valuation of employee stock options, and Huddart and Lang (1996) is an empirical analysis of the exercise of employee stock options.

Risk management is an important area of study in modern finance. *The Economist* (1996) is a crisp survey of the state of the art. Froot, Scharfstein, and Stein (1993) and (1994) and Tufano (1996a) and (1998b) provide motivation for why managers should be concerned about total risk. Tufano (1996b) discusses the strategic uses of derivatives thinking.

Merton (1990) and Chapter 1 of Crane et al. (1995) introduce the functional approach to risk management. See also Kulatilaka and Lessard (1998) for a synthesis of total risk management.

A Web site devoted to introducing the concepts of risk management to corporations is www.contingencyanalysis.com. The section on corporate controls is particularly good.

Chapter 5

The use of the real options approach to support and enhance corporate strategy is a promising but relatively new area. The collection of papers in Foss (1997) captures recent academic thinking on the art of strategy creation and its current limitations. This volume contains many references to the same issues addressed by the real options approach. The strategic importance of contracts in corporate strategy is highlighted by the collection of papers in Buckley, Michie, and Coase (1996).

The concept of competencies, or capabilities, gained prominence with the work of Hamel and Prahalad (1994). Hamel (1996) and (1997) push the concept further, into areas where a firm might influence market outcomes through the capabilities it develops. Kogut and Kulatilaka (1994a) links the concept of capabilities and real options. Womack, Jones, and Roos (1990) and Sabbagh (1996) describe capabilities development in the auto and aircraft industries.

Arthur (1994) is the leading book on the economics of increasing returns industries, and Arthur (1996) is a very accessible introduction to this topic.

The authoritative resource for the economic implications of modular design is Baldwin and Clark (forthcoming). An introduction to this rich body of research is Baldwin and Clark (1997).

Chapter 6

The material in this chapter is largely derived from our experience in teaching the real options approach to students and working with corporate clients. McDonald (forthcoming) looks at how standard corporate rules of thumb for capital budgeting can be reinterpreted in the light of real options insights.

Chapter 7

Dixit and Pindyck (1994) and Trigeorgis (1996) survey and synthesize the academic literature on real options. Mason and Merton (1985), Kulatilaka and Marcus (1988), and Kulatilaka (1995) contain models of multiple real options. Grinblatt and Titman (1998) has a good discussion of current techniques used to value real assets.

The corporate risk profile is analogous to the value-at-risk concept in the financial options literature. See Jorion (1997).

Chapter 8

Black and Scholes (1973) and Merton (1973) are the original references for the Black-Merton-Scholes option pricing model. Cox, Ross, and Rubinstein (1979) introduced the binomial model. Hull (1997) and Luenberger (1997) are good overviews and syntheses of the material.

Smithson, Smith, and Wilford (1995) has a practical focus in its overview of derivatives and contains an excellent guide to the history of option pricing, including extensions to the Black-Scholes model. Hull (1997) and Stoll and Whaley (1992) give mathematical details of the option pricing models that are accessible at the MBA level. For a more advanced and rigorous treatment, refer to Merton (1992).

Hull (1997) is an excellent introduction to the numerical procedures used in option pricing. Additional detail about the numerical methods used in academic papers can be found in Dixit and Pindyck (1994). Schwartz and Moon (forthcoming) contains a clear description of a numerical method used to value a sequence of options with multiple sources of uncertainty. Varian (1996) contains useful information about computational techniques. Important references from the field of engineering include Bertsekas (1976) for dynamic programming and Kushner (1967) for stochastic control. Campbell, Lo, and MacKinlay (1997) and Dixit (1990) are good references on optimization with references to financial applications. Campbell, Lo, and MacKinlay (1997) also has a good treatment of the estimation of volatility and the use of implied volatility estimates.

Chapter 9

Siegel and Siegel (1990) and Edwards and Ma (1992) have good discussions on convenience yields in commodity markets. Gibson and Schwartz (1990) bridges the financial options literature and real options literature on this topic. Schwartz and Smith (1997) provides a very general model linking convenience yields to short-term and long-term price dynamics. Their bibliography also references the prominent papers in this area in the finance literature. An early article in this area is McDonald and Siegel (1984).

Pindyck has completed a large body of research on the economics of industry dynamics, commodity price fluctuations, and convenience yields. See his (1984), (1993b), and (1994) papers.

Hull (1997) provides additional mathematical detail on the option calculations shown in this chapter and on calculating convenience yields from newspaper quotes.

Chapters 10 and 11

Sahlman (1997) shows how investors evaluate the nature of the growth options contained in start-up ventures. Gompers and Lemer (forthcoming) summarizes the link between the options in start-ups to the contractual forms used by venture capitalists, and integrates a large body of empirical findings on venture capital investment and valuations.

Kester (1984) introduced the notion of growth options to the general management audience. Brealey and Myers (1996) also has a good discussion of growth options. Faulkner (1996) applies the concept of growth options to the valuation of R&D.

Chapter 12

Oil exploration was one of the first applications of the real options approach. Paddock, Siegel, and Smith (1988) values off-shore petroleum leases after accounting for the subsequent exploration options. Dixit and Pindyck (1994) has a detailed discussion of this paper and other related academic work. Bjorstad, Hefting, and Stensland (1989) lays out a contingent claims model for oil exploration. Tufano and Moel (forthcoming) shows how a real options analysis of exploration efforts can influence bidding strategy.

There is a long history of the use of decision analysis in oil exploration, although often without consideration of oil price uncertainty. Newendorp (1975) is a standard reference. Harbaugh, Davis, and Wendebourg (1995) also uses a dynamic programming/decision analysis approach. Two forthcoming papers by Smith and McCardle look at modifying oil exploration inputs in a decision analysis framework to obtain results consistent with the real options approach. Murtha (1995) uses simulation analysis to evaluate exploration decisions.

Chapter 13

The pharmaceutical industry is undergoing sweeping changes that are increasing the importance of the real options way of thinking. These changes are detailed in *The Economist* (1998b). Nichols (1994) is an interview with Judy Lewent, the chief financial officer of Merck, on the use of the real options approach for investment decision making. Schwartz and Moon (forthcoming) develops a real options application for drug development. Myers and Howe (1997) evaluates the risk profile of an entire portfolio of drugs in development.

Chapter 14

The material in this chapter is based on on-going research at the Systems Research Center, Boston University. Additional material on this case study is available at their Web site at www.busrc.org. An interview with Professors John Henderson and Nalin Kulatilaka about insights from the real options approach for information technology investment appeared in *PC Week*, March 25, 1995.

Chapter 15

Grinblatt and Titman (1998) contains an excellent overview of the use of the real options approach for real estate. An early article in this area is Titman (1985). McDonald and Siegel (1986) is a first paper on the option to wait to invest. Grenadier (1996) examines real estate investment strategy using the real options approach, while Grenadier (1995) values real estate contracts. Quigg (1993) is an empirical examination of real estate transactions, with findings consistent with investors' use of the real options approach. Case, Shiller, and Weiss (1993) proposes new financial instruments for the real estate market, indexed-based futures and options.

Chapter 16

This chapter is largely based on Kulatilaka (1993). Margarbe (1978) first modeled the option to switch from one asset to another. Other applications of switching options include Triantis and Hodder (1990), Kogut and Kulatilaka (1994b), Fine and Freund (1990), and Chapter 12 of Dixit and Pindyck (1994). Trigeorgis and Mason (1987) and Upton (1994) use the same type of arguments to value managerial flexibility.

Chapter 17

Merton (1990) introduced the concept of a "virtual refinery." Risk (1995) has numerous examples of financial contracts based on refinery operations, including operating a refinery while contracting on the crack spread. Moel and Tufano (1998) provides empirical evidence on the band of inertia present for the temporary closures of gold mines. The use of financial contracts to complement operating strategies is also the subject of Tufano (1996a) and (1998a). Additional detail on the work presented in this chapter can be found in Yi (1997).

Chapter 18

McGahan, Vadasz, and Yoffie (1997) is a recent review of the personal digital assistant (PDA) product market.[1] Kulatilaka and Perotti

(1998) has a more formal model of the issues considered in this chapter. Other papers on preemptive investment under uncertainty that use the real options approach are Grenadier and Weiss (1997) and Smit and Trigeorgis (1995). Baldwin and Clark (forthcoming) examines technology investments to shape industry outcomes in the context of modularity.

Chapter 19

The application of the real options approach to technology licensing is relatively new. See www.cadence.com for information on the real options approach to licenses for intellectual property in the semiconductor industry. In related work, Tufano and Moel (forthcoming) analyzes the effect of contractual features on bidding strategy.

Chapter 20

Organizational constraints can prevent the full option value from being captured. We believe this is an important subject of future research and an area in which real options thinking can add enormous value. Good references on the types of organizational issues that affect the value of real options include Brickley, Smith, and Zimmerman (1997), Buckley, Michie, and Coase (1996), Kogut and Kulatilaka (1997), and Tufano (1998b).

Notes

Chapter 1

1. "A Survey of the Pharmaceutical Industry," *The Economist*, February 21, 1998, p. 16.
2. "Andy Grove: Man of the Year," *Time*, December 29, 1997, p. 72.
3. "Opportunity Walks," *Red Herring*, February 1998, p. 98.
4. "Introduction: Rethinking Innovation in a Changing World" in Brown (1997), p. ix.
5. Dixit and Pindyck (1995), p. 107. See the appendix to this book for a quick introduction to net present value (NPV).
6. Myers (1984), p. 13.
7. This example is taken from *The Economist*, February 16, 1991, p. 59.
8. Lucent currently generates $1.60 per share in annual earnings. Using a 20% discount rate (a cost of capital appropriate to the electronics industry) and assuming that the earnings continue forever, a quick valuation of Lucent is $8.00 = $1.60 / .20.
9. Grove (1996), p. 75.
10. For surveys of how each industry is dealing with the transactions challenge, see *The Economist*, February 1998, and *Red Herring*, February 1998.

Chapter 2

1. Thanks to Kevin McCurry for the notion of decision making by "managerial charisma."
2. We learned of the term "cone of uncertainty" from a quote by Paul Saffo. For example, see "Mirror, Mirror: Paul Saffo Peers into the Future," *Red Herring*, July 1997, p. 160.
3. Ibid.
4. We use the cone of uncertainty to create an intuitive picture of volatility and uncertainty. Part II of this book provides a more formal description.
5. A more precise definition of volatility is ". . . the standard deviation of the return provided by the asset in one year when the return is expressed using continuous compounding." Hull (1997), p. 262.
6. Peter Bernstein writes in a history of modern finance: "Options enable investors to control risk and to shape the outcomes they face: at a cost, losses can be limited while upsides can be magnified. This is the most attractive feature of options." Bernstein (1992), p. 6.
7. Baldwin and Clark (1994) argue that U.S. firms using traditional valuation tools missed the growth opportunities in their industry in the 1970s and 1980s.
8. Similarly, venture capitalists, who specialize in investments with high growth potential but significant risk, are careful to evaluate the exit opportunities before investing in a start-up.

9. Estimates of gold price volatility can be obtained from option contracts, and the market's forecast of gold prices can be obtained from futures contracts. See Chapter 9 and the appendix to this book for further details.

10. However, we voice a note of caution about strategic investments that appear hugely valuable. What is the source of value: grounded realism or analytical optimism?

11. Bernstein (1996), p. 15.

12. See Womack, Jones, and Roos (1990).

13. See Brealey and Myers (1996), Chapter 21.

Chapter 3

1. Bernstein (1992), p. 227.

2. Net present value (NPV) is one form of discounted cash flow analysis. See the appendix for a detailed example. We use the term "discounted cash flow" throughout, because one could make the argument that real options is an expanded form of net present value.

3. Here's another example: Return to the three-year harvest option held by Forest Products introduced in Chapter 2. Suppose that the price of lumber is very low two years and nine months from now. Knowing that only three months are left on its option, Forest Products would probably give up because there would be no chance of a harvest. The payoff is then certain, at zero, and independent of further fluctuations in the price of lumber. However, if the price of lumber is fairly high, Forest Products would start to plan on a harvest and would watch the price of lumber closely. Before the harvest date, the risk of the payoff varies with the price of lumber and how much time is left before the harvest date. Any discount rate used must reflect the varied levels of risk throughout the cone of uncertainty, an impossible task.

4. For a history of the option valuation model breakthrough and the state of the academic literature before the breakthrough, see Bernstein (1992) and Smithson, Smith, and Wilford (1995).

5. The biggest difference between a traded option contract and a warrant is that when the warrant is exercised (cashed in), the company issues a new share of stock. When an option is exercised, payment is made from an already outstanding share of stock.

6. Smithson, Smith, and Wilford (1995, p. 318) write: "A differential equation is simply an equation that contains (calculus) derivatives. If there is a single independent variable, the derivatives are ordinary derivatives and the equation is an ordinary differential equation. . . . If there are two or more independent variables, the derivatives are partial derivatives, and the equation is called a partial differential equation."

7. Bernstein (1992), p. 210.

8. Ibid., p. 217.

9. Ibid., p. 223.

10. Note that we do not talk about volatility increasing, but about levels of volatility. We argue throughout this book that volatility is relatively stable and its estimates fairly robust. Our experience is that magnitude of volatility seldom changes in real options applications.

11. See Cox and Ross (1976) and Cox, Ross, and Rubinstein (1979).
12. The inputs are covered in more detail in Chapters 4 and 9.
13. This last input is discussed in more detail in Chapters 4 and 9.
14. This vignette is taken from the Ph.D. thesis of Martha Schary Amram. See Schary (1987, 1991).
15. A simple way to approximate the value of continued operations is to assume that the mill will run forever. The value of continued operations can be calculated as the profits divided by the risk-adjusted discount rate.
16. The mill's stock price will include the value of continued operations and the option to abandon, but it can be used in a tracking portfolio because the stock price is highly correlated with the value of continued operations.
17. *Time*, December 29, 1997, p. 72.

Chapter 4

1. "Economists are puzzle solvers," an interview with Robert Merton on winning the Nobel Prize, *Harvard Business School Bulletin*, December 1997, pp. 6 and 7.
2. See Kulatilaka and Marcus (1994) and Huddart and Lang (1996).
3. For simplicity, we do not include the convenience yield to holding sugar inventory in this example. We show how to include this input in Chapter 9.
4. The precise language in finance is that real options have risks that are not *spanned by* the set of traded securities.
5. See "Storage and natural gas risk management" in *Risk* (1995), pp. 206 and 207.
6. See Merton (1997) for further details and references.
7. See Cuny (1993).
8. See *Risk* (1995) and (1997).
9. See Rienhardt (1993, 1995), Walsh (1994), and Byrd and Zwerlin (1993).
10. See Ellerman and Montero (1996) and Joskow, Schmalansee, and Bailey (1996).
11. See "Storage and natural gas risk management" in *Risk* (1995), pp. 206 and 207.
12. See "Transactions Summary" at the EPA Web page, www.epa.gov/ ardpublc/acidrain/allsys.html and Joskow, Schmalansee, and Bailey (1996).
13. See Tufano (1989).
14. Scholes (1997), p. 16.
15. *The Economist*, January 31, 1998, p. 75.
16. For example, the magazine *Red Herring* reports an index of 100 high-tech companies that have gone public in the previous 18 months.

Chapter 5

1. See Myers (1984).
2. Bernstein (1996), p. 197.
3. For example, see Figure A.1 in the appendix, which shows how poorly Internet stocks fared on Wall Street in 1997.

4. In the venture capital business, the sales forecast is often called a hockey stick because the revenue curve is flat and then upward sloping once sales begin.
5. © 1998 The VC. All rights reserved. Used with permission. See www.thevc.com for this and other comic strips about venture capital.
6. Steven Burrill, *Financial Times*, March 25, 1996.
7. Sources for this example are: the *Boston Globe*, December 4 and December 12, 1997; and *The Wall Street Journal*, February 2, 1998.
8. Brown (1997), p. xix.
9. Fast Company, June:July 1998, p. 104.
10. Arthur (1996), p. 10.
11. Lerner (1995).
12. This analysis is shown in Figures 14.1 and 14.2.

Chapter 7

1. "The World According to Robert Jarrow," *Derivatives Strategy*, April 1997.
2. The distribution of stock prices and its impact on option pricing have been an active area of research. Hull (1997) has a review of the relevant literature.
3. A standard deviation is the square root of the variance.
4. Figure 7.3 shows one possible process from the class of mean-reverting processes, more formally known as the Ornstein-Uhlenbeck processes.
5. Pindyck and Rubinfeld (1998) describe the statistical tests for discriminating between mean-reversion and log-normal price evolution. Also, note that when the asset has a convenience yield, specification of the statistical test requires additional assumptions, such as whether the convenience yield itself is mean-reverting.
6. *Derivatives Week*, August 18, 1997, p. 2.
7. See Pindyck (1993b) and (1994) for analyses of markets exhibiting this behavior.
8. GARCH stands for generalized auto-regressive conditional heteroscedacity, an approach introduced by Engle (1982) and Bollerslev (1986). A good first reference is Hull (1997).
9. In fact, options models can be checked as follows. Set all volatility inputs equal to zero. Is the total value of the asset equal to the discounted cash flow result? The answer should be yes, because without uncertainty there are no contingent decisions, and discounted cash flow method gives the correct answer.

Chapter 8

1. Explicit finite difference methods have a set of equations that define a relationship between one value of the option at time T and three possible changes in value. Explicit finite difference methods use the principle of dynamic programming to fold back values and are equivalent to a trinomial (or three-branched) option valuation model. Implicit finite difference

methods have a set of equations that define the relationship among three possible current values of the option and one future value at $T + 1$.

2. For example, an application with three sequential binary decision points will explode into eight paths. In general, computational burden increases substantially with each decision point.

3. Continuous compounding is used in option valuation for modeling convenience, not a desire to increase the precision of results. Option valuation models are based on continuous dynamic tracking, and the number of periods (within a given length of time) in the binomial model can be increased until the underlying asset moves continuously. The frequency of compounding should match the frequency of movements of the underlying asset, so the binomial model is in its most general form with continuous compounding.

4. Usually these expressions are written for short time periods of length Δt, and the value of r is scaled by Δt and σ is scaled by the square root of Δt.

5. Similar contractual features are found in price support programs for agricultural commodities and in loan guarantees.

6. In fact, because the $55 million will only be received in 6 months, while the option value is in current dollars, the current value of the sale is the present value of $55 million less $8.06 million.

7. Sometimes complex mathematical expressions are broken into more simple components. The Black-Scholes equation is usually written as three separate expressions. See Figure 8.7.

8. We have changed the common notation for the underlying asset from S to A to highlight the use of the Black-Scholes equation for real options valuation.

9. See the Guide to Literature for full citations.

10. The phrase "elegant and practical" has been used by Merton in several places when describing the Black-Merton-Scholes breakthrough. For example, see Merton (1997).

Chapter 9

1. A word of warning. Sometimes analysts get confused about the required adjustment to the option valuation model. Options have contingent cash flow: If things look good, we'll put in cash and reap the benefits. Option valuation models must be adjusted for noncontingent cash flows from the underlying real assets, the leakage: We've got to make this payment regardless of what we do about our options.

2. See Dixit and Pindyck (1994), pp. 178–179 for a more formal exposition.

3. Analytical approximations to the Black-Scholes equation could be used. See Chapter 11, Hull (1997).

4. A standard binomial tree with n time steps will result in $n + 1$ nodes in the last period, but a nonrecombining tree will result in 2^n nodes.

5. See Pindyck (1993b) and (1994).

6. Note that the source of the mean-reversion has implications for the application frame. Mean-reversion in prices is already captured in the option valuation model because option valuation is done relative to the price of

the underlying asset. Mean-reversion in convenience yields requires an adjustment to the option valuation model.

7. Location and quality of inventory also determine the convenience yield, blurring this interpretation a bit.

Chapter 10

1. Our next case study includes private risk of a start-up, while this case study includes only market-priced risk.

2. Portlandia is privately held so its shareholders demand a return that compensates for holding the *total risk* of the company. Portlandia's volatility is 40%, the market volatility is 20%, and the market risk premium is 8%. Solving the following expression for x gives a risk premium of 16% (8 / 20 = x / 40). Adding the 5% risk-free rate of interest gives Portlandia a discount rate of 21%.

Chapter 11

1. As in the previous case study, it is important to choose firms that are representative of the future business model. More data points could lead to noise, not precision.

2. Mary Meeker, a noted Internet analyst on Wall Street, summarizes: "You can't value these new IPOs on a price-to-earnings basis because a lot of them don't have earnings. You can't value them on a discounted cash flow basis because it's hard to figure out the guaranteed cash flow. So what people are doing is asking: How big is the market opportunity? What kind of share can this company have?" *Fortune*, December 29, 1997, p. 114.

Chapter 12

1. This case study treats chance of success as a strictly geological source of uncertainty. Other uses of the term often include an economic component, defining the chance of success as the geological possibility of pulling oil out of the ground if justified by a "first pass" on the economics.

2. The learning ratio is a term summarizing a richer model of the updating in which each investment is a draw from a set of distributions, given certain constraints. This is known as Bayesian updating, and a good description of its application to oil exploration is in Bjorstad et al. (1989).

Chapter 13

1. Myers and Howe (1997).

2. Figures in this case study are from Myers and Howe (1997) and *The Economist* (1998b).

3. Research by Grabowski and Vernon (1994) traces drug revenues through their decline from years 26 to 32.
4. There is more than one suitable application frame. Ours differs from others published in the real options literature in that we include marketing as well as drug development expenditures and we explicitly model the option to stop sales. See Schwartz and Moon (forthcoming) and Myers and Howe (1997).
5. See Pindyck (1993), Dixit and Pindyck (1994), and Schwartz and Moon (forthcoming).
6. Pindyck (1993) first introduced this type of private risk.
7. These probabilities have been compiled by a number of authors. See Myers and Howe (1997) and the references therein. *The Economist* (1998b) reports a cumulative probability of 10%.
8. Industry insiders often believe that particular investments will increase the chance of passing an FDA test. This would change the application frame, linking the probability of success to costs already incurred.
9. Schwartz and Moon (forthcoming), p. 29.
10. See *The Economist* (1998b).

Chapter 15

1. Developers generally watch the price per square foot of local developed property because it better captures the specifics of the very local market; REITs can be too broad an index for the key worry of "location, location, location." However, REITs capture the broad set of forces affecting the value of developed land. The difference between fluctuations in a local index and an REIT can be treated as basis risk.
2. A modeling alternative is to assume that the orchards have an infinite life, which gives the pde a closed form solution. An example of this approach is McDonald and Siegel (1986).
3. This result was first noted by Titman (1985).

Chapter 16

1. This is easily checked by repeating the analysis with the other fuel chosen.
2. See Kulatilaka (1993) for details of this type of estimation.

Chapter 17

1. Depending on the relative prices of the possible outputs, New Jersey Refining could vary its mix of outputs within some limits. For example, it commonly produced more heating oil in the winter, when heating oil prices were high, and more gasoline in the summer. We ignore this additional flexibility in this application.
2. The market's forecast of the crack spread is contained in crack spread futures contracts.

Chapter 18

1. Hamel (1997), pp. 72–73.
2. See Kulatilaka and Perotti (1998).
3. Preemptive investment can confer a strategic advantage in several ways. Investments in research or pilot projects create more lead time for learning and technological development. Investments in marketing, distribution channels, and advertising create early brand identification and name recognition. Investments in capacity or logistics may lower the cost of capacity. In many of these cases, investments may also create a time-to-market advantage.
4. Kulatilaka and Perotti (1998) obtain the result shown in a model in which investment creates a cost advantage vis-à-vis a single potential entrant.
5. *Red Herring*, April 1998, p. 72.

Part IV

1. John Browning and Spencer Reiss, *Wired*, February/March 1998, p. 98.

Appendix

1. The P/E ratio is the stock price of a publicly traded company divided by its earnings per share. The ratio measures how much you would be willing to pay to obtain $1 of earnings in perpetuity. P/E ratios typically cluster between 10 and 30, but reported P/Es span a wide range of values.
2. ISDEX is an equal-weighted index of 35 companies tracked by Mecklermedia Corp. Data used with permission. See www.internet.com.
3. See Hull (1997) and Grinblatt and Titman (1998).

Guide to Literature

1. A recent history of the industry is chronicled in "The Next Small Thing," *Fast Company*, June:July 1998, pp. 97–110. The emerging competition in the industry is described in "Palm-to-Palm Combat," *Time*, March 16, 1998, pp. 42–44. "Pilot Pals," *Fast Company*, April:May, 1998, p. 60, describes the cluster of products available as add-ons for PDAs.

References

Arthur, W. (1994). *Increasing Returns and Path Dependence in the Economy.* Ann Arbor: University of Michigan Press.

Arthur, W. (1996). Increasing returns and the new world of business, *Harvard Business Review,* July–August.

Baldwin, C., and K. Clark (1992). Capabilities and capital investment: New perspectives on capital budgeting, *Journal of Applied Corporate Finance,* Summer, 67–87.

Baldwin, C., and K. Clark (1994). Capital-budgeting systems and capabilities investments in U.S. companies after the second World War, *Business History Review,* Vol. 68, Spring, 73–109.

Baldwin, C., and K. Clark (1997). Managing in an age of modularity, *Harvard Business Review,* September–October, 84–93.

Baldwin, C., and K. Clark (forthcoming). *Design Rules: The Power of Modularity.* Cambridge, Mass.: MIT Press.

Barnaud, F., and J. Dabouineau (1995). The oil market, in *Managing Energy Price Risk.* London: Risk Publications, 169–188.

Becker, R., and V. Henderson (1997). Effects of air quality regulation on decisions of firms in polluting industries, National Bureau of Economic Research, Working Paper No. 6160.

Berger, P., E. Ofek, and I. Swary (1996). Investor valuation of the abandonment option, *Journal of Financial Economics,* Vol. 42, No. 2, 257–287.

Bernstein, P. (1992). *Capital Ideas: The Improbable Origins of Modern Wall Street.* New York: Free Press.

Bernstein, P. (1996). *Against the Gods—The Remarkable Story of Risk.* New York: John Wiley and Sons.

Bertsekas, D. (1976). *Dynamic Programming and Stochastic Control.* New York: Academic Press.

Bjorstad, H., T. Hefting, and G. Stensland (1989). A model for exploration decisions, *Energy Economics,* July, 189–200.

Black, F., and M. Scholes (1973). The pricing of options and corporate liabilities, *Journal of Political Economy,* No. 81, 637–659.

Bodie, Z., and R. Merton (1998). *Finance.* Upper Saddle River, N.J.: Prentice Hall.

For additional references on the application of the real options approach, see www.real-options.com.

Bollerslev, T. (1986). Generalized autoregressive conditional heteroscedasticity, *Journal of Econometrics*, Vol. 31, No. 2, 307–327.

Boyle, P. (1977). Options: A Monte Carlo approach, *Journal of Financial Economics*, Vol. 4, May, 323–338.

Brealey, R., and S. Myers (1996). *Principles of Corporate Finance*, 5th ed. New York: Irwin McGraw-Hill.

Brealey, R., S. Myers, and A. Marcus (forthcoming). *Foundations of Corporate Finance*, 2d ed. New York: Irwin McGraw-Hill.

Brennan, M., and E. Schwartz (1985). Evaluating natural resource investment, *Journal of Business*, Vol. 58, No. 2, 135–157.

Brennan, M., and L. Trigeorgis, eds. (1998). *Flexibility, Natural Resources and Strategic Options*. Oxford: Oxford University Press.

Brickley, J., C. Smith, Jr., and J. Zimmerman (1997). *Managerial Economics and Organizational Architecture*. New York: McGraw-Hill.

Brown, J. (1997). *Seeing Differently: Insights on Innovation*. Boston: Harvard Business School Press.

Buckley, P., J. Michie, and R. Coase, eds. (1996). *Firms, Organizations and Contracts: A Reader in Industrial Organization*. Oxford: Oxford University Press.

Byrd, J., and T. Zwirlein (1993). Environmental protection and forward contracts: Sulfur dioxide emission allowances, *Continental Bank Journal of Applied Corporate Finance*, Vol. 6, No. 3, Fall, 109–110.

Campbell, J., A. Lo, and A. MacKinlay (1997). *The Econometrics of Financial Markets*. Princeton, N.J.: Princeton University Press.

Case, K., R. Shiller, and A. Weiss (1993). Index-based futures and options markets in real estate, *Journal of Portfolio Management*, Winter, 83–92.

Clark, K., and S. Wheelright (1992). *Revolutionizing Product Development*. New York: The Free Press.

Clemson, R. (1990). *Making Hard Decisions*. Belmont, Calif.: Duxbury Press.

Copeland, T., T. Koller, and J. Murrin (1994). *Valuation: Measuring and Managing the Value of Companies*. New York: John Wiley and Sons.

Cox, J., J. Ingersoll Jr., and S. Ross (1985). An intertemporal general equilibrium model of asset prices, *Econometrica*, Vol. 53, No. 2, 363–384.

Cox, J., and S. Ross (1976). The valuation of options for alternative stochastic processes, *Journal of Financial Economics*, Vol. 3, No. 2, 145–166.

Cox, J., S. Ross, and M. Rubinstein (1979). Option pricing: A simplified approach, *Journal of Financial Economics*, Vol. 7, September, 229–263.

Crane, D., et al. (1995). *The Global Financial System: A Functional Perspective*. Boston: Harvard Business School Press.

Cuny, C. (1993). The role of liquidity in futures market innovations, *The Review of Financial Studies,* Vol. 6, No. 1, 57–78.

Cusamo, M., and R. Shelby (1995). *Microsoft's Secrets.* New York: The Free Press.

Deng, S., B. Johnson, and A. Sogomonian (1998). Exotic electricity options and the valuation of electricity generation and transmission assets, Working Paper, School of Engineering, Stanford University.

Dixit, A. (1990). *Optimization in Economic Theory,* 2d ed. Oxford: Oxford University Press.

Dixit, A. (1992). Investment and hysteresis, *Journal of Economic Perspectives,* Vol. 6, No. 1, 107–132.

Dixit, A., and R. Pindyck (1994). *Investment under Uncertainty.* Princeton, N.J.: Princeton University Press.

Dixit, A., and R. Pindyck (1995). The options approach to capital investment, *Harvard Business Review,* May–June, 105–115.

The Economist (1996). A survey of corporate risk management, February 10, special section.

The Economist (1998a). An earthquake in insurance, February 28, 73–75.

The Economist (1998b). A survey of the pharmaceutical industry, February 21, special section.

Edwards, F., and C. Ma (1992). *Futures and Options.* New York: McGraw-Hill.

Ellerman, A., and J. Montero (1996). Why are allowance prices so low? An analysis of the SO_2 emissions trading program, Kennedy School of Government, Harvard University, Working Paper No. 96-001.

Engle, R. (1982). Autoregressive conditional heteroscedasticity with estimates of the variance of the United Kingdom inflation, *Econometrica,* Vol. 50, 987–1007.

Faulkner, T. (1996). Applying 'options thinking' to R&D valuation, *Research Technology Management,* May–June, 50–56.

Fine, C., and R. Freund (1990). Optimal investment in product-flexible manufacturing capacity, *Management Science,* Vol. 36, No. 3, 449–466.

Fitzgerald, J., and J. Pokalsky (1995). Storage and natural gas risk management, in *Managing Energy Price Risk.* London: Risk Publications, 189–211.

Foss, N., ed. (1997). *Resources, Firms and Strategies: A Reader on the Resource-Based Perspective.* Oxford: Oxford University Press.

Froot, K., D. Scharfstein, and J. Stein (1993). Risk management: Coordinating corporate investment and financing policies, *Journal of Finance,* Vol. 48, No. 5, 1629–1658.

Froot, K., D. Scharfstein, and J. Stein (1994). A framework for risk management, *Harvard Business Review,* November–December, 91–102.

Gibson, R., and E. Schwartz (1990). Stochastic convenience yield and the pricing of oil contingent claims, *Journal of Finance,* Vol. 45, No. 3, 959–976.

Gompers, P., and J. Lerner (forthcoming). *The Private Equity Cycle.* Cambridge, Mass.: MIT Press.

Grabowski, H., and R. Vernon (1994). Returns to R&D on new drug introductions in the 1980s, *Journal of Health Economics,* No. 13, 384–406.

Grenadier, S. (1995). Valuing lease contracts: A real-options approach, *Journal of Financial Economics,* Vol. 38, 297–331.

Grenadier, S. (1996). Strategic exercise of options: Development cascades and overbuilding in real estate markets, *Journal of Finance,* Vol. 51, No. 5, 1653–1679.

Grenadier, S., and A. Weiss (1997). Investment in technological innovations: An option pricing approach, *Journal of Financial Economics,* Vol. 44, No. 3, 397–416.

Grinblatt, M., and S. Titman (1998). *Financial Markets and Corporate Strategy.* New York: Irwin McGraw-Hill.

Grove, A. (1996). *Only the Paranoid Survive.* New York: Currency Doubleday.

Hamel, G. (1996). Strategy as revolution, *Harvard Business Review,* July–August, 69–82.

Hamel, G. (1997). Killer strategies that make shareholders rich, *Fortune,* June 23, 70–84.

Hamel, G., and C. Prahalad (1994). *Competing for the Future.* Boston: Harvard Business School Press.

Harbaugh, J., J. Davis, and J. Wendebourg (1995). *Computing Risk for Oil Prospects: Principles and Programs.* Tarrytown, N.Y.: Pergamon.

Hayes, R., and D. Garvin (1982). Managing as if tomorrow mattered, *Harvard Business Review,* May–June, 71–79.

Huddart, S., and M. Lang (1996). Employee stock option exercises: An empirical analysis, *Journal of Accounting and Economics,* Vol. 21, No. 1, 5–43.

Hull, J. (1997). *Options, Futures, and Other Derivatives Securities,* 3d ed. Englewood Cliffs, N.J.: Prentice Hall.

Hull, J. (1998). *Introduction to Futures and Options Markets,* 3d ed. Englewood Cliffs, N.J.: Prentice Hall.

Ibbottson, R., and R. Sinquefeld (1997). *Stocks, Bonds, Bills and Inflation.* Chicago: Ibbotson Associates.

Johnson, B., and A. Sogomonian (1997). Electricity futures, in *The U.S. Power Market.* London: Risk Publications, 83–98.

Jorion, P. (1997). *Value at Risk.* New York: McGraw-Hill.

Joskow, P., R. Schmalansee, and E. Bailey (1996). Auction design and the market for sulfur dioxide emissions, National Bureau of Economic Research, Working Paper No. 5745.

Kester, W. (1984). Today's options for tomorrow's growth, *Harvard Business Review,* March–April, 153–160.

Kogut, B., and N. Kulatilaka (1994a). Options thinking and platform investments: Investing in opportunity, *California Management Review,* Winter, 52–71.

Kogut, B., and N. Kulatilaka (1994b). Operating flexibility, global manufacturing, and the option value of a multinational network, *Management Science,* Vol. 40, No. 1, 123–139.

Kogut, B., and N. Kulatilaka (1997). Capabilities as real options, Proceedings of the Conference on Risk, Managers, and Options in Honor of Edward Bowman, Reginald H. Jones Center, Wharton School of Business, University of Pennsylvania.

Kulatilaka, N. (1993). The value of flexibility: The case of a dual-fuel industrial steam boiler, *Financial Management,* Vol. 22, No. 3, 271–280.

Kulatilaka, N. (1995). Operating flexibilities in capital budgeting: Substitutability and complementarity in real options, in *Real Options in Capital Investments: Models, Strategies, and Applications,* ed. by L. Trigeorgis. Westport, Conn.: Praeger, 121–132.

Kulatilaka, N., and D. Lessard (1998). Total risk management, Working Paper, Sloan School of Management, MIT.

Kulatilaka, N., and A. Marcus (1988). General formulation of corporate real options, *Research in Finance,* Vol. 7, JAI Press, 183–199.

Kulatilaka, N., and A. Marcus (1992). Project valuation under uncertainty: When does DCF fail?, *Journal of Applied Corporate Finance,* Fall, 92–100.

Kulatilaka, N., and A. Marcus (1994). Valuing employee stock options, *Financial Analysts Journal,* November–December, 46–56.

Kulatilaka, N., and S. Marks (1988). The strategic value of flexibility: Reducing the ability to compromise, *American Economic Review,* Vol. 78, 574–580.

Kulatilaka, N., and E. Perotti (1998). Strategic growth options, *Management Science,* Vol. 44, No. 8, 1021–1031.

Kushner, H. (1967). *Stochastic Stability and Control.* New York: Academic Press.

Law, A., and W. Kelton (1991). *Simulation and Modeling Analysis.* New York: McGraw-Hill.

Lerner, J. (1995). Pricing and financial resources: An analysis of the disk drive industry, 1980–88, *Review of Economics and Statistics,* Vol. 77, No. 4, 585–598.

Luehrman, T. (1992, 1995). Arundel partners: The sequel project, Harvard Business School Case No. 292–140 and Teaching Note 295–118.

Luehrman, T. (1997). What's it worth? A general manager's guide to valuation, *Harvard Business Review,* May–June, 132–142.

Luehrman, T. (1998). Investment opportunities as real options: Getting started with the numbers, *Harvard Business Review,* July–August, 51–64.

Luenberger, D. (1984). *Linear and Nonlinear Programming,* 2d ed. Reading, Mass.: Addison-Wesley.

Luenberger, D. (1997). *Investment Science.* Oxford: Oxford University Press.

Lund, D., and B. Øksendal, eds. (1991). *Stochastic Models and Options Values.* New York: North-Holland.

Majd, S., and R. Pindyck (1987). Time to build, option value, and investment decisions, *Journal of Financial Economics,* Vol. 18, No. 1, 7–27.

Margarbe, W. (1978). The value of an option to exchange one asset for another, *Journal of Finance,* Vol. 33, No. 1, 177–186.

Mason, S., and C. Baldwin (1988). Evaluation of government subsidies to large-scale energy projects: A contingent claims approach, *Advances in Futures and Options Research,* Vol. 3, 169–181.

Mason, S., and R. Merton (1985). The role of contingent claims analysis in corporate finance, in *Recent Advances in Corporate Finance,* ed. E. Altman and M. Subrahmanyam. Homewood, Ill.: Richard D. Irwin, 7–54.

Mason, S., R. Merton, A. Perold, and P. Tufano (1995). *Cases in Financial Engineering: Applied Studies of Financial Innovation.* Englewood Cliffs, N.J.: Prentice-Hall.

Mauer, D., and S. Ott (1995). Investment under uncertainty: The case of replacement investment decisions, *Journal of Financial and Quantitative Analysis,* Vol. 30, No. 4, December, 581–605.

McDonald, R. (forthcoming). Real options and rules of thumb in capital budgeting, in *Flexibility, Natural Resources and Strategic Options,* ed. M. J. Brennan and L. Trigeorgis. Oxford: Oxford University Press.

McDonald, R., and D. Siegel (1984). Option pricing when the underlying asset earns a below-equilibrium rate of return: A note, *Journal of Finance,* Vol. 34, No. 1, 261–265.

McDonald, R., and D. Siegel (1985). Investment and the valuation of firms when there is an option of shut down, *International Economic Review,* Vol. 28, No. 2, June, 331–349.

McDonald, R., and D. Siegel (1986). The value of waiting to invest, *Quarterly Journal of Economics,* Vol. 101, November, 707–727.

McGahan, A., L. Vadasz, and D. Yoffie (1997). Creating value and setting standards: The lessons of consumer electronics for personal digital assistants, in *Competing in the Age of Digital Convergence,* ed. D. B. Yoffie. Boston: Harvard Business School Press, 227–265.

Merton, R. (1973). Theory of rational option pricing, *Bell Journal of Economics and Management Science*, Vol. 4, No. 2, 141–183.

Merton, R. (1976). Option pricing when underlying stock returns are discontinuous, *Journal of Financial Economics*, Vol. 3, No. 1, 125–144.

Merton, R. (1990). Financial system and economic performance, *Journal of Financial Services Research*, Vol. 4, No. 4, 263–300.

Merton, R. (1992). *Continuous-Time Finance*, rev. ed. Cambridge, Mass.: Basil Blackwell.

Merton, R. (1997). Applications of option-pricing theory: Twenty-five years later, Nobel Lecture, December 9.

Milgrom, P., and J. Roberts (1991). *Economics, Organization and Management.* Englewood Cliffs, N.J.: Prentice-Hall.

Moel, A., and P. Tufano (1998). When are real options exercised? An empirical study of mine closings, Working Paper, Harvard Business School.

Morck, R., E. Schwartz, and D. Stengeland (1989). The valuation of forestry resources under stochastic prices and inventories, *Journal of Financial and Quantitative Analysis*, Vol. 24, No. 4, 473–487.

Murtha, J. (1995). *Decisions Involving Uncertainty: An @RISK® Tutorial for the Petroleum Industry*, self-published (contact number: 713-266-4592).

Myers, S. (1984). Finance theory and financial strategy, *Interfaces*, Vol. 14, January–February, 126–137.

Myers, S., and C. Howe (1997). A life-cycle financial model of pharmaceutical R&D, Working Paper, Program on the Pharmaceutical Industry, Sloan School of Management, MIT.

Myers, S., and S. Majd (1990). Abandonment value and project life, *Advances in Futures and Options Research*, Vol. 4, 1–21.

Newendorp, P. (1975). *Decision Analysis for Petroleum Exploration.* Tulsa, Okla.: PennWell Books.

Nichols, N. (1994). Scientific management at Merck: An interview with CFO Judy Lewent, *Harvard Business Review*, January–February, 88–99.

Paddock, J., D. Siegel, and J. Smith (1988). Option valuation of claims on real assets: The case of offshore petroleum leases, *Quarterly Journal of Economics*, Vol. 103, August, 479–508.

Pindyck, R. (1984). Uncertainty in the theory of renewable resource markets, *Review of Economic Studies*, Vol. 51, April, 289–303.

Pindyck, R. (1988). Irreversible investment, capacity choice, and value of the firm, *American Economic Review*, Vol. 78, No. 5, 969–985.

Pindyck, R. (1993a). Investments of uncertain cost, *Journal of Financial Economics*, No. 34, 53–76.

Pindyck, R. (1993b). The present value model of rational commodity pricing, *The Economic Journal,* Vol. 103, No. 3, 511–530.

Pindyck, R. (1994). Inventories and the short-run dynamics of commodity prices, *Rand Journal of Economics,* Vol. 25, No. 1, 141–159.

Pindyck, R., and D. Rubinfeld (1998). *Econometric Models and Economic Forecasts,* 4th ed. New York: McGraw-Hill.

Quigg, L. (1993). Empirical testing of real option-pricing models, *Journal of Finance,* Vol. 48, No. 2, 621–640.

Reinhardt, F. (1992, 1993). Acid rain: The Southern Company (A), (B), and Teaching Note, Harvard Business School, Cases No. 9-762-060, 9-793-040, and 5-794-043.

Risk (1995). *Managing Energy Price Risk.* London: Risk Publications.

Risk (1997). *The U.S. Power Market.* London: Risk Publications.

Ross, S. (1995). Uses, abuses, and alternatives to the net present value rule, *Financial Management,* Vol. 24, No. 3, 96–102.

Rubinstein, M. (1995). On the accounting valuation of employee stock options, *The Journal of Derivatives,* Fall, 8–24.

Sabbagh, K. (1996). *Twenty-First Century Jet: The Making and the Marketing of the Boeing 777.* New York: Scribner.

Sahlman, W. (1997). How to write a great business plan, *Harvard Business Review,* July–August, 98–109.

Samuelson, P. A. (1965). Rational theory of warrant price, *Industrial Management Review,* Spring, 13–39.

Schary (Amram), M. (1987). Exit from a declining industry, Ph.D. thesis, Sloan School of Management, MIT.

Schary (Amram), M. (1991). The probability of exit, *Rand Journal of Economics,* Vol. 22, No. 3, 339–353.

Scholes, M. (1997). Derivatives in a dynamic environment, Nobel Lecture, December 9.

Schwartz, E. (1998). Valuing long-term commodity assets, *Financial Management,* Vol. 27, No. 1, 57–66.

Schwartz, E., and M. Moon (forthcoming). Evaluating research and development investments, in *Flexibility, Natural Resources and Strategic Options,* ed. M. Brennan and L. Trigeorgis. Oxford: Oxford University Press.

Schwartz, E., and J. Smith (1997). Short-term variations and long-term dynamics in commodity prices, Working Paper, Fuqua School of Business, Duke University. Contact author Smith at jes9@mail.duke.edu.

Siegel, D., and D. Siegel (1990). *Futures Markets.* Dryden Press: Ft. Worth.

Siegel, D., J. Smith, and J. Paddock (1987). Valuing offshore oil properties with option pricing models, *Midland Corporate Finance Journal,* Spring, 22–30.

Smit, H., and L. Trigeorgis (1995). Flexibility and competitive R&D strategies, Working Paper, Columbia University.

Smith, J., and K. McCardle (forthcoming). Valuing oil properties: Integrating option pricing and decision analysis approaches, *Operations Research.*

Smith, J., and K. McCardle (forthcoming). Options in the real world: Lessons learned in evaluating oil and gas investments, *Operations Research.*

Smith, J., and R. Nau (1995). Valuing risky projects: Option pricing theory and decision analysis, *Management Science,* Vol. 41, April, 795–816.

Smithson, C., C. Smith, and D. Wilford (1995). *Managing Financial Risk.* Chicago: Irwin Professional.

Stoll, H., and R. Whaley (1992). *Futures and Options: Theory and Application.* Cincinnati: Southwestern.

Titman, S. (1985). Urban land prices under uncertainty, *American Economic Review,* Vol. 75, June, 505–514.

Triantis, A., and J. Hodder (1990). Valuing flexibility as a complex option, *Journal of Finance,* Vol. 45, No. 2, 549–565.

Trigeorgis, L., ed. (1995). *Real Options in Capital Investments: Models, Strategies, and Applications.* Westport, Conn.: Praeger.

Trigeorgis, L. (1996). *Real Options—Managerial Flexibility and Strategy in Resource Allocation.* Cambridge, Mass.: MIT Press.

Trigeorgis, L., and S. Mason (1987). Valuing managerial flexibility, *Midland Corporate Finance Journal,* Spring, 14–21.

Tufano, P. (1989). Financial innovation and first mover advantages, *Journal of Financial Economics,* Vol. 25, No. 2, 213–240.

Tufano, P. (1994). Enron Gas Services, Harvard Business School Case No. 294–076.

Tufano, P. (1996a). Who manages risk? An empirical examination of risk management practices in the gold mining industry, *Journal of Finance,* Vol. 51, September, 1097–1137.

Tufano, P. (1996b). How financial engineering can advance corporate strategy, *Harvard Business Review,* January–February, 136–146.

Tufano, P. (1998a). The determinants of stock price exposure: Financial engineering and the gold mining industry, *Journal of Finance,* Vol. 53, pp. 1015–1052.

Tufano, P. (1998b). Agency costs of corporate risk management, *Financial Management,* Vol. 27, No. 1, 67–77.

Tufano, P., and A. Moel (forthcoming). Bidding for Antamina: Incentives in a real options context, in *Flexibility, Natural Resources and Strategic Options,* ed. M. Brennan and L. Trigeorgis. Oxford: Oxford University Press.

Upton, D. (1994). The management of manufacturing flexibility, *California Management Review*, Winter, 72–89.

Varian, H., ed. (1996). *Computational Economics and Finance: Modeling and Analysis with Mathematica®*, New York: Springer-Verlag.

Walsh, M. (1994). Potential for derivative instruments on sulfur dioxide emission reduction credits, *Derivatives Quarterly*, Fall, 32–39.

Womack, J., D. Jones, and D. Roos (1990). *The Machine That Changed the World*, New York: Harper Perennial.

Yi, C. (1997). Real and contractual hedging in the refinery industry, DBA dissertation, School of Management, Boston University.

Index

About the Authors

Martha Amram is a principal at Onward Inc., a consulting and software development firm in Mountain View, California, where she heads the real options practice area. She has led teams in a number of industries, including pharmaceuticals, oil exploration, electric power generation, and semiconductor design, that have developed tailored applications of the real options approach for valuation, decision making, and corporate strategy. Dr. Amram is frequently asked to speak to senior management and academic audiences on a diverse set of issues including valuation and use of intellectual property, strategic alignment of R&D portfolios, oil exploration strategies, and technology valuation and licensing.

Dr. Amram holds a Ph.D. in Applied Economics from Massachusetts Institute of Technology, a B.A. in mathematics and a B.A. with Honors in economics from the University of Washington. She was previously a faculty member at the School of Management at Boston University and the vice president at Analysis Group/Economics, where she worked on litigation regarding the valuation and risk profile of derivative securities. She is the author of published academic research on mergers, bankruptcy, and the cost of capital, and a casebook on corporate finance.

Nalin Kulatilaka is Professor of Finance at Boston University School of Management and is a senior faculty member of the Boston University Systems Research Center. He received his B.Sc. in electrical engineering from Imperial College, London, his S.M. in decision sciences from Harvard University, and his Ph.D. in applied economics from Massachusetts Institute of Technology.

His primary teaching activities are at the executive MBA level, and in 1998 he was honored with the Russell Award for his excellence in executive teaching. He works closely with corporate members of the Systems Research Center on issues of valuation and strategic implementation of information technology.

Professor Kulatilaka has published widely on real options, risk management, and international finance, and his work has appeared in the profession's top journals, including the *American Economic Review, Journal of Finance, Management Science, Review of Economics and Statistics, Journal of the Royal Statistical Society,* and the *California Management*

Review. His research on employee stock options won the 1994 Graham and Dodd Award from the Association for Investment Management and Research.

He has addressed executive audiences throughout the world and has consulted to governments, banks, and corporations on applications of risk management, valuation, and real options in energy markets, telecommunications, and information technology. Professor Kulatilaka sits on the board of directors of Lanka Internet Services Ltd. and has been a senior advisor to several start-up firms.